P

'Thought-provokin

'A superb follow-up to the fir ... ncing
lyrical prose with intense th ... ed,
must-read novel' – **Leanna, *The Crime Review***

'Khan delivers an action-packed police procedural complemented by strong characters with believable motives' – ***Associated Press***

'Exceptionally fine… A heartfelt novel for lovers of crime fiction and anyone interested in the complexities of living as a Muslim in the West today' – ***Library Journal*** (starred review)

'*The Language of Secrets* is as much an examination of the complicated social, political and religious aspects of the war against terrorism as it is a crime procedural'
– **Carol Memmott, *Washington Post***

PRAISE FOR *THE UNQUIET DEAD*

'*The Unquiet Dead* is a powerful and haunting story'
– **Laura Wilson, *The Guardian***

'Stunning, both for its beautiful writing and for the visceral brutality and terror of its subject matter, *The Unquiet Dead* reads more like fine literature than standard crime novel. This book is an experience, not just a novel, and deserves a close reading' – ***The Crime Review***

'There's much to admire in this well-plotted Canadian debut' – **Karen Robinson, *Sunday Times Crime Club***

'Compelling and challenging, this is a beautifully written and powerful story of inhumanity and justice' – **Leigh Russell, bestselling author of the DI Geraldine Steel series**

'a powerful and absorbing debut novel' – **Peter Murphy, author of the Ben Schroeder series and former counsel at the ICTY**

'Compelling and hauntingly powerful… Anyone looking for an intensely memorable mystery should put this book at the top of their list' – ***Library Journal***

ALSO BY AUSMA ZEHANAT KHAN

The Unquiet Dead
The Language of Secrets
A Death in Sarajevo (novella)

The Khorasan Archives Fantasy Series
The Bloodprint

AMONG THE RUINS

An Esa Khattak and Rachel Getty Mystery

AUSMA ZEHANAT KHAN

NO EXIT PRESS

First published in the UK in 2018
by No Exit Press,
an imprint of Oldcastle Books Ltd,
Harpenden, UK

noexit.co.uk

 A CIP catalogue
record for this book is available from the British Library.

ISBN
978-0-85730-195-6 (print)
978-0-85730-196-3 (epub)

Typeset in 11pt Minion Pro and 10pt Frutiger
by Avocet Typeset, Somerton, Somerset, TA11 6RT
Printed in the UK by Clays Ltd, Elcograf S.p.A.

For the green birds of June.
Don't give up, don't give in – you are many.

For Nader, who hopes one day to return.

For my Iranian family, who share the dignity and beauty of their culture with ceaseless generosity.

And for Sane, whose father asked us to remember.
May you and the others find justice and peace.

A Time Line of Modern Iran

1905–1911
After a promising beginning, Iran's Constitutional Revolution is thwarted by Russian and British intrigue. With some democratic concessions, the Qajar Dynasty emerges as Iran's preeminent power. The ideals of this democratic moment remain a reference point for democracy advocates in Iran throughout the twentieth century.

1925
Reza Khan, a military officer in Persia's Cossack Brigade, names himself Shah of Persia after staging a coup against the Qajar Dynasty. His authoritarian rule is characterized by an ambitious campaign to modernize the country, similar to the secularizing and modernizing polices of Mustafa Kemal Ataturk in Turkey.

1935
Persia is officially renamed Iran. By the mid-1930s, political dissent against the Shah's authoritarian policies begins to emerge.

1941
Reza Shah declares Iran a neutral power during the Second World War, but his refusal to break ties with Germany leads to his ousting by Allied forces. Russia and Britain jointly occupy Iran. Reza Shah's son, Mohammad Reza Shah Pahlavi, succeeds to the throne. Parliament is allowed to function and civil society

is revitalized. With the backing of the Great Powers, a brief period of political opening begins.

1951
Prime Minister Mohammad Mossadegh is democratically elected. Mossadegh attempts to nationalize the British-owned oil industry. He is removed from power by the Shah, but regains office through an outpouring of popular support. Mohammad Reza Shah exits Iran. Iran's confrontation with Britain leads to an economic blockade.

1953
A CIA coup topples the Mossadegh government. Mohammad Reza Shah returns to Iran. A new pro-Western, modernizing authoritarian regime emerges. Iran's second democratic opening of the twentieth century comes to an end.

1957
American and Israeli intelligence officers work with Mohammad Reza Shah to set up SAVAK, an Iranian intelligence organization later blamed for the torture and execution of thousands of political prisoners.

1963
The Shah implements 'The White Revolution,' an aggressive campaign of social and economic Westernization that is met with intense popular opposition. Popular religious nationalist Ayatollah Khomeini is arrested and sent into exile, in one of many crackdowns on the Shah of Iran's opponents. By the late 1960s, the Shah relies regularly on SAVAK to quell political dissent.

1976
In one of a series of reforms that alienates a largely religious populace, the Shah replaces the Islamic calendar with an 'imperial' calendar, dated from the founding of the Persian Empire. The Shah's close alliance with the West is buttressed by growing corruption, and together with widespread political repression undermines the legitimacy of his rule.

1978
Mass demonstrations and strikes erupt in response to the Shah's rule. Martial law is imposed.

1979
January 16 The Shah flees Iran amid intensifying unrest.
February 1 Ayatollah Khomeini returns from his exile in France. He emerges as the leader of the revolution.
April 1 After a national referendum, Iran declares itself an 'Islamic Republic.'
November 4 Students storm the U.S. Embassy in Tehran, taking fifty-two Americans hostage. They demand that the Shah return from the United States to face trial in Iran. Khomeini applauds their actions. A crisis is ignited between the United States and Iran.

1980
April The United States and Iran sever diplomatic ties over the hostage crisis. The U.S. Embassy becomes a training ground for the Revolutionary Guards Corps.
July Mohammad Reza Shah dies in exile in Egypt.
September Iraq invades Iran. The eight-year war that follows claims more than a million lives on both sides.

1981
American hostages are released after 444 days of captivity. Supporters of Khomeini win the post-revolutionary power struggle, and take full control of the country.

1985
The United States covertly seeks to sell arms to Iran in exchange for the release of hostages held by Iran-backed militants in Lebanon, prompting the Iran-Contra scandal.

1988
Iran accepts United Nations Security Council Resolution 598, leading to a cease-fire in the Iran-Iraq War.

1989
February British author Salman Rushdie's book *The Satanic Verses* causes uproar among fundamentalist Muslims, and Ayatollah Khomeini places a fatwa (religious edict) on the writer, calling his book 'blasphemous against Islam.' A three-million-dollar bounty is placed on Rushdie's head.
June Khomeini dies. An elected body of senior clerics known as the Assembly of Experts chooses the outgoing president of the Islamic Republic, Ali Khamenei, to succeed Khomeini as Iran's Supreme Leader.
August Ali Akbar Hashemi-Rafsanjani, the speaker of the National Assembly, becomes president of Iran.

1993
Rafsanjani wins re-election.

1995
The United States imposes oil and trade sanctions on Iran, accusing Iran of sponsoring terrorism, committing human rights abuses, and seeking to sabotage the Arab-Israeli peace process.

1997
Political reformer, Mohammad Khatami, is elected to Iran's presidency in a landslide victory. Khatami promises social and economic reforms.

2000
Pro-reform candidates and allies of President Khatami win 189 of the 290 seats in parliament, setting the stage for reformers to control the legislature for the first time since the Islamic Revolution of 1979.

2001
President Khatami wins re-election. Conservatives begin a crackdown on the Reform Movement through their control of the courts and the Revolutionary Guards Corps.

2002
In his January State of the Union speech, American President George W. Bush refers to Iran as part of an 'axis of evil,' accusing Iran of pursuing weapons of mass destruction. The speech is met with anger in Iran.

2003
Iran admits to plutonium production, but the International Atomic Energy Agency finds no evidence of the development of nuclear weapons. Iran agrees to rigorous U.N. inspections of nuclear facilities.

2004
Conservatives reclaim control of Iran's parliament after controversial elections are boycotted by reformists. The new Iranian government declares its intention of restarting a nuclear program.

2005
Hardline mayor of Tehran, Mahmoud Ahmadinejad, campaigns as a champion of the poor and pledges to return to the values of the 1979 Revolution. He defeats one of Iran's elder statesmen in the presidential election.

2007
The United States announces new economic sanctions targeted at Iran's military and its disputed nuclear program.

2009
Iranian President Mahmoud Ahmadinejad is declared the landslide victor in presidential elections, sparking protests by supporters of reformist candidate Mir Hossein Mousavi, who was widely expected to win. The Green Movement is launched and protests rock Iran for the next six months. Severe repression and mass arrests crush the movement.

2010
Iran's relationship with the international community deteriorates further over its nuclear program. Additional international sanctions are imposed.

2011
Fearing the spread of the Arab Spring, the Iranian regime places Green Movement leaders Mir Hossein Mousavi, Zahra Rahnavard, and Mehdi Karroubi under house arrest. The regime welcomes popular revolt in Bahrain, Egypt, and Tunisia but opposes it in Syria, where it backs Assad's rule.

2013

Hassan Rouhani is elected on a reformist platform that promises to end Iran's hostile relationship with the West. Nuclear negotiations between Iran and the P5+1 begin. Civil society restrictions are slightly eased.

2015

A nuclear agreement is reached. Sanctions against Iran are gradually lifted, but Iranian hardliners crack down on civil society. Iran's Supreme Leader rejects diplomatic relations with the United States. Leaders of the Green Movement remain under house arrest.

Who killed these youngsters in their own country?
I wish they would answer.

Parvin Fahimi, mother of Sohrab Arabi
Killed June 15, 2009, age 19

1

Esfahan nesf-e jahan.

Esfahan is half the world. Wouldn't you agree, Inspector Khattak? You've been in my city for weeks now, abandoning the urgency of Tehran for Esfahan's twilight peace. Exploring its attractions, ambling along its boulevards, pausing to read in the gardens of Chahar Bagh. How many times have I seen you under the plane trees, a book in your hands, occasionally lifting your head into the wind? I thought you were reading in your own language, perhaps making a study of a tour book that would tell you about the secret passages behind the Grand Mosque, or the Shaking Minarets of Junban. But when I drew closer, I saw you had set yourself a more delicate task, taking your time to uncover the mysteries of the great Persian poets. But not Rumi for you, no. He's too often misquoted by too many would-be Sufis. And if we're honest with each other, as I hope we will always be, English translations are so utterly without grace, so empty of any meaning. I knew a man of your reputation could not be content with translations of Rumi, so I thought, perhaps Sadi or Hafiz? It is Hafiz who extends the invitation, after all: I lay my wings as a bridge.

Yes, Inspector Khattak, think of these letters as a bridge. Between my world and yours, between my thoughts and yours, between my suffering and your unattainable freedom. If you had a taste for irony, you would conclude we are bound up together, chained.

But you aren't reading Hafiz either. You've brought your own book, you travel your own closed circuit. You carry the words of our exiles, a dangerous book to carry on your person – but so many books are dangerous in Iran, so many paragraphs treason, these letters I write to you folly. Hide them for they will condemn us.

Don't be frightened, Inspector Khattak. I can't be anything but glad that you've come – come to take up my burden –

You will soon have a story to tell.

2

The small town of Varzaneh was a two-hour bus ride from the imperial capital of Esfahan. The bus wound through sand dunes along a rugged road, the early morning light describing the dunes in dust-pink whorls. Esa had been told to visit Varzaneh by Nasih, the proprietor of his guesthouse in Esfahan.

'I see you in the teahouses or gardens all day,' Nasih said. 'You need a change of scene. There are places to visit nearby, but if you want to see something a little different, take the bus to Varzaneh, and visit the Salt Lake. You'll like the pigeon towers, and you must walk along the Old Bridge. The people are friendly, though only a few may understand your Persian.'

Esa smiled.

'Is my Farsi as unintelligible as that?'

'You have an accent,' Nasih said. 'I can't place it, but I like it. Go.' And then surprising Khattak with his knowledge of the English proverb, 'A change is as good as a rest.'

So Khattak had found himself on the first bus out of Esfahan, bumping along the eastern road to a town that seemed as if the desert had swallowed it up and spit it back out again, the dun-colored dwellings absorbed into the surrounding terrain. He had dutifully listened to the guide's explanation of Varzaneh's attractions: its history of Zoroastrianism, its faithful adherence to the middle Persian language, the craftsmanship of women skilled in weaving the traditional tablecloth of the *sofreh*.

'You must go down to the river, you will see them laying the *sofreh* out.'

Khattak had visited the six-hundred-year-old Jame Masjid first, standing beneath the minaret the guide had boasted of, its sandcolored brick rising to a height of sixty-five feet, over the old town and dunes. At its summit, the diamond-patterned brickwork was interrupted by a pair of loudspeakers, out of place in this desert setting. Some distance from the spire, the blue dome made a modest statement, patterns of desert and sky echoed in the old mosque's architecture and in the inlaid tilework of the blue mihrab.

Khattak paused to read the inscription surrounding the mihrab. Shah Rukh, the son of Tamerlane the conqueror, had captured Esfahan in 1417, inscribing his plea for heirs on the mihrab's blue *kashani* tiles. When Esa finished reading, he noticed a screen of tiny, symmetrical crosses reflecting a pattern on the floor, the crosses picked out against a wash of light.

As he turned, two women in white chadors stepped over the pattern, the crosses mottling the fabric of their shawls. It was an arresting image – the blue mihrab, the sandy walls, the rose-gold crosses on a field of white. It took him a moment to realize the women had turned from the screen to face him, the dials of their faces framed by their shawls.

The woman on the left stared back at him, her dark eyes huge in a clear, young face. She was indescribably lovely with high arched brows and softly flushed cheeks, but he was struck most by an impression of sorrow.

She's damaged, he thought. And just as quickly, *I haven't come here to solve anyone's problems but my own.*

He didn't know what prompted the thought. The woman didn't speak to him, didn't ask for anything, but neither did she look away, as if the space between them was weighted with intangible desires. She was looking at him, he couldn't be sure she was seeing him.

He transferred his gaze to her companion. She might have been in her twenties, though it was difficult to tell with the enveloping chador that left her face half-hidden. She smiled at him, her glance bold and inquisitive, her eyes and lips tilted up at the corners, a cast to her features that hinted at an impish nature. There was a beauty mark beside her left eyebrow, and underneath this a tiny sickle-shaped scar.

The call to the mid-day prayer sounded. He remembered his manners and glanced away, murmuring a greeting. The women murmured back, one reaching for the other's hand. They disappeared down a narrow arcade, their figures diminishing under a succession of arches, elegant in their simplicity. He wasn't thinking of the arches, or the light or the splendid mihrab.

He was left with the impression of dolorous eyes.

Later, in the *chaikhaneh* teahouse across from the mosque, Esa drank tea from a gold-rimmed glass, a sugar cube between his teeth. He liked strong, milky chai, but he'd learned to adapt in the weeks he'd spent in Iran. He could hear the muted sound of the river rushing past, a gently throbbing loneliness. He felt the welling sweetness of the air against his face, and wanted nothing more than to relax into its embrace. But he knew why he'd followed Nasih's advice and come to Varzaneh. He was seeking a distraction from the letter.

You will soon have a story to tell.

It read to him like a threat. He'd had a sense of being watched, the letter confirmed it. Someone was following him through the streets of Esfahan, someone who'd come close enough to read the title of the book he carried in his pocket. He'd felt the shadow of a watcher ever since he'd arrived in Esfahan three weeks ago. He'd assumed it was an official minder, sent to act as his detail by a member of the Iranian government, even though he'd applied for a tourist visa with his Pakistani passport, instead of his Canadian one. He'd claimed an interest in making a pilgrimage to various sites of worship, and paid for a tour visiting the cities of Mashhad, Qom, and

Shiraz. Esfahan, the city of poets, philosophers, pilgrims, and kings, had been last on his list. He'd thought to reflect on his experiences in the city's peaceful gardens, but the arrival of the letter had changed that.

Nasih had brought him a book on the Alborz Mountains, written in Farsi, the Persian language. Esa's name was printed in a small, neat hand on the cover leaf. Pleased and surprised, he'd thanked Nasih for the gift.

'No, no,' Nasih said. 'I found it on the doorstep when I went to the market. I don't know who left it for you.'

Puzzled, Esa paged through the book in the privacy of the courtyard, stationed at his chair beneath the quince tree. When he'd opened the book, soft yellow rose petals had fallen out, along with the folded letter. Holding the letter to his face, he smelled the perfume of the roses. He wondered at first if the book with the rose petals was a gesture in some secret rite of courtship.

But when he read the letter, he knew it for a threat.

Whether from agents of the regime, or from a provocateur, the letter was intended to disrupt the peace he'd found in Esfahan's early spring.

We are bound together, chained.

He didn't want to be.

He hoped the letter was a prank of some kind, meant to scare him, or perhaps to startle him out of his lethargy. Though lethargy was an unusual change of pace.

The Drayton inquiry had come to a close after a protracted hearing, vindicating his choices about that desperate night on the Bluffs. The public outcry against the government had been so strong that in the end, the Minister of Justice had paraded Khattak before the cameras as a solution to his problems.

'Yes, we didn't act on information we had about Drayton, but look what Khattak did to set things right.'

Tom Paley's missing file on Drayton had turned up as mysteriously as it had disappeared.

In its aftermath, he'd received a cryptic note from his former partner, Laine Stoicheva.

You're welcome, Esa.

As soon as he'd gotten his visa, he'd left for Iran with a brief stop along the way.

He was still on administrative leave, awaiting a decision on the fate of his stewardship of Community Policing. He hadn't seen Rachel in weeks, though he called and emailed her as often as he could. But every time they talked, they couldn't bring themselves to discuss the outcome of the case that had resulted in his being placed on administrative leave.

He'd killed a man.

And though he'd sensed Rachel's willingness to listen, he hadn't wanted to revisit that night at Algonquin Park. Enough that it haunted his dreams, he didn't need to bring the nightmare out into daylight to examine it. He wasn't ready, though the weeks he'd spent in Esfahan, not thinking of that night in the woods, had helped.

Until the letter had arrived to disturb his sense of calm.

Because either the letter was a threat or it was a demand.

And he wasn't prepared for either.

He crumpled the letter up, ready to drop it in a dustbin.

Sober second thought gave him pause.

These letters I write are folly. Hide them for they will condemn us.

There was a loose brick in the wall behind the quince tree.

He thought of burning the letter so it would leave no trace, but with a policeman's instinct, he folded it into a fragment of itself, and placed it behind the brick with care.

Then he realized something else.

These letters I write are folly.

This was only the first.

As he sipped his tea, taking a slow pleasure in it, women in white chadors swept through the mosque's courtyard and dispersed down to the Old Bridge, a sea of fluttering doves on the breeze. The image charmed him, the white veils unique to Varzaneh, a sight Nasih had urged him not to miss.

These poems now rise in great white flocks.

The letter had turned his thoughts to Hafiz.

He followed the progress of the women along the seven arches of the Old Bridge, the river below surging with browns and blues. At the first arch, two slender young women broke away from the flock. One of them waved to him, it was the woman with mischievous eyes. She blew him a kiss with full, pouting lips.

Mildly scandalized, Khattak looked around. No one had noticed the kiss. The young woman looped her arm through her friend's, bringing her friend to Khattak's notice.

It was the woman with sad, dark eyes.

Don't, Khattak thought. *Don't come any closer.*

He raised his tea glass and nodded his head, returning his attention to the mosque. His heart was beating unaccountably fast. He pretended to study the crumbling minaret of the mosque. If he looked toward the river, he knew the woman's eyes would still be on him. He thought of rising quickly, paying his bill and returning to the station to catch an earlier bus. But he didn't know why the thought of two young women should frighten him.

Again he had the sense of being watched, that prickling of his nerves. But apart from the mosque-goers who were headed to the river, no one else was in view.

His eyes scanned the mosque. He had exited from the door on the left, and walked along the alley at the rear to view the dome's exterior profile. The chipped-away bands of ceramic glowed turquoise in the sun. Now huffing around the corner from the exit came a heavyset woman with a bright pink scarf that seemed destined to escape the collar of her smock.

It was a painter's smock with several strategically placed

pockets. She fished through the pockets, muttering to herself, discarding matchbooks, a cell phone, cigarettes. A prolonged search produced a piece of paper. She studied it, grimacing.

The hair bunched thickly on her forehead was a sandy blond touched with gray.

She looked up and met Khattak's eyes, holding out the piece of paper. After a moment, she lifted her hand in a wave, her shoulders slumping in a gesture of relief.

Despite her haphazard attire, there was an air of officialdom about her.

She'd been searching for Khattak, and she'd found him.

His sojourn in Paradise was over.

3

The Sonata

No one says anything in the car. I know they're Basiji, and I know we're not headed to Evin. I turn my head to look out the window, one of the Basiji catches me. He cuffs my head with his fist. The violence is a shock, even after Evin. 'Keep your head down,' he says. 'Where are you taking me?' I ask. I'm ready for the blow this time, my arms up to protect my face. These men are frightening, but they aren't much older than me. 'Please,' I say. 'My family will want to know where I am.' The Sonata turns south, away from the mountains. The driver grunts something over his shoulder. 'Shahr Ray,' he says. My stomach drops at the name. Sweat breaks out on my body, I lose control of my hands. My heart feels like a stone in my chest, I swallow, and I can't speak.

I'm going to Kahrizak.

4

They walked along the Old Bridge together, enough of a distance between them as they walked to deny an association if they needed to. The woman hadn't presented a business card or any other form of identification, and Khattak didn't ask for one. He slowed his pace to accommodate her limp. She was overweight and favored her left knee as she walked. The piece of paper she'd held up to examine was a photograph of Khattak clipped from a Canadian newspaper.

'My name is Helen Swan, but call me Touka, everyone does.'

She spoke in a distracted manner with the hand gestures to match, but her gray eyes were sharp and direct. They widened with appreciation as they ranged over Khattak's face.

'I've been touring Iran for a few weeks – mostly up north, at the sea. I love this country, I come back every year.'

He didn't ask how she managed to obtain the visa. He suspected he didn't want to know.

He was following the progress of the young women who'd crossed the bridge ahead of them. The ground below was covered with the *sofreh* the weavers had left out to dry, geometric patterns that cut across the river's banks in colorful, even patches.

'Mostly, I buy souvenirs for resale – carpets, ceramics, even turquoise. But every now and again, I run errands on behalf of our government.'

Khattak didn't know what to make of this. There was no formal relationship between the governments of Canada and Iran. Canada had closed its embassy in Iran in 2012, expelling

Iranian diplomats from its own territory at the same time. There wasn't even a pretense at consular relations between the countries. Aware of this, Khattak cut to the heart of the matter.

'The Iranians must have a file on you, then.'

'Perhaps.' She made a harried gesture with her hands. 'What does it matter? I'm in a position to do favors for certain people and to withhold favors from others, which makes me useful. Especially now there's been an election in Canada. With the new government, who knows how things might change?'

Khattak suspected Touka Swan knew quite well if relations between Canada and Iran were about to change with the election of a new prime minister.

'Ms. Swan –'

'Touka,' she interrupted. 'You're here on holiday, I understand that. And you were clever about getting your tourist visa, so you've managed to keep yourself out of the spotlight.'

It was Khattak's turn to interrupt.

'I'm on leave,' he said. 'I've no interest in whatever you've come to speak to me about.'

'But you know Zahra Sobhani.'

Touka Swan came to a halt above one of the arches. She studied the *sofreh* spread out on the banks.

'Maybe I should get into buying and selling *sofreh*,' she mused.

'Ms. Swan –'

'Inspector Khattak,' she said firmly. 'You are not at liberty to refuse your duty. It would be nothing for me to drop a word in the ears of the wrong people, and bring your visit to this country to an end. I don't like making threats, but I expect you to hear me out.'

Khattak leaned against the railing. The women he was idly tracking had reached the far end of the bridge. They were talking to a serious young man with an air of grievance who was in the business of renting out tour bikes. Esa thought they would ride to the other side of the Zayanderud River and disappear from his view. Instead, they wheeled the bikes in his direction. The sad-eyed woman had exchanged her chador for a manteau and head scarf. As she rode past him, its tail whipped over her shoulders, the white cloth bordered by a band of swallows. It was whimsical and pretty, at odds with his impression of the woman's magnetic eyes.

'I know Zahra Sobhani by reputation only,' he said at last. 'We've never met.'

Sobhani was a well-known Canadian filmmaker. Her documentary on Iran's 2009 election had swept the awards season, winning accolades for its originality, a story told without commentary or subtitles, the music written by Zahra's son, the musician Max Najafi, acclaimed in his own right.

The documentary was called *A Requiem for Hope*. Khattak had seen it at the Toronto International Film Festival, and had attended the discussion with mother and son that followed. Zahra Sobhani had struck him as a fiercely capable woman, bold and unafraid, burning with unresolved questions. Her son had spoken about his music. When pressed to comment on the politics of the film, Max Najafi had said simply, 'Iran *is* the music, that's all I have to say.'

Khattak had been impressed by the somber mood of a young man gifted with exceptional talent, a man without the need for words. The next time he'd viewed the film, he'd understood a little better. The film was personal to Max, the music intimate, reflective – sorrowful.

It had penetrated Esa's defenses, making him think of that dark night in the woods.

And other things he wished to forget.

A gun in his hand. The sound of a body thudding against the ice.

He felt its echo in Esfahan, so far away from home.

He looked at Touka Swan and knew she had come to tell him Zahra Sobhani was dead.

'What happened?' he asked quietly.

Not far from Varzaneh, seasonal birds invaded the Gavkhuni wetland. Though climate degradation had eroded their numbers, a few straggling pelicans dotted the banks of the river, their beaks bullet gray against turbulent flashes of green.

'She insisted on returning to Iran. She was welcomed at the airport like a conquering hero –'

'Like a daughter of Iran,' Khattak interposed. It was a phrase he loved.

Touka Swan shot him a swift glance. She went on as if he hadn't spoken.

'She must have thought that made her safe. Or that no one in the government would take notice of her. You remember her documentary about the election?'

Khattak nodded.

The stolen election of June 2009 and its slogan, *Where Is My Vote*, had dominated international headlines for a time, the death of a young protester named Neda Agha Soltan captured on a cell phone to harrowing effect and sent around the world.

Elections were stringently conducted within Iran: candidates were required to receive the Guardian Council's approval before they were granted permission to campaign. When widely supported reformist candidates had met these requirements, their subsequent, categorical loss was viewed by the public as electoral fraud.

Neda Agha Soltan and millions of others had poured into the streets to protest what they called the embezzlement of their votes: the regime had responded with violent repression, the mass arrest of protesters, and in some cases, its forces had meted out death.

'Then you remember how the film ended,' Touka continued.

'Yes. There was a selection of photographs. An "In Memoriam" section for the students killed during the protests that followed the vote.'

'It was also a memorial for the living. Zahra came back on behalf of the living.'

'I find it strange that the government allowed her to return.'

'She raised an international outcry, painting the Iranian regime in the worst possible light, when they were trying to sanitize their image. They must have weighed the risks of letting her return.'

A flock of starlings rose up from under the bridge. Khattak watched their wings beat against the sky before they spun away into the desert emptiness. To Khattak, the sky seemed cumbrous.

'Wouldn't she have realized it was still a risk?'

'That's why she didn't allow her son to come. She intended to use her platform to demand the release of all of Evin's political prisoners. She was planning to make a follow-up documentary.'

Khattak didn't want to hear the rest. He had tremendous respect for Zahra Sobhani's determination. Evin prison was notorious for its abuse of human rights, its state-sanctioned cruelties a well-known lexicon of torture.

The smallest act of personal defiance could gain an ordinary citizen months of discretionary detention without recourse to due process of the law. The interrogators, the wardens, the prosecutors, the judiciary, the Ministry of Intelligence and Security – these were arms of a long-churning machinery of repression.

'I'm surprised the regime allowed her anywhere near Evin. Photography is forbidden at the prison, she must have known that.'

'She didn't ask anyone's permission. She dodged her official minders. A few pictures leaked from her camera would have raised the profile of the prisoners held there. But I admit, I'm surprised she risked it. She normally proceeded through the appropriate channels.'

Khattak was beginning to understand why Touka Swan had sought him out.

'If she was willing to take such a risk, she must have gone to see someone who mattered to her. Personally.'

'Haven't you been reading the news?'

Khattak waved away a man who approached him with the offer to rent a jeep to drive over the dunes. They exchanged pleasantries, the tour guide delighted to meet a visitor who was fluent in his language.

Touka Swan looked at him with interest.

'You speak Farsi.'

'My father taught me.' She already knew this, he thought. He moved away from Touka, careful to look in the opposite direction. The tour guide's friends were gathering behind them. 'I don't think we should be seen together. I don't know who you represent, and I don't want to find out. Whatever you've come to tell me about Zahra, you could be next. Or I could.'

Touka gave an inelegant snort.

'Your profile isn't high enough to worry the Ministry of Intelligence. All you've done is read a slightly subversive book.'

Khattak's hand went to his breast pocket.

'It's foolish of you to carry it around with you.'

'It was you?' he asked. 'You've been following me? Was it you who sent me the letter?'

He had a difficult time reconciling the dreamlike phrasing of the letter with the matter-of-fact woman beside him.

Touka scratched her head.

'I've been keeping an eye out for you at the request of our government, but I don't know what you're referring to. The first rule of traveling in Iran is not to put anything in writing. I've come to you because our government is trying to – balance – its interests in Iran.'

'I have no idea what you mean.'

She sighed deeply, reaching into her pocket for her cigarettes. Without asking Khattak if he minded, she lit a cigarette and expelled the smoke over the river. She coughed for several moments before speaking again.

'One week ago, Zahra Sobhani was arrested for taking photographs at Evin prison. Two days ago, her body was delivered to her family's doorstep in Tehran.'

The hollowness that had cut away at Khattak since that night in the woods now opened into a chasm. He felt himself clawing at the edges of it, a wetness behind his eyes.

'They murdered her?' he asked.

'She was tortured, raped, and beaten to death.'

Touka stubbed out her cigarette, her knee buckling at the action. She gripped the deck of the bridge with her hands. They were powerful hands, the skin chafed and raw, the knuckles dark red. They looked like the hands of a fisherwoman.

His mind racing, Khattak said something he hated himself for saying. It laid his selfishness bare.

'How does this concern me? She made a dangerous choice, she's paid for it, there's nothing I can do.'

'We need a name,' Touka said. 'We need to know who's responsible.'

Khattak shook his head. He couldn't understand why.

'It could be any one of the interrogators at the prison,' he said. 'A prison I have the sense to avoid.'

The noise of the crowd was growing behind them. Khattak felt a prickling at the back of his neck. He knew he should walk away without hearing anything else, take the next bus back to Esfahan, then to Tehran, pack up his things and leave. He knew nothing good waited for him in the streets of the capital or at the outskirts of Evin prison.

'We think Barsam Radan is directly implicated. All we need is proof.'

Khattak knew the name, as did anyone who followed news of Iran. Radan was a senior official at the Ministry of Intelligence and Security. He frequently attended Evin to take part in the interrogation of political prisoners, a catch-all phrase for students, labor organizers, artists, intellectuals, and journalists. He'd reigned over the most ruthless period of repression in the history of the prison, with a special fire reserved for those who'd protested the stolen election.

The name Barsam meant 'Great Fire.' Prisoners in Evin's infamous Ward 209 whispered to each other of his coming – *the Great Fire is here to burn us down.*

The tour guide approached Khattak again. This time Khattak made a lengthy request. The guide listened, his head cocked to one side. When Khattak finished, the guide waved to his friends. They departed as a group for the *chaikhaneh.*

When they were out of earshot, Khattak asked, 'Why? What could that possibly gain you? The Iranian government rarely admits culpability in these cases. At most, they'll hold a low-ranking interrogator to account. You won't be able to get Radan. You know he's much too powerful.'

He didn't want to ask why the Canadian government would want such proof or what they intended to do with it. He could sense the shadowy presence of an intelligence agent behind Touka Swan's façade.

Touka's smile was tight.

'That's why we need him. Radan is an operator, he runs a network of spies and informants. He has a finger in every pie. If he's implicated and we can prove it, that's a significant blow to the entire apparatus. And it would protect dual citizens like Zahra.' Sensing Khattak's skepticism, she continued. 'That's not our primary focus. Our government has a problem on its hands. We're on the brink of resuming diplomatic relations. The prime minister is planning to reopen our embassy in Tehran. And Canadian businesses have been waiting for the chance to invest. There's a lot at stake here – politically, financially. But we won't be able to do any of these things if we don't demand accountability from Tehran. And not a low-level interrogator, as you suggested. Zahra's son has managed to capture the attention of the press. He would never accept that as a solution.'

Khattak cut her off.

'Would you, if it was someone you loved?'

'There are other ways of seeking justice, Inspector Khattak. Didn't you decide that in the Drayton case? I believe that's what you said at the inquiry.'

Khattak looked at her quickly. How long had he been on Touka Swan's radar? And just how thorough was her dossier on him?

'Even if everything you say is true, how could I get you proof of Radan's involvement? What kind of inquiries could I make? I have no authority here, and I certainly have no jurisdiction.'

At his words, Touka Swan relaxed a little. She must have sensed he was giving in.

'Don't worry about jurisdictional issues, you won't be saying or doing anything in an official capacity. You speak Farsi, you'll blend in, and you know how to be careful. We've heard a rumor there's a video.'

Khattak was appalled. 'Of the interrogation? Or the murder?'

He didn't know which would be worse.

But Touka was shaking her head, ash-gray hair drifting into her eyes.

'I don't know. If I can locate it, I'll want you to take a look at it. Someone will contact you if I can get my hands on it. If you have sources you can work in Canada, do so. Have your partner visit Max Najafi. It would help to track Zahra's movements before she left for Iran.'

Khattak felt a quick lift of his spirits. He wouldn't be alone. He knew he could ask anything of his partner, Rachel Getty, and she would be there to help.

With a small sigh of defeat, Khattak said, 'I won't go to Evin. I won't put my family through what might happen to me there.'

'You won't need to,' Touka said, assured now of her victory.

'Zahra has a stepdaughter from her husband's second marriage. Roxana Najafi is the prisoner she went to Evin to free. Roxana's family is under house arrest in Esfahan. Start there and tell me what you find.'

When Khattak seemed to hesitate, she added, 'I know your résumé better than you think. You're on leave because of what happened in Algonquin. You've also had your share of difficulties with the press. If you deliver Radan, I can make that go away.' She waited a beat. 'And if you don't, you might find your difficulties worsen.'

Khattak raised his head. He looked straight at Touka, holding her with his gaze.

'If I did, that wouldn't be the reason. If you've been keeping tabs on me, you should know that about me by now.'

The blush that rose to Touka's face made her a little less formidable.

As she walked away without a word, her left leg dragging on the road, Khattak placed his hand over the spot where she had rested hers on the bridge, covering the card she'd left behind. A phone number was typed on its surface in black ink. And under this she had written in a minuscule hand, *Yes, you are being followed.*

The guide returned with his friends and a supply of bottled water, carrying several steaming paper bags. *Lavash* bread and kebabs, accompanied by small containers of a yogurt mixture called *mast-e khayar*, along with grilled tomatoes and onions, a snack for an afternoon picnic.

He'd asked Fardis, the guide, to drive him to see the Salt Lake, a salt flat that spread out from the southwestern part of the wetlands, a striking contrast between hot blue sky and boundless earth. Fardis chatted on about this and the wonders of the Black Mountain, a magma formation that signaled the beginning of the wetlands. Much was being done to promote tourism in the region, to offset the drying up of the marsh and the extinction of wetland species. Fardis's friends showed Esa photographs from their trips to visit the lake.

When they reached the lake, Esa witnessed its wonders for himself. A vast white plain, a heartbreaking sky, the salt gathered like shabby mounds of snow.

As he drank from the bottled water Fardis had poured into a glass, Khattak thought again, *These poems rise in great white flocks.*

The women in chadors, the flurries of salt foam, the rose-gold crosses on a dusty floor – what a stark and beautiful country this was.

Fardis quoted Hafiz with gentle pride.

Even after all this time the sun never says to the earth, you owe me.

A love like that lights the whole sky.

He wondered if the words expressed Zahra's feeling for her country. Was it the reason she'd risked her safety to return to Iran, to fight for Roxana Najafi? Had she loved Roxana like a daughter of her own? So much so she couldn't bear the thought of her broken and misused body? Had she risked a worse fate for herself in order to spare Roxana?

He shook his head at the stupidity of the regime, at its mindless and needless savagery. Left to herself, Zahra Sobhani would have raised her voice in support of Iran's political prisoners. Obstructed by the petty tyrannies of the state, she would have returned to her home in Canada to be with her only child.

The murder and defilement of Zahra Sobhani would become an international incident, a diplomatic nightmare with long-lasting consequences. The voices of protest that had gone underground, the attention of the world's media that had moved on to other tragedies would now return. The spotlight was back. The regime had created the very thing it wished to suppress.

And now Esa thought of the poet Rumi.

The wound is the place where the light enters you.

Staring out at the salt flat, he raised his glass to Zahra's memory.

5

Everything I do violates a law.

I sing, I draw, I speak, I write – everything I do violates a law.
But what kind of law cleaves us like a sword?
What kind of law pounds us like a stone?
What kind of law hangs us from a crane?

They've killed our mother – the mother of all the children of Iran, her death a stone, a ripple in the pond, a crack in the wall, a crack in the regime – the place where the fortress is breached, a treasure among the ruins.

I slip through the crack to find you, borne along on a sea of light.
I have so many stories to tell you, but I find I have so little time.
Before the guards come, there is something you must do.
You must find out what Zahra wanted with the letters.

6

Khattak placed the second letter behind the brick in the courtyard. Nasih had brought it to him inside a tea cozy in a box addressed to Khattak. And he wondered whether Nasih was beginning to suspect there was more to these gifts than readily appeared. Why would Khattak, a stranger to Iran, be receiving gifts from someone he didn't know? It would make anyone curious.

Though the second letter was a more dangerous possession than the first, Esa couldn't bring himself to destroy it. The letter read as if it had been written by a prisoner at Evin, possibly Zahra's stepdaughter – if any of what Touka Swan had told him was true, something he'd ask Rachel to verify.

As painful as the circumstances of Zahra's death were, he found himself relieved to be shaking off the sense of lethargy that had immobilized him during his stay in Iran. There were two possibilities to consider. The first was that Touka Swan was not who she claimed to be and he was being set up for reasons unknown. The second possibility mirrored the first: the letters were sent not from any political prisoner or jailed activist, but rather by an agent of the Ministry of Intelligence, as a means of entrapment. And Nasih could be that agent, though Khattak found it hard to suspect him of anything more than an interest in Khattak's well-being.

But the fact remained: Khattak was a high-ranking police officer, a status he'd kept to himself when he'd applied for his pilgrimage visa, so he could see the potential for trouble, perhaps even detention – he could be used as a bargaining chip. But he cautioned himself as well. He was an insignificant player in the larger scheme of things, he'd attended the pilgrimage sites faithfully and with vivid interest – and a Canadian officer of any stripe was not of the same value to the regime as an American.

It was possible Touka Swan was an emissary of the Canadian government. But that didn't answer the question of the letters. He couldn't envision a scenario where a prisoner inside Evin would have the freedom to write these letters, and arrange to have them sent to his lodgings. The letters indicated knowledge of his movements. By what means could a prisoner inside Tehran's notorious prison have gained such knowledge?

The letters were a blind of some kind.

And what had the letter writer meant by telling him Zahra had been seeking the letters?

Were there more to come?

And if there were, how could Zahra have known about them?

It was circular logic that made little sense.

He realized if Rachel was able to confirm the basic facts of Zahra Sobhani's death, the most sensible course to pursue would be to return to Tehran to speak with Zahra's mother, and to arrange a viewing of the body, both of which were dangerous propositions. Perhaps that was why Touka had suggested he seek out Roxana's family in Esfahan first.

He looked up at the sound of ice cubes clinking inside a glass. The spring weather was temperate, the trees coming into blossom, a wide variety that included willows, hackberries, walnut trees, and elms. And the Chahar Bagh gardens were famous for their *chinar* plane trees.

Nasih was approaching him, a cold glass of juice on the tray before him. It was an inspired concoction of watermelon and lemonade, made with Shirazi lemons. He invited Nasih to join him beneath the quince tree, wanting to assess how the proprietor of the guesthouse might be connected to the letters.

'Agha Nasih,' he began, making use of the respectful form of address, 'I don't know who is bringing me these gifts. Did you happen to see anyone this time?'

Nasih nodded. His sunburned face was set in welcoming folds. His manner had become less formal in the weeks Khattak had spent in Esfahan, and he answered Khattak with warmth. And without, as far as Khattak could discern, a trace of deception. But that could be a cover, if Nasih was an agent of the Ministry of Intelligence, instead of just the host of his guesthouse.

'It was a young man who left it at the desk. His name was Ali. He said a man paid him to bring you the box, he wasn't told the man's name.'

A request for a description met with little success. Ali was possibly in his twenties or early thirties, dark-eyed, dark-haired, smooth in manner.

And Ali as a name in Iran was as common as Jacob or Matthew in Canada.

Esa thanked Nasih, finished his drink, and decided to walk over to the gardens of Chahar Bagh to make his call to Rachel in private. The time difference wasn't extreme, unless he needed to call her in the evenings, but he did wonder if it was possible that his phone calls were being monitored. The disturbing sensation of being watched had vanished. He didn't recognize anyone in the park as someone he'd spotted before, or observe anyone lingering close enough under the trees to overhear his call.

Rachel's voice was bright with welcome and tinged with surprise.

'Sir, how are you? Have you been enjoying the break?'

They spent several minutes catching up – enough time to learn that his friend, the prosecutor Sehr Ghilzai, was doing well at her new job and seemed happy, a thought that gladdened him. He found himself thinking of Sehr more often these days, a fact that caught him by surprise. He asked after Nate and Audrey Clare, and about Rachel's brother, Zachary. Neither of them mentioned

Esa's sister Rukshanda. Ruksh had asked her brother to leave the family home as soon as their mother had returned from Pakistan, and Esa hadn't spoken to her since. It was a situation he needed to rectify, but he found himself needing time to reflect before he could begin to earn back his sister's trust.

'Can I do anything for you, sir? Send you anything?'

Esa's response was careful. 'I'd like to be kept up to date on the news if you don't mind. There must be many developments I would find interesting, especially as I'm in Esfahan. Nate could probably give you a sense of what I'd like to hear.' And before Rachel could ask for specifics, he hurried on, 'Don't use your personal account, be creative. And be aware that I may also call you from other numbers at odd times, depending on where I'm traveling.'

There was a long pause on the line. He could almost hear Rachel thinking, just as he could hear her munching something over the phone.

'I can do that, sir. But you should come home. Now, without delay.'

So Rachel had heard about Zahra Sobhani's murder. And she was as sharp as ever at putting the pieces together. She was warning him about the severity of the Canadian government's reaction to Zahra's death. A change in the wind had seemed possible with the lifting of sanctions against Iran and the election of a new prime minister in Canada; now relations between both governments would harden. Unless he was able to satisfy Touka Swan's demands, demands that were beginning to seem more urgent.

'There are a few remaining sights I'd like to see, visits I still have to make – but I don't expect to be here much longer.'

'Ah.'

Neither of them spoke Zahra Sobhani's name.

'The sun is bright here, though it's not officially spring.'

'Don't tell me that, sir. Not to be indelicate, but we're freezing our buns off in Toronto.'

Khattak grinned to himself. He rather enjoyed Rachel's unvarnished style of expression.

'You'd be surprised at how important a symbol the sun is in Persian culture. I've learned that it dates back to Zoroastrianism.'

He waited for Rachel to catch on.

'All right,' she agreed. 'Maybe it's time I broadened my horizons. Explored a little bit, asked a few historical questions.'

Well done, Esa thought. She'd realized he wanted her to speak to Max Najafi.

'I'll follow up soon.'

'Fair enough. Don't overdo things, all right?'

Esa thanked her. In their roundabout way, they'd discussed a safer means of communication. He'd reminded her to use her anonymous email accounts, while she'd warned him not to overstep his bounds in a country where their government sustained no diplomatic relations.

He was thinking of his Pakistani passport.

And wondering about the distance to the border.

7

The Container

It happens quickly. Forty boys in a container designed for ten. The pro-democracy activists, the ones who lined up for hours to vote and then to protest the results of the vote. We are terrified. We rattle off our family names. A younger boy, he may be fifteen, has urinated on himself. The stink fills the container. Out of politeness, no one looks. At the beginning, we're all polite. From my name, they can tell what I am, and everyone looks sorry. 'Just tell the truth,' I say. 'Tell them you're not political.' I try to smile, the others look away. 'Tell them you don't know me, you never met me before this minute.' The sad thing is it's the truth. But the truth won't help them now.

8

Rachel rang the doorbell at Winterglass, a house she'd fallen in love with. Its weathered stone and ordered garden gave way to a wildness of lake and sky at the back. The tarnished stone rose from the Bluffs, a temple against a cinereal sky.

Nathan Clare was waiting for her, dressed in shabby tweeds and a jacket he'd buttoned over his sweater. He'd wound a thinly striped scarf about his neck, in a shade that mirrored the bronze of his glasses. He welcomed her with a smile, his warm hands enveloping hers, a gesture that discomfited Rachel. She shoved her hands into the pockets of her parka, following Nate through the grand entrance to a room that led off the kitchen.

Nate had arranged a breakfast of coffee and pastries. Beside these, she could see he'd collected the morning papers and folded them back. He'd been reading the coverage of Zahra Sobhani's death.

Rachel hung her parka over the back of a chair. She helped herself to a slice of cheese strudel as Nathan poured their coffee. The pastry was delicious. She wondered if he'd flown it in from Vienna because the other options were plum cake with hazelnut crumble or apricot-flavored Punschkrapfen fondant. Nothing at Winterglass was served on an ordinary scale.

'You ever hear of this place, Esfahan?'

Rachel enjoyed spending time with Nate, though the opportunities to do so had been few. An old and dear friend of Khattak's, Nathan Clare was a well-known writer and public figure. His father, Loveland Clare, had been an icon of the foreign policy establishment. And the distinction of the Clare name, coupled with Nate's own public stature, had resulted in Nate being asked to serve as an informal envoy, representing the nation's interests at various cultural festivals and summits. Though he'd declined to do so more and more of late, Nate still maintained an influential network of contacts.

Rachel could appreciate why Nate had chosen to distance himself; he valued his independence as a critic of government policy. Over the past few years, he'd argued against the proposed Charter of Values in Quebec, and had made clear his opposition to the Conservative government's stance on the admission of Syrian refugees.

'Let's not take a step back in fear,' Nate had said about the refugee crisis. 'We've come too far, and worked too hard to build our reputation. And then there's the question of decency.'

Rachel wondered if Nathan Clare, whose pedigree placed him in the category of what the former prime minister had termed an 'old stock' Canadian, would have argued so strongly for a multicultural Canada if he hadn't grown up with Esa Khattak, a man whose parents were from Pakistan. The work Loveland Clare had done in his post as ambassador, the work his children were doing now, suggested the answer was yes.

Their paths had crossed several times since Rachel had first met Nathan during the course of an investigation. Initially, she'd been nervous around him, intimidated by his fame, but their relationship had since progressed to an easy camaraderie that made Rachel realize Nate had decided on her as a friend.

Not a girlfriend, she thought, remembering with a blush the hints she had dropped to her father. And she wasn't sure how she felt about the closing off of romantic possibilities. In addition to everything else, Nathan Clare was undeniably charming.

When she'd called Nate to ask about Zahra, he'd invited her to Winterglass, the Clares' magnificent house on the Bluffs.

And now they were seated in the morning room, a tray of

coffee between them, the room a late addition to the glass-and-silver kitchen. An oak table was set before a window enclosed by columns. The white spires of birch trees cast their shadows on the window. The waves of the lake blossomed in the distance, seagulls skimming the surface. It was a cold spring morning, the long grass soaked by a heathery snow.

On a wall to one side, bookcases rose to the ceiling, the room made intimate by the amiable presence of books. Nate's laptop hummed on a writing desk between the bookcases, a vase of ivory tulips beside it. A photograph of Zahra Sobhani flickered from the screen.

'Esfahan,' Nate mused. 'An imperial capital of Persia, at least twice in its fascinating history. I've never been there, but I understand it's an architectural wonder.'

'The boss says he's been hanging out in the gardens. Must be nice to have a real spring.'

Rachel's ardent passion for winter began to wane by the middle of March. Six months was more than enough time to indulge in her fondness for winter activities. She caught Nate's eye. She'd dressed for this meeting with care, pairing a tailored cream blouse with matching slacks, the effect undercut by the giant blue parka hanging over her chair. But she felt fresh and feminine, eager to tackle the challenge of a new case, and no longer over-awed by Nate, lulled by his old-world charm.

'I knew Zahra,' he went on. 'We met at the film festival last year and stayed in touch. She was a fascinating woman. I can't believe this has happened to her.'

Rachel nodded. She couldn't imagine the starkness of a place like Evin prison. She'd seen the dead, she knew the human heart was capable of a monstrous darkness, but she'd never seen the dead brutalized. Or imagined the fragility of a Canadian passport.

It made her all the more worried for Khattak.

When she'd asked him to come home, she'd meant it. He

wasn't just her boss or her partner at Community Policing. He was a measurable part of her life.

'What can you tell me about Zahra? What was she like?'

Nate thought about this, his coffee cup half-raised to his mouth.

'She was lovely. And I don't mean that in the way most men talk about women.'

He spoke as if Rachel understood, Rachel who'd never heard a man describe a woman as lovely. These days you were either hot or not, womanhood reduced to a basic equation Rachel hadn't been able to figure out and didn't see why she should. She wanted to be attractive, everyone did, but it was the smallest part of who she was.

'She was thoughtful and decent, but I don't think anyone would describe Zahra as comfortable. A discussion of culture or film could turn into something urgent. She held you accountable for what you chose to do with your life.'

'That *does* sound uncomfortable. I wonder if it made her any enemies.'

'You're thinking like a detective,' Nate cautioned. 'Wasn't this a political crime?'

'I'm not sure.' Rachel weighed her words. After their call, Khattak had sent her a brief email about the letters left for him at his guesthouse.

Find out what Zahra wanted with the letters.

She'd made a quick guess that proved sound upon reflection.

There were two different sets of letters. The ones Khattak had received, and the ones in Zahra Sobhani's possession. Either she or Khattak would have to track Zahra's letters down.

'What were you able to find out?' she asked Nate.

'You've seen the news, you know there's been an international outcry. It would lead you to think something's being done, that demands are being made on the family's behalf.'

'They're not?'

Nate tilted his head to one side.

'Our government has no formal relationship with the Iranian regime. All diplomatic ties were severed some years ago and haven't been renewed. Publicly, the government is expressing its outrage with some firmness. Privately, it will do nothing.'

'That's not what I've been hearing,' Rachel said.

'Ah, you mean the thaw? The plans to reopen our embassy in Tehran? Yes, I'd heard that, too. There were rumblings – all of which depended on the terms of the nuclear agreement being upheld and sanctions being lifted. Things would have progressed,' he mused. 'Canadian companies are keen to get back to business in Iran, something Zahra's death will complicate.'

'What about this woman the boss mentioned in his email? Where does she fit into things?' Rachel checked her phone. 'Touka Swan. Helen.'

'The next time you hear from him, ask him to send you a photograph. I've asked around. Her name is not unknown in diplomatic circles. She has no official standing that anyone will admit to, so she may be intelligence. And Touka Swan may be an alias. I wonder if she was sent ahead to smooth the way – for the day the doors of our embassy reopen.'

Rachel thought this was possible. Khattak had described a sense of being threatened to cooperate by Touka. And of being bribed. Rachel smiled inwardly at the thought. Clearly, this woman knew nothing about Khattak.

'Then what do we actually know about Zahra Sobhani's murder? Why would Swan want proof of this character Radan's involvement, if we're hoping to rebuild an official relationship with Iran? Wouldn't it be better to sweep things under the rug?'

Nate flipped through a notebook in his hands. 'Max Najafi is raising a stink, which is only to be expected. He's calling his mother's murder an extra-judicial killing and demanding the government intervene. He's said he'll take it to the International Criminal Court. The court won't have jurisdiction over

Zahra's murder, but it's an embarrassment for our government nonetheless. Pursuing Radan may be a way of keeping him quiet while working to re-establish diplomatic ties.'

Rachel took a long sip of her coffee, thinking this over.

'Not if you can't do anything with Radan once you have him. It seems flimsy to me. And it seems like Zahra was inconvenient.'

Nate nodded his agreement.

'It could be for leverage, then. To be used at a later date when something critical is at stake – perhaps a business opportunity or trade deal that favors us.'

Rachel looked at the photograph on the laptop screen.

'The murder of a human rights advocate seems critical to me.' Behind Nate's shoulder, Zahra's expression in the photograph was lively, her mouth smiling, the expression of her eyes commanding. She was as well-known for her films as she was for the clarity behind them.

The state should not murder its own citizens.

Rachel shook her head in disgust. 'I wouldn't have had the guts to make those films. She must have thought she had the government's protection, but we seem quick to trade her away.'

'We don't know that for sure, though I've learned not to doubt your instincts.'

Nate leafed through his notebook again. When Rachel had called for his help, she'd asked him to sound out his friends at the Department of Foreign Affairs.

No one had warned him off. That didn't mean it wasn't a matter of time.

'She arrived in Iran at the end of December. She made the rounds that every family member of a detainee makes: the Ministry of Intelligence, the judiciary, the prosecutor's office, the police chief of Tehran, the offices of human rights groups that haven't been shuttered. Ten days ago, she was able to obtain an interview with a representative of the Supreme Leader.'

Rachel snorted into her coffee.

'Sounds like he should be running an army in North Korea.'

Nate didn't laugh.

'No one holds more power in Iran. To have gotten that interview, Zahra must have had some highly placed contacts.'

'Do we know why she wanted to meet him?'

'She asked to discuss the case of Roxana Najafi – her ex-husband's daughter from his second marriage.'

Rachel mulled this over. Maybe that wasn't the only thing Zahra had hoped to discuss. Maybe she'd been searching for the mysterious letters. Or used the letters to some end they didn't know. She wished Khattak's secret correspondent had been less oblique.

'Three days later, she was detained at Evin. Maybe there's a connection there. If she was granted that meeting –' She looked at Nate, the question in her eyes.

'She was,' he confirmed.

'I wonder if connections were what got her that meeting.'

'What do you mean?'

'I doubt the office of the Supreme Leader grants interviews on the welfare of political prisoners. I'm wondering if Zahra had some leverage of her own. If she got the meeting because she had something over them. Or if she knew something that was of interest to the Supreme Leader's office. And that's what got her killed. That's what put her at Evin, where someone wanted her dead. And if that's the case – we'll have to figure out why. What did she know that someone found so dangerous?' In short, sharp sentences she told Nate about Esa's letters.

'Esa's burning the letters, I hope.'

'I hope so, too.' Though in Khattak's position, Rachel would have thought of the letters as evidence, she wouldn't have destroyed them.

She stood up, stuffing herself back into her parka.

'Where are you going?' Nate put his notebook away.

'You're coming with me,' she said. 'The only way we'll figure out how she got that meeting is if we arrange to speak to her son.'

Nate gathered up his things while Rachel took their mugs to the sink.

'You think Max Najafi will talk to you?'

She gave him a breezy smile.

'Maybe, maybe not. But given that he's trying to get the government's attention, I'd lay odds he'll want to talk to you.'

9

The Welcoming Committee

You know what to expect at Evin. They beat your feet, you walk the gauntlet past the locked cells to the interrogation building. They keep you for hours, then you're thrown into a cell to scratch your name into a wall, or possibly to sleep. At the interrogation, a man walks behind you out of sight, clicking his beads between his fingers, while another man asks questions by thumping his fists on the table. They may or may not beat you, the violence is psychological. But in Kahrizak, things are different. The beatings begin at 6:00 a.m. and continue until the sun sets. No one is stronger than anyone else, everyone cries, everyone bleeds. And as our bones crack and organs burst, the guards begin to laugh.

10

Max Najafi shared a home with his mother in Summerhill, a Toronto neighborhood near the old railway station, characterized by Edwardian-style homes and the occasional renovated property.

Zahra Sobhani's house was in a state of mild disrepair, lending a scruffy charm to a beautifully landscaped garden yet to come into bloom. Kaffir lime trees bordered the stone driveway. A flat-bottomed swing attached by a set of metal chains hung from the sturdiest branch of an oak tree in the center of the garden.

As Rachel and Nate stood side by side on the porch waiting for an answer to the doorbell, Rachel couldn't shake the feeling they were bearers of bad tidings, though Max had already been informed of his mother's death. And he hadn't been left to grieve on his own. A line of cars was parked on the street in front of his house, the driveway blocked by three more.

When he answered the door, she recognized him from his picture in the newspaper. She flashed her ID and introduced Nate.

Max was dressed in black, his face unshaven, his eyelids puffy with lack of sleep. Past him down a long corridor, Rachel could see a room filled with visitors. Men and women dressed in black, their faces somber with the courtesies of grief, while a young woman in a black dress offered a tray of tea glasses around the room.

Candles were lit on a side table before a portrait of Zahra. The windows were open, and two men stood near them, smoking and speaking in low voices. A television program ran mutely in the background. From time to time, a woman would sob aloud.

Max invited them into a cold and spacious room at the front of the house, where a pair of rattan chairs were flanked by a low-cushioned seating area, broad enough for several people to stretch out. Persian string instruments reminiscent of sitars were stationed at intervals around the room, along with a drum called the *tombak*. In pride of place at the center of the room was an exquisitely restored Bösendorfer piano, the underside of its lid painted a creamy white. Against this backdrop, a flight of blue starlings encircled a vegetal vine. On either side of the piano's fallboard, two sets of initials were inscribed in inlaid panels. *MN* and *RN*.

Above this, a scrollwork held an unfinished composition.

Nate wandered over to it, his gold eyes flinty with concentration. Rachel could sense how badly he wanted to touch the keys.

When Max called to the other room in Farsi, a young man served them tea without milk. Rachel examined Max's face. He gripped his glass, staring at Rachel in turn.

'Why have you come?' He frowned over at Nate, still lingering at the piano. 'I don't see how the local police can help me.'

In the photographs Rachel had studied while bringing herself up to date on Zahra's murder, Max Najafi had seemed possessed of an inarticulate, dreamlike quality, like a stargazer searching the skies. She'd seen the look before, on her mother's face, when Lillian had played the piano sequestered in the basement.

The basement was Lillian's retreat. Seated before a shabby piano, she would play Schubert, Liszt, Tchaikovsky, the Polish composer Karol Szymanowski. Rachel would sit at her mother's feet, enthralled, until her father's return from work signaled the end of their private rapprochement. If the piano had been out of tune, if the pages of Lillian's sheet music were out of order, neither of them had minded.

And as Lillian had played, a familiar look would come into her eyes – a look Rachel had mistaken for abstraction. Max's eyes held that same ethereal quality: he was hearing the music in his head.

Nate had taken a seat on the piano bench. At a brief nod of permission, his fingers strayed over the Bösendorfer's keys, in a delicate run of notes.

'I'm very sorry for your loss, Mr. Najafi. Given your mother's talents, it's a more than ordinary loss.'

Max was distracted by Nate's desultory wanderings at the piano. Rachel recognized Chopin's Nocturne in C-sharp Minor, its soft introduction followed by broken portamento chords that Nate intentionally dampened. She was glad he hadn't chosen 'Tristesse' or Ravel's 'Pavane for a Dead Princess', too close to Max Najafi's pain. Halfway through, Nate broke off – perhaps recognizing the music as an intrusion into another's sorrow, rather than a tribute.

Max drew a sharp breath. He turned his head from the piano.

'No loss is ordinary,' he said.

'Tell me about your mother. I know she was a gifted filmmaker. Is that why she was in Iran? To make another film?'

Najafi seemed to consider many different responses before he answered.

'It was her life's purpose. She wanted to do a follow-up to the last film. She said the regime had broken the bones of the movement.'

'What was there to follow up?' Rachel asked cautiously. 'Do you mean a sequel to *A Requiem for Hope*? Would the Iranian authorities have allowed her to make such a film, given the reception to the first one?'

The widely lauded film had been a damning indictment of the regime's repression of human rights, embarrassing the nation on the world's stage and isolating it further.

'The story wasn't finished.'

'Of course it wasn't,' Nate agreed. He was studying the sheet music in his hands. 'The election was just the beginning. Your mother must have wanted to know the fate of the protesters. She must have hoped there was something more she could do.'

Rachel took this up. 'I believe she was asking about your stepsister. I understand your mother had a meeting at the office of the Supreme Leader.'

Najafi's face went blank.

'You mean my *sister*, Roxana.' And then a note of excitement crept into his voice. 'How could you know this?' he demanded. 'Do you have sources in Iran? Someone who could help?'

This was a question Rachel preferred not to answer, she wished she'd been more discreet. She nodded at Nate, who began to play the untitled composition, his fingers tentative as they worked through the notes.

'We have sources here, Mr. Najafi. But we'd be in a better position to help if we knew a little more about what your mother was doing in Iran. She couldn't have expected cooperation from the Iranian government in making a film that documents their abuses. Do you know why she wanted the meeting? Or what she was doing at Evin?'

Max placed his glass on the table, giving the impression of a man whose strength was held in check, so finely restrained were his movements.

'Roxana has been in and out of Evin since the stolen election. She was a member of the opposition, one of the first to join the Green Movement. She thought her green bracelet gave her magical powers, powers of invincibility. It didn't take her long to find out otherwise. The Greens believe in non-violence. The regime takes advantage of that. So, of course, my mother was seeking Roxana's release. When we visited Iran, Roxana would always stay with us. She wanted to be close to us. My mother mentored her, she loved her as if she were her own daughter. They shared a deep love of Iran.' Max's face clouded over. 'And the same independent spirit. They were determined to bring about a change.'

'Is that why Roxana was imprisoned? Did she protest the election results?'

The melody Nate was playing raised the hairs on the back of Rachel's neck, a supernal quality to its dreamlike pianissimo. If she didn't know better, she would have called it a mild strain of optimism.

Max answered Rachel with an effort that appeared to cost him something. He was listening to Nate play, his musical sense engaged.

'She was a protester like many others,' he admitted. 'But she also put her talents at the service of the movement.' Pride colored his voice. 'Roxana is a musician in her own right – we worked closely together, shaping each other's music. She was tired of "Yar-e-Dabestani" as an anthem, so she wrote her own songs for the movement. The entire nation was lifted by her music. Everyone knew – knows Roxana.'

Rachel looked at the initials inscribed on the piano's fallboard.

MN

RN

Max Najafi, Roxana Najafi. But why the name Max? It didn't sound like an Iranian name to Rachel. When she asked him, he scowled.

'I want nothing that belongs to Iran, nothing that comes from the mullahs. My father called me Mahmood, you should call me Max. I left Mahmood behind with my father.'

'Where is your father now?' Rachel asked.

'I don't know, and I don't care.'

'Your sister didn't come to Canada with you?' At the piano, Nate was doing something to the melody, something she wasn't sure she liked, turning its soft notes dark.

Max noticed, too.

'Why did you play that? The piece isn't finished.'

Nate let his hands fall away from the keys.

'I'm sorry,' he said, his gold eyes as languorous as the music he'd played. 'I didn't mean to offend you. The direction of your composition seemed to suggest it. I was thinking of your mother,' he added. 'And it just happened.'

Max looked from Rachel to Nate.

'I know you,' he said, rising to his feet. 'You're not with the police. You're Nathan Clare, the writer. My mother spoke of you to me.'

'Yes,' Nate said. 'I've come to pay my respects.'

The fogginess of Max's grief sharpened into focus.

'Please,' he said. 'You have to help me, Mr. Clare. You can raise the profile of this, I know the government will listen to you – you often work on their behalf.'

Nate removed himself from the piano. He gripped the hand Max extended to him.

'Of course, I'll help in any way I can. I'm just not sure what you think I can do.'

'The Iranian authorities.' Max's eyes were wet. 'Please,' he said again. 'You must ask the Canadian government to insist on a confrontation. You must ask them to have my mother's body released so we can hold her funeral here.'

'I thought her body was returned to her family in Tehran.'

Max nodded in earnest. 'It was. And my grandmother and my uncles had a doctor perform an examination. That's how we learned how she'd died.' He swallowed painfully. 'We knew they had brutalized her. But as soon as we made the news public –'

He lurched away, his back to Rachel.

The girl in the black dress appeared at the doorway. She murmured in Farsi, a soft-spoken plea of some kind. Max shrugged her off. But when Nate put one hand on his shoulder, he turned back to them.

'Before I could make arrangements to transport my mother's remains, agents from the Ministry of Intelligence appeared at my grandmother's house. They went to the morgue and confiscated the body.'

His black eyes burned with an impotent eloquence.

'My mother has disappeared.'

They stayed for several minutes, though Max could tell them little else. Nate made promises to inquire with his contacts in government, while Rachel followed up on Roxana's status.

'Anything you can tell me would be helpful. Did your mother mention any letters to you?'

Max looked surprised. 'You know about the letters? What do they have to do with my mother's murder? It's clear she was killed by agents of the regime.'

Nate and Rachel exchanged a glance.

'We don't know,' Rachel said with care. 'We thought the letters may have been the reason she wanted to meet the Supreme Leader. Perhaps there was something in the letters that would have helped secure your sister's release.'

Max shook his head. 'No, they were nothing, a tangent. They've been missing for many years – letters from a former prime minister of Iran to one of his closest friends, a writer and opposition activist. They had nothing to do with Roxana. If my mother *had* found the letters, it would have been the talk of the whole country.'

'Who was the activist?' Nate asked. 'Who was the prime minister?'

From the suppressed excitement in his voice, Rachel thought Nate had some idea of the answer.

'They were Mossadegh's letters to Dariush Forouhar. Does that mean anything to you?' Max's voice ripened into scorn. 'Of course not. They're no more relevant than my mother's obsession with the Shah of Iran. Before she left for Iran, she requested archival footage of the Shah's coronation from the library. The coronation was fifty years ago – it has nothing to do with my mother's death.'

He moved to a rosewood desk behind the Bösendorfer, rummaging through its drawers. After a minute, his search proved fruitful. He extended the card in his hand to Rachel.

'I don't know why it matters, but you're not the only one to ask about my mother. You should speak to this woman, I told her about the letters and the coronation. But you'll remember, won't you? Time is moving against us.'

Nate bowed his head. He understood what Max was saying – the longer they took to act, the less chance there was of recovering Zahra's body.

'You must come back,' Max said. He fingered the sheet music Nate had left on the rack. 'I would like to discuss my composition with you, in memory of my mother.'

Nate promised he would.

Rachel read the name on the card. She supposed she shouldn't have been surprised.

It was Vicky D'Souza, a reporter Khattak knew.

Rachel realized she should ask if she could search the house for Zahra's personal effects: a diary or her notes on the sequel to her film. Perhaps she'd written about the letters or the Shah's coronation.

Max had taken Nate's place at the piano.

Slumped against the music, he began to cry.

11

This is a path of long and grave suffering.

I say this in parentheses to myself. They expect encouragement from the writer's child, so to them I'm optimistic. I tell them my cell has a window – it allows me to measure the days. I tell them the world is changing – they've been the ones to change it.

I sing them that same old, pointless song – Roxana's song – the song that brought us to this pass, like the letters no one will speak of, the letters that were burned.

I sense your reluctance to act, but this isn't what I've been told of you. I've heard you're a man of conscience. I've learned our lives matter to you, you won't turn the other cheek, although your name is Esa.

Do my jokes surprise you? It's not possible to spend one's life in tears, even in a place as dismal as Evin. My father's strength infuses me – he died and lived behind these walls, why should I do any less? He'd want me to do more.

So I look for the light, Inspector Khattak.

I look for the Light and I find it.

12

Naqsh-e Jahan, the pattern of the world.

Khattak made his way through Naqsh-e Jahan square, the second-largest public square in the world, named for the architectural glories stationed along its perimeter.

It housed the finest jewels of the Safavid empire, the Masjid-e Shah and the Masjid-e Sheikh Lotfallah competing for glory with the Qaysarieh Portal and the mystifying geometrics of the Kakh-e Ali Qapu, each a monument to the imagination of Shah Abbas the Great.

Everywhere Khattak's eye fell, there was beauty. From the turquoise domes inscribed with floral motifs, to the elderly husband and wife feeding stray cats in the alleyways opposite the square.

Khattak thought of his visit to the tomb of Rumi in Konya, some years before. A blue-ribboned tower had paid homage to the sandy dome above the tomb. And in the building that housed the tomb, a sense of pressure and inclusion, tourists and worshippers entwined. At dusk, he'd played soccer with children in the park across from the tomb, intrigued by the notion that the dead were a welcome presence among the living.

The Naqsh-e Jahan captured something of that feeling, the centuries inching along, the glories of long-dead empires a commonplace of the present.

Fountains played in the afternoon light, families thronging the souvenir shops set up on either side of the arcades that ran along the square. Khattak passed through the Qaysarieh Portal at the north-east end of the square, seeking the domed arcades known as *timchehs* that housed the bazaar's trades. He was in search of a gift appropriate to a bereaved family, he thought white flowers were befitting. But he wondered if Roxana Najafi's family were grieving Zahra's death or only Roxana's imprisonment.

Zahra was the former wife. It was unlikely Khattak's intervention or his questions would be welcomed by her ex-husband's second family. Touka Swan had told him to try.

He felt a hand tug at his elbow.

When he turned, a woman was standing in a shaft of light that spilled from the apertures of the bazaar. The woman stepped closer, his vision cleared, and he realized it was the young woman from Varzaneh, the woman with the sickle-shaped scar at her eyebrow, the one who'd blown him a kiss. At once, he was wary of the coincidence.

She began to walk along the handicrafts lane, moving in and out of broad strips of light that lanced the arcade. She crooked her fingers behind her back, beckoning Khattak to follow. He matched her pace, keeping a little away. She stopped at a display of blue ceramics, locked in a breakfront cabinet. Khattak watched her reflection in a mirror behind the artisan's head.

A chic black head scarf had slipped all the way back, a fringe of black hair artfully styled across her forehead. She wore a tight black jacket and matching skirt over her leggings, without a chador, a messenger bag strapped across one shoulder. Her cheeks and lips were tastefully rouged. He was close enough to smell her ambergris perfume.

She exchanged a few words with the tradesman. He held out a tulip-shaped vase for her inspection. She concluded her bargaining in a matter of minutes, though the vase was too unwieldy to be carried. She smiled at Khattak, indicating he should help her.

Now they walked along together, the young woman offering her thanks.

'You've been following me?' Khattak murmured in English.

'Or perhaps your stars have aligned, and wherever you go, the women of the city fall into your arms.'

She spoke in English as well, teasing him.

Khattak could think of nothing to say in response.

She gave him the impish smile again.

'I hear you've been looking for something.' She fiddled with the latches on her bag. 'My name is Taraneh, I might be able to help you.' When he didn't say anything, afraid to commit himself, she went on, 'Of course, it's not me you're interested in, it's my friend, Nasreen.'

Khattak made his face a blank.

Was Nasreen the woman with mournful eyes? And how had he given himself away when he'd scarcely glanced at her?

Taraneh unlatched her bag. She took a book from it, its title obscured from Khattak's view.

'Don't worry,' she said airily. 'It's the most natural thing in the world for a man to notice a woman. If it's any comfort, she noticed you as well.'

Khattak shifted the package with the vase in his hands.

'I don't know what you mean,' he said, a faint color in his face.

She grinned. 'Of course you do, but that's a matter for another time. Take the book, Inspector Khattak, and give me the vase. But be careful with it, won't you? It's not the kind of thing you should carry around.' She nodded at his jacket. 'It's far more dangerous than your little book of poems.'

Her hands brushed his as she made the exchange, quite deliberately, Khattak thought.

He looked at the title of the book.

It was a hardbound translation of the sociologist Ali Shariati's famous essay.

On the Plight of Oppressed People.

He looked up.

'Did you send me the letters?' he asked, his voice sharp.

Taraneh's smile acquired a fixed quality.

'You were looking for this,' she repeated. 'If you want to talk about the essay with like-minded friends, you can find us at the Hezar Jarib dovecote on Saturday. We're always there, just after dawn when the light is best. Ask the gatekeeper to let you in, he's happy to accommodate tourists.'

She took the vase from him and disappeared down the arcade. Within minutes, she was lost to view but not before he'd heard her whisper.

'I'm a messenger, Inspector Khattak. I don't know of any letters.'

He moved out of the light of the main arcade, finding his way to the embellished entrance of the Qaysarieh Portal, a symphony of blue tiles against the faded stone. When he opened the book Taraneh had given him, rose petals fell into his hands. He let them flutter to the ground, searching for another letter. Something shifted within the book.

Keeping his shoulder to the wall, Khattak shielded the contents of the book with his hands. A thin plastic sleeve peeked out between the pages. It contained a flash drive. He closed the book with a snap, slid it inside his jacket pocket, shifted away from the wall, and ambled away. He found himself in the lane of the carpet-sellers, scanning the crowd.

He stopped for a drink of pomegranate juice, then turned down another aisle. No one followed. He purchased a mother-of-pearl box from a nearby vendor, declining an invitation for tea with a smile, his heart beating fast.

Taraneh knew his name and his profession, just like the author of the letters.

None of it had been a coincidence, perhaps not even the drive to Varzaneh. It was possible someone had told Nasih to suggest the bus ride through the desert to Esa. Just as it was possible Nasih knew who was leaving the letters at the guesthouse. The young women at the mosque in Varzaneh, poised inside his line of vision – planned, also – but why?

He felt the weight of Shariati's book in his breast pocket, and understood its significance. Shariati had been a sociologist of religion, whose views were often described as a branch of liberation theology. A prominent intellectual of the twentieth century, Shariati had been an advocate for social change, until his mysterious death in exile in England. He was an enormously popular teacher; his lectures had politicized a generation of students who yearned for a modernist reading of Islam, but his thoughtful critique of his own society had earned him an eighteen-month prison term in solitary confinement.

Shariati's writings were among the most widely known of his period, eloquent in the religious argot of his society, while influenced by his studies in the West. To Shariati, the struggle for a just society was meant to be ongoing – it hadn't ended at the battle of Karbala in A.D. 680, with the martyrdom of Hossein, the most significant figure of Shia Islam.

Hossein had refused to bow to the tyranny of Yazid, the corrupt usurper of the caliphate, and he and his family had been killed at Yazid's order. To invoke the battle of Karbala, as Shariati had done, was to be conscious of suffering wherever it took place, and to take up the struggle in Hossein's place.

Every day is Ashura, every place is Karbala.

Shariati's adoption of this maxim had led to his life of imprisonment and exile. *On the Plight of Oppressed People* was his most personal essay, morally exacting, lyrical in expression.

Why had Taraneh given it to Esa?

Touka Swan had told him someone would contact him, she may have sent Taraneh to him, without mentioning the young woman during their meeting. She may have been testing his interest in Zahra's death, or his commitment to resolve it – a reworking of her earlier threat.

He had to remind himself of the dangers of intercession. He had lied to the Iranian government by omission and could easily be deemed a foreign agent. There were others languishing in

Iranian prisons whose actions were more innocent than his own.

He retraced his steps through the gardens, the scent of wisteria hanging heavy. The visit to Roxana's family would have to wait. First he had to see what was on the drive.

And as always at such times, he wished Rachel were with him.

Esa was disingenuous with Nasih. He didn't regret it. It would protect Nasih, if he was asked to account for Esa's activities in Esfahan. And if Nasih was involved with the Ministry of Intelligence, the less he guessed about Esa's activities, the better.

He asked Nasih if he could borrow a copy of the Turkish drama *The Magnificent Century* that was currently the rage in Iran. To watch it, Nasih would have to loan him a laptop, as Esa had chosen not to travel with his own. His host was happy enough to do so. He suggested Khattak watch the program in the privacy of his room, out of the sunlight in the courtyard.

Esa wondered if Nasih had seen through his ruse, if Nasih was involved with the letters in some way or was connected to Taraneh and Nasreen. But he was finding it more and more unlikely. Another letter had come for Esa during his visit to the square, printed in the same hand as the others. Nasih told him a young man had left a box of melons at the door. The letter had been stapled to the underside of the paper that lined the box – the paper hadn't been disturbed.

Looking at Nasih's open and trusting face, Khattak had beseeched him to accept the gift of fruit. The polite demurrals had gone back and forth in the rituals of *taruf* – something Khattak's parents would have called *thakaluf*, based on the same principle of hospitality. Khattak's request for the Turkish drama had settled the issue. Nasih could accept the gift because it was in his power to bestow another.

Khattak retreated to his room with the laptop.

He attached the flash drive, conscious he was holding his breath.

Without warning, a series of black-and-white images appeared on the screen. There was no menu or introduction. At first, he wasn't sure what he was seeing. Then the angle of the camera shifted to reveal a concrete barrier topped by spikes that stretched beyond the lens. At the foot of the barrier, a few men and a group of women in black chadors milled against the barrier. Beyond them, on a rugged mound, several women were seated together, their hands fastened about picture frames, their faces turned to the wall.

The camera focused on a gatehouse.

Yazdashtagah Evin, Khattak read.

Evin House of Detention.

A car pulled up to the group of women, disgorging another woman in a black chador. The camera zoomed in on the woman's face, and Khattak recognized her as Zahra Sobhani.

He could just make out the canvas strap that cut across her chador. It looked like Taraneh's messenger bag. When she moved away from the car, he saw the professional camera slung around her neck. She lifted it with both hands and pointed it in a rapid-fire barrage of photography – at the women near the gatehouse, the women at the barrier. When she tilted the camera up, he realized she had aimed it at the watchtower.

The contraband nature of the footage became clear.

He was watching the security feed from the watchtower of Evin prison.

A throng of women began to gather round, crowding Zahra, importuning her with pleas, having guessed she was a person of importance, someone who could challenge the authorities.

Then others came. Men from the crowd, other men with guns. There was a shout from the watchtower, movement along the perimeter. The camera bounced from Zahra's hands, the strap yanked from her neck. She put a hand to her neck, testing the abrasion, panic shadowing her face. The security feed stayed focused on her.

The car that had driven her to the gates honked its horn, six staccato bursts.

Zahra tried to break away. She was reaching for someone, her hands stretched out, her lips whispering. More noise. Cries of dismay, orders shouted from the gates.

The entrance to the gatehouse opened, dislodging four guards with guns and a tall man in a suit that fit him like a glove. They began to push through the crush of people, the camera panning over them. Veils flapped in the wind like spiraling shrouds. Some of the women fell, others beat at their breasts, sending up a lamentation. In seconds, Zahra was surrounded. Hands that struggled to free her were beaten back.

Zahra stood her ground, gesticulating with her hands. One hand pointed to the watchtower. She shouted indistinctly at the camera. An arm snaked around her throat, pressing back. She was handcuffed, a hood thrown over her head.

Two of the guards turned on the group of women, beating them back with sticks.

One woman held up the picture of a boy, sixteen or seventeen years old. She cried out when the guards ripped the photograph from her hands. The woman collapsed in the midst of the others. Arms reached out to catch her.

In the noise and confusion, Zahra disappeared. Esa skipped the footage back and checked the picture again. The camera hadn't shifted, Zahra was no longer there.

Its tires screaming, the car in the background reversed and sped away.

The driver had never gotten out.

Esa watched the footage a dozen times over. He knew now it was footage of Zahra's last day of freedom, the last time anyone outside Evin had seen her alive. He couldn't decipher the sound on the drive, intuiting the course of events from the crowd's increasing clamor.

The guards had moved swiftly, well versed in the transitioning of prisoners from the space outside the prison to the other side of the gatehouse. They must have taken Zahra to Ward 209, to run the gauntlet of Evin's interrogators.

He wondered if Zahra had made demands. Or if her interrogators had considered her formidable reputation before setting in motion the chain of events that had led to her death.

One week ago, Zahra had been pursuing the question of Evin's political detainees, arguing for Roxana's release. Now Zahra was dead, and Roxana's fate was unknown.

If the regime had murdered Zahra, whose international renown and dual citizenship should have kept her safe, what hope was there for Roxana? Political detainees were powerless, buried behind the walls of prisons like Evin.

In Esfahan, Esa had been at peace as the days passed like a dream, while in a prison on a hill, others were subjected to incalculable cruelty, sealed off in the muffled places of the world, forgotten by all save those who loved them. Though he'd worked as a police officer nearly all his adult life, it seemed remote from Esa's experience, incomprehensible and opaque. He felt a sickness in his stomach at the thought of what Zahra had endured, what so many prisoners endured at the hands of men trained to break and kill.

He wondered if Zahra had ever asked herself the question he found himself facing now.

What do strangers owe each other in this life?

He had a laptop and an internet connection, but he knew better than to search for information on Zahra or the prison. The connection could be traced, the host at his guesthouse endangered. The footage on the drive hadn't been doctored, he'd studied it closely, analyzed the movement of the images, the sound.

There were men in the video – guards, but also participants in the crowd, some of whose faces he couldn't see. From Zahra's documentary, he knew the people gathered outside the prison would be petitioners whose loved ones had been detained. Originally built to house a few hundred prisoners, Evin now detained close to fifteen thousand inmates: those convicted of crimes such as theft, rape, or murder, along with high-profile political detainees.

Evin had been used to break the back of the Green Movement, to silence criticism of an election the government denied had been stolen, despite announcing Ahmadinejad's victory before the polls had closed. However broken the system, Iranians had prized their right to vote, expecting their ballots to count. But even with a hastily conducted recount, widely favored reformist candidates had failed to win their ridings. If nothing else was understood about the election, this much was clear: the votes of the Iranian people had been dismissed, the result foreordained.

And the storm that had swept the country in the election's aftermath had galvanized the Green Movement. Popular candidates like Mir Hossein Mousavi and Mehdi Karroubi – who had been leading figures of the 1979 revolution – became closely aligned in the aftermath of the election. Mousavi had used the color green as his emblem: it signified democratic change within an Islamic framework. The use of the color green had been a carefully calibrated strategy. As the color of Islam, the regime had been challenged where it was most vulnerable: in its claim to embody Islamic authenticity.

Mousavi's message had resonated with nearly every segment of Iranian society. And for six months after the election, Iranians had come together to protest the theft of their votes, cohering into a national movement. One year later, Mousavi and Karroubi had published a charter for the movement.

The Green Movement's charter stated its foremost goals as freedom, social justice, and the formation of a legitimate national government that represented the will of the people. It referenced Iran's earliest constitutional iterations, dating back to 1906. It called for the rejection of totalitarian rule, and the strengthening of civil society. Its chief values were human dignity and the advocacy of change through non-violence.

It referred to itself as the Green Path of Hope.

And as such, it was an existential threat to the regime.

Zahra had worked tirelessly for the release of members of the Green Movement from Evin. But she'd been defeated by Iran's Orwellian judicial system, where attorneys were not permitted to meet with their clients, and the charges brought against protesters allowed scant opportunity for defense. These charges included insulting the holy sanctities, colluding to harm national security, and spreading propaganda against the system. Any activity could fall within these parameters, while for the prosecutor's office, the accusation alone was enough – there was no demonstrable standard of proof required, leaving protesters' families without recourse.

Zahra must have known she wouldn't have been allowed to record Evin's notorious abuses. Had she been hoping to find a friend among the stone-faced men at the prison? Or had she been promised a meeting with Roxana? Why, then, had she taken her camera?

The one thing Esa knew was the drive couldn't stay in his possession. Nor could he leave it at the guesthouse, Touka had confirmed he was being watched. And since it was too dangerous to keep, he would need to send the footage to Rachel: she might find something he'd missed.

Barsam Radan is implicated, Touka had said. *We just need proof.*

He didn't know what Radan looked like, but there was no such proof on the drive. His presence on the footage wouldn't establish a clear link to Zahra's murder, it wasn't a smoking gun, it had no power to change the status quo.

There was the most recent letter to consider as well.

This is a path of long and grave suffering.

He recognized the line from a famous ruling of Ayatollah Montazeri's, a reformist cleric who'd lived long enough to witness the total failure of the 1979 revolution he'd once championed. After the election, Montazeri had issued a groundbreaking fatwa: he'd argued that a political system was automatically annulled the moment it lost the people's trust. Nor was it the people's burden to establish the misconduct of their leaders, as they lacked the power and resources of the state. Rather, it was the ruling regime that was faced with the burden of demonstrating its legitimacy.

Ayatollah Montazeri was the Green Movement's conscience.

Khattak considered what it meant that his correspondent had referenced Montazeri's ruling. This most recent letter and the others as well, he presumed, were encoded. There were clues for him to pick out, clues that would point him to a revelation.

He pondered the mention of letters that threatened the government.

Were they connected to Zahra's murder?

The recent string of events that had interrupted his stay in Esfahan were probably connected. Zahra Sobhani's death. Touka Swan. The appearance of Taraneh and Nasreen, the two women from Varzaneh. The mysterious letters and the young man who delivered them. And the security footage from Evin.

He watched it again, this time focused on Zahra. And this time, he caught it. A hurried movement, a sleight of hand just before the camera was yanked from her neck.

She had pressed her hand to her neck for a reason.

But he couldn't quite see what had happened next.

He debated what step to take.

He would have to call Rachel, this was too much to put in an email. And he needed to hear from her in turn, but there was also more. If he was going to trust Touka Swan, he would need to show up at the dovecote. Taraneh was the key to a much larger puzzle.

Or the young woman was an agent of the regime.

13

The Cell

We're packed together in the cell. We sleep standing up, warming each other's bodies. We whisper to each other, we make promises. We assure each other our families are strong, no one is wailing at a grave site, beating at his chest. We say our families are searching for us, the guards won't dare to beat us. Someone says his father took him to the police to demonstrate his innocence. The Green Movement knows – they're working on our behalf. There are lawyers at the prosecutor's office, Karroubi has written to the judges, Mousavi is convening a press conference, and so on. The innocent boy starts sobbing. He's the one who pissed himself, the youngest in the cell. I tell him, he's the first who'll go home. 'But remember, you don't know me, you've never met me – it's what's keeping you alive.'

14

Following Nasih's instructions, Khattak purchased a phone at a corner market four blocks from the guesthouse. It was late evening, and the temperature had dropped. He was grateful he'd worn his coat, not least for its many pockets. A pretty girl at the counter smiled at him. When he smiled back, she blushed ruby red, startled into dropping his change on the counter. A wave of his hand indicated she should keep it.

He turned south, away from the store, walking several more blocks from his usual haunts. He crossed the magnificent square again, this time ducking into a restaurant in the shadow of the Masjid-e Shah. It was noisy and boisterous, packed with tour groups drawn to its traditional courtyard and gorgeous ornamentation – a fountain at play, a painted ceiling with a mirrored inlay, a wall of breathtakingly blue *kashani* tiles under a vaulted roof.

Khattak welcomed the noise. It would drown out his conversation with Rachel. He ordered *khoresht-e alu*, chicken stewed with plums, and waited for Rachel to answer her phone. She sounded groggy when she did. It was 3:30 in the morning in Toronto. When she recognized Esa, her voice warmed up.

'Are you all right, sir?'

He took a sip of mint tea, bringing her up to date on recent events without mentioning names. Her voice dropped when she heard about the women in Varzaneh, and his encounter with Taraneh at the bazaar.

'Normally, you being stalked by attractive women wouldn't

surprise me, sir, but this is Iran. They're hardly going to hand you a phone number on a napkin.'

Esa was both warmed and embarrassed by the compliment.

'Iran is no different from anywhere else, except that young people have to be more creative when it comes to expressing their interest.'

'You don't say, sir. What form does that interest take, then?'

He caught the sardonic note in Rachel's voice and chuckled.

'I'm afraid to ask what you're imagining, Rachel. What about rose petals pressed between the pages of a book?'

He thought of them not just because of the secret letters. Taraneh had also used them as a cover. But he was reminded of his favorite film, Mohsen Makhmalbaf's *A Moment of Innocence*, where a similar courtship had taken place. The director favored a neo-realist style of filmmaking, and he'd instructed his amateur actors to recreate an incident from his personal history.

As a young man, Makhmalbaf had tried to steal a policeman's gun at a protest against the Shah of Iran, using his female cousin to distract the policeman's attention. Makhmalbaf had ended up stabbing the policeman and spending five years in jail for the crime. Asked to reprise that moment of violence, the actors had made a stunning artistic choice.

The final frame of the movie was considered one of the most moving in modern cinema.

He told Rachel none of this, there would be time enough later. He wanted to keep the call short. As he'd known she would, she cautioned against him accepting the invitation to the meeting at the pigeon towers in Mardavij Square. Rachel thought it was a trap.

'You've got to get rid of everything, sir, and I do mean everything.'

But he caught her hesitation. It was difficult for a police officer to contemplate destroying evidence. And they agreed the security footage could serve as valuable leverage in the hands of the Canadian government, perhaps going some way to fulfilling Touka's goals. He tried to disregard her accompanying threat: *do this or your difficulties will get worse.*

Listening to Rachel, Khattak no longer believed his little nook in the courtyard wall behind a loose brick was a safe hiding place. He'd dug a hole for the flash drive at the opposite end of the courtyard and placed a planter pot on top of it, though there was no reason to believe the new hiding place was any safer.

'Any way you could get me that footage?' Rachel asked.

Khattak waited a beat as his food was served. He'd ordered only stew. The server had brought him four or five more dishes besides, a beatific smile upon his face.

When he'd left, Khattak answered, 'I've been thinking about that. Let's see if my new friends have any answers. What did you find out about the letters?'

'The person in question *was* looking for letters – a very old correspondence between friends. But I've been told they didn't matter.'

They would matter like hell if they possessed the power to earn Zahra a meeting with the Supreme Leader, he thought. He wanted to know the names, and he knew Rachel would have to send them through one of her anonymous accounts.

'Dig deeper. Let me know what you turn up.'

'Sir,' she said. 'There's something else. The person who told me about the letters also told me our friend was searching for footage of a coronation. Quite a glamorous one.'

Now Khattak was truly puzzled. Could Rachel be hinting at the coronation of Reza Pahlavi, the Shah of Iran? The coronation had taken place nearly fifty years ago. There had been no coronations since, history interrupted and then re-formed by the Iranian revolution.

The Shah had been in power for more than twenty-five years, his rule increasingly despotic, his SAVAK police a terror. Opposition to his rule had grown over the years –

the people demanding a change. When the Shah had left the country on a vacation in 1979, his departure had sparked the Iranian revolution. Long in exile, Ayatollah Khomeini had been welcomed back to Iran with a national outpouring of support.

Ten days later, the Shah's regime had fallen. And Khomeini's framework of Islamic governance had transformed the country from a monarchy to a republic.

'All right,' Esa said. 'Spring is an excellent tracking season.'

He meant for Rachel to search for the footage and consider the question of why it had interested Zahra. There was no clear line from the reign of the Shah and his secret police to the present terrors facing supporters of the Green Movement. Other than that the Shah had made torture conventional, a tactic now employed by the regime.

'That it is,' Rachel said. He heard the doubt in her voice. 'Sir. It looks like our friend has vanished again, and no one seems to care. What should I do about that?'

Khattak took a moment to work this out.

Zahra Sobhani had died at Evin, her body delivered to her family.

If she'd disappeared twice, it meant the authorities had returned to claim her body.

To impound it.

Because the flesh and bones of the dead told tales, a book of secrets laid bare.

'Tim Horton has nothing to say?'

It was his way of referencing the prime minister. Rachel bit off a laugh.

'Ask Nate to use his influence, but if it's legalities you're concerned with –' He thought carefully, wondering about the wisdom of his next suggestion. He'd hardly been a harbinger of good news for his friend, the prosecutor. 'The Crown might be the right person to ask.'

He meant Sehr Ghilzai, a friend and colleague who'd worked a former case with him.

There was a stretch of silence on the phone. He guessed there were many things Rachel wanted to say that circumstances prohibited. This was no way to conduct an investigation. Neither of them could speak openly, they couldn't exchange ideas or draw encouragement and insight from each other, they were stuck on their own. And he found it a lonely place to be. He missed Rachel, missed her warmth and smart-mouthed tenacity.

He was ready to go home. He wanted to see her again.

'Yeah,' she said at last. 'I'll do that. But if it looks like the weather's not agreeing with you, I recommend you catch the first flight home.'

While you can.

The words remained unspoken between them.

He felt a surge of affection for her.

'I will,' he said. 'I've been here long enough.'

From the whoosh of Rachel's breath, it was clear she missed him as well.

As a precaution, Khattak removed the SIM card from his phone and crushed it beneath his heel. He'd purchase a new one tomorrow, and would hide the phone in the meantime.

When he finished his meal, there were signs that pointed the way to the rooftop terrace. He paid his bill and made his way to the roof. The night was leavened by the dim glow of stars, a string of lights floating above a low stone wall. There was a haze of pollution over the city, lending the dome and minaret of the neighboring Masjid-e Shah a dusty romanticism.

In one corner of the roof, a man and woman murmured to each other in hushed voices. A few feet away from Khattak, another man stood with his face wreathed in smoke, the tip of his cigarette flaring orange at his lips. A peculiar tang of smoke struck Khattak's nostrils, spicy and strange, like tree bark and rich earth burning together.

He sneezed twice.

The smoker muttered an apology. He brushed past Khattak to the stairs, dropping his cigarette as he passed, leaving Khattak to grind out the burning ember.

He hadn't seen the other man's face – a thin man of middling height and smoke-heavy breath. When the man had gone, Khattak sought a place on the roof where he could hide his temporary phone.

Behind the couple in the corner was an ornamental woodstove, a bundle of Persian buttercups poking through its lid. He couldn't think of a better place. He waited for the couple to finish their conversation, his fingers idly tracing his pocket.

Its shape and weight were different.

He plunged his hands in his pockets to find his new phone was gone.

There was no point in looking for the smoking man now, he should have paid closer attention on the roof. The man must have preceded him to the roof. He must have watched Esa and eavesdropped on his conversation. Thankfully, Esa and Rachel had barely been able to hear each other, their muddy code understood best by themselves.

He would have to be more careful. He felt a sharp anxiety about the letters hidden behind the brick. He should have photographed them and mailed the images to Rachel. Too late now. And if the smoking man was following him, it would be a mistake to return to the guesthouse and reassure himself the letters and the drive were undisturbed. What he could do was burn the two books – the poems of Iran's exiles and, for extra measure, the book Taraneh had given him, not because reading Shariati was dangerous, but because the book connected him to Taraneh.

He should have done it already.

He wandered back to the restaurant and cut across the square.

He remembered that torches were lit at the exit of the smaller Jame mosque. If the caretaker was gone, he could drop the books inside the bracket of the torch.

He meandered along the perimeter, retracing his steps several times. The door to the mosque was untended, the torches high and bright with fire. He palmed Shariati's essay and dropped it into the flames. When the pages had crackled into embers, the poems followed suit.

Something twisted inside him.

He'd never had to worry his thoughts or political inclinations could condemn him, something he now recognized as the careless presumption of privilege. There were places he hoped to travel, Iran with its history and architecture had been at the top of his list, a crossroads of empire, a civilization whose vocabulary was threaded through his own. The Urdu language was heavily influenced by Persian, just as there'd been a long and fluid interchange between successive Persian and Turkic empires and the Indian subcontinent: culture, customs, and goods weaving a tapestry of exchange.

He had loved Persia without knowing Iran. After these long weeks in Esfahan, his love had grown richer, deeper – bearing out his lifelong interest. It had allowed him to ignore other truths simmering beneath the city's beauty. Like Zahra Sobhani, he'd thought himself protected by the privileges of citizenship, but as he watched the words of Shariati burn, he became aware the tentacles of authoritarianism could reach far enough, deep enough, to cause him to second-guess his own thoughts, his choice of reading materials, his private communications, his public conversations.

These risks may have been worth taking on his own behalf; he wouldn't have permitted Rachel to assume them in his place.

Should I come? he could imagine her saying. *Do you need me there with you?*

Zahra Sobhani had been killed by agents of the regime, agents who were now tracking Esa.

You shouldn't come, he thought.

This city has fallen from grace.

15

Interrogation

'Do you have a computer? Do you have a mobile phone? What are you doing in this country? Why are you colluding against the government? You're a foreigner. You came from Turkey, you're a peshmerga. You're a traitor, you're a spy, you're a foreign agent. Tell us the truth. Tell us where the weapons are. Tell us where the money is.' I sob, I weep, I beg, I tremble. I speak my native tongue. 'Do you have a computer? Do you have a mobile phone? What are you doing in this country? Where are you from? Where do you belong?'

Iran, Iran, Iran.

16

The snow had given way to rain, the skies above Winterglass stormy, the waves of Lake Ontario dashing a doomed course against the shore. Even the Bluffs looked battered, their chalky outline misty and dull.

Rachel honked her horn, and Nathan Clare appeared at his door, his elegance suborned by a hooded jacket made of heavy plastic. Though she had an umbrella in the car, Rachel had no intention of braving the rain to preserve Nate's impractical choice of outerwear.

'You did see the forecast today?' she commented as Nate slid into her car, adjusting the passenger seat to make room for his long legs.

He glared at the umbrella in the backseat, and Rachel grinned.

'You could have brought your own. And why on earth are you wearing plastic? I'm guessing Audrey didn't buy that for you.'

He'd told Rachel his sister was responsible for his usual sartorial splendor. The Clare siblings were exceptionally close, as Rachel had once been with Zach.

'It's not plastic,' Nate said, affronted. 'It's the same material mountain climbers use for protection at high altitudes.' Droplets of rain beaded away from the weave of the jacket, finding their way to Rachel's passenger seat.

'Hmm,' she said. 'You know Toronto's almost at sea level, right? And that your hair is wet?' Then sweeping her car round the circle: 'Which way? Where are we meeting Sehr?'

'Liberty Village. She has an appointment with a client who

works at a boutique there. She said she can fit us in after.'

Sehr's career had taken a new direction. She'd had a distinguished career as a Crown prosecutor, achieving the rank of senior counsel at a young age, through enormous dedication. It was a career path that burned women out, leaving little time for the demands of family life, if there wasn't a partner to share the load. Rachel had the impression this wasn't a problem for Sehr. She hadn't gotten to her position without a full complement of ambition in her makeup.

Sehr's new job was as in-house counsel to a small women's NGO called Woman to Woman. Nate's sister, Audrey, ran the organization, and just as Sehr had seemed at a loss for a new career direction, Audrey had found herself short of legal representation for the NGO's clients. Sehr was a quick study. She'd familiarized herself with Canadian refugee policy in short order, putting her skills at the service of Audrey's clientele. And like Nate, she was becoming more outspoken in her views. Rachel wondered if Sehr had political ambitions.

Just like she wondered how the opening at Woman to Woman had so neatly aligned with Sehr's search for a new position. She suspected Khattak had made a phone call to Nate, and the rest had fallen into place. Sehr was an old friend of the Khattaks and the Clares, a chummy little club where Rachel still felt very much on the outside.

She liked them all but couldn't quite find her place among them. If she had a place.

The drive from the Bluffs to the boutique took an hour in the rain, the traffic slow and mostly careful. Rachel used the time to bring Nate up to speed on events in Iran, dismayed by his frowning response. She'd been right to think that Khattak was in danger, right to warn him against the meeting at the dovecote.

They drove past the Canadian National Exhibition. When they'd crossed the train tracks into Liberty Village, Rachel parked along a side street, leaving her police ID on the dashboard.

She didn't like the changes to the industrial neighborhood, now a thoroughfare of steel-and-glass apartment buildings, the loft spaces of the old factories home to a new wave of media and design companies. The old buildings had character. The new façades didn't.

Sehr waved to them from the front door of one of these, stepping down to the rain-slicked pavement, dressed for the weather in a trench coat and leather boots. She held a matching umbrella over her head, and Rachel's own Maple Leafs umbrella seemed decidedly out of place as they walked to a coffee shop called the Roastery at the corner of a redbrick factory. Shaking rain from their umbrellas, they ordered their lunch, Nate waiting patiently at the counter.

Setting her umbrella down, Sehr smiled at Rachel.

'You look well, Rachel. It's good to see you again.'

'You too.'

The former Crown prosecutor did look well, her russet hair longer, her intelligent face calm and worry-free. Rachel regretted she would be the one to change that. She had begun to develop some idea of Sehr's feelings for Esa Khattak.

Quickly, she went over the facts of Zahra's death. She asked Sehr if she'd ever met Max Najafi or his mother.

Sehr shook her head as Nate brought their food to the table.

Rachel was cold. She'd ordered a hearty onion soup with sourdough bread. She soaked the bread in the soup, listening to the others talk as she ate, grateful they weren't picking away at salads. Sehr had chosen a seafood pasta, Nate a spicy bowl of chili.

'I don't know them, no. But I've been following the story, of course. It's such a terrible thing. And we have no leverage, no way of calling the Iranian government to account. There's been an opening after the nuclear deal, the possibility of renewing relations between our countries. Zahra's murder will scuttle all that.'

Rachel and Nate exchanged a look. One of Sehr's eyebrows went up.

'Have I missed something?'

'Najafi told us the Ministry of Intelligence has confiscated Zahra's body. He wants it back, to bury his mother in Toronto. He asked if we could help.'

'You know why, of course. They want to bury the evidence of what was done to Zahra. I imagine they're exerting tremendous pressure on the family in Iran to cover things up.'

'So they'll force the burial?' Rachel asked. 'There's nothing we can do?'

Sehr put her fork down.

'I'm not a diplomat or an Iran expert –'

Rachel waved this away. 'Just tell us what you think.'

'It's been a week, yes, since Zahra was murdered? How long ago was her body seized?'

'Two or three days,' Nate said.

'They'll have buried her by now. The diplomatic costs are too great otherwise, our government won't want to squander this opening. Max Najafi, the Sobhani family – they just haven't been informed yet.'

'What about an exhumation? What if Max went to Tehran?'

'We're talking about an authoritarian state. As it relates to political detainees, the entire judicial process is a sham. Zahra would have been detained without charge, interrogated without counsel present, and denied contact with her family. She didn't make it to a trial, but if there'd been a trial, it would have resembled a Stalinist show trial, complete with a forced confession.'

Sehr turned to Nate. 'You're better versed in diplomacy than I am. You know there's no chance of getting the body back, there's no possibility of redress for Zahra's murder. Unless there's a change in the regime, but even that wouldn't be enough. The entire structure would have to be dismantled before detainees at Evin or other prisons would be released. And the idea of a national accounting?' She shook her head. 'Honestly, I don't see it.'

'What about the Green Movement?' Rachel asked. 'What about the film Zahra made and the sequel she was planning?'

Sehr looked doubtful.

'Was she planning a sequel? Had she raised any funds, did she have a script? Did she really think she could gain filming permits inside Iran? Everything I've read about her doesn't sound like she would be ignorant about these things.'

Rachel took a final sip of her soup, letting it trace a long, hot trail to her stomach.

'What are you saying?'

Sehr looked from Rachel to Nate.

'I know I haven't given you any news you wanted to hear. I can't help in getting Zahra's body back. If there was any road to doing so, it would have to be through Nate's political contacts. But I can tell you if Zahra had returned to Iran, it wasn't for a film.'

'Yes,' Rachel said impatiently. 'We know. She was there to visit her stepdaughter. She was trying to get her out.'

'I don't think so. Or at least, that was only part of her reason. Zahra would have had greater influence outside the country – by raising the profile of her stepdaughter's case. Wouldn't you agree, Nate? If she'd returned to Iran, she must have had another reason.'

Rachel pondered this. She realized there were several questions she had failed to ask Max Najafi, sidelined by his grief.

'If she wasn't making a follow-up documentary, what do you think she was doing?'

They had dropped their voices, as if the subject matter of their conversation could somehow implicate them.

'I really don't know. And if her son doesn't know, we would need to follow her trail in Iran. But I don't see how we could.'

Nate cleared his throat. Rachel didn't bail him out. She didn't want to be the one to say it.

'Esa's in Esfahan,' he said. 'He could follow that trail.'

'What?' Sehr whispered. 'What is he doing there? Why didn't you tell me?'

Nate looked embarrassed. Rachel wondered if he'd guessed at Sehr's interest in Esa. Or if he knew more about Sehr and Esa's history than she did.

'He's taken some time off. He was approached by someone in the Canadian government, and told to sniff around. The government wants something on Barsam Radan. They think he's involved in the murder.'

Sehr began to gather her things. Her lips were stiff, and her eyes had darkened.

She didn't ask who Radan was, which meant she was familiar with the name.

'Wait,' Nate said, his voice warm with compassion. 'Let me get some coffee.'

When he was at the counter, Sehr spoke to Rachel.

'I suppose you think I'm a fool. Esa didn't tell me he was going to Iran, so obviously we're not that close. Nate already knows, he's being gentle with my feelings.'

Rachel had female friends, but she wasn't versed in the art of sharing personal confidences. Mostly, her friends were a rough-and-tumble group of women like herself, who talked about sports and their jobs. Rachel had only recently begun to mention her brother, Zachary. And that was because Zach had asked to move in with her, and she didn't want her friends to think she was keeping him a secret.

'The boss doesn't talk about himself,' she responded. Then because that sounded like she didn't care either way, she added, 'I wouldn't know how to ask him something personal.'

'So he doesn't mention me.'

Rachel shook her head, raindrops finding their way from her

ponytail to the side of her neck. She shivered at the touch.

'He was upset at himself for dragging you into our last case.'

Sehr's face softened. She was really very lovely, Rachel thought. Intelligent and sophisticated, the kind of woman who would have no trouble attracting attention if she wanted it. And if she didn't want it, was that because she was tied up in knots over Khattak? Rachel felt a pang as she asked herself the question. If a woman as intriguing as Sehr couldn't interest him – she shut the thought down, not liking where it was headed. She caught sight of Nate at the counter, watching them both with an air of anxiety, shrinking inside his ridiculous jacket.

Rachel found herself flushing. She'd never meant to give the impression that Khattak was more to her than a friend.

'We were friends,' Sehr said. 'Samina and I. Really close friends.' She was speaking of Khattak's wife. 'I introduced them. Sometimes I wish I hadn't, but it wouldn't have made any difference.' Her eyes glanced away from Rachel's. 'He never thought of me in that way, and now I just remind him of her death. I can't make him see me in any other light.' She sighed. 'I did try, and I don't regret it – what I regret is the way things are now.'

Nate joined them again, bearing a tray of coffee.

'I'm not sure what you mean.'

Rachel wasn't sure if she or Nate felt more awkward at this moment.

'He went to Iran to distance himself from me.'

The whole thing was tangled and unpleasant. And as much as she missed Khattak, Rachel wanted to think about the case, she didn't want to play the role of Sehr's confidante.

She glared at Nate.

Get me out of this, the glare said.

To oblige her, he redirected the conversation.

'So there's nothing we can do for Max Najafi?'

Sehr stirred sugar into her coffee, thinking.

'You'd need someone on your side, someone highly placed who could put pressure on the Iranians – the Minister of Foreign Affairs, a director at CSIS, maybe someone at the RCMP.'

Rachel set down her coffee cup with a thump, sloshing dark liquid onto the table.

Nate looked at her in horror.

They'd thought of the same name.

The RCMP's Outreach Coordinator, Laine Stoicheva.

'Don't do it,' Rachel said in the car. Laine had turned Nathan's life inside out.

They were driving down the expressway, headed to the Film Reference Library on King Street. The rain and the lake ran together, a turbulent gray on the periphery of Rachel's vision. The lake was her comfort, her home, the boundary of all she knew and loved, pleasing to her in every season. Her wipers flew across the windshield.

'You have plenty of other contacts, she's not that highly placed, she's going to mess with your head, and she'll probably mess with what we're trying to do while she's at it.'

'She might know something about the letters,' Nate said, his face turned to the lake.

'Why would she? She's no Iran expert. Didn't Max tell us – the whole thing is fifty years old, we're probably grasping at straws and all because we're trying to figure out what Zahra was up to before she was killed.'

Nate studied her, his fingers drumming against the passenger door. It was a nervous gesture that gave him away.

'Isn't that how you normally pursue a murder investigation? By tracing the victim's last movements?'

'That's not what's happening here. Zahra was a political dissident. Those kinds of politics get you killed.'

'Look at what Sehr just told us,' he said reasonably. 'She doesn't think Zahra went to Iran to make a documentary. It would have been next to impossible.'

Words stuck in Rachel's throat. She was thinking of Khattak's safety, but she was also thinking of the compulsions that had driven Zahra.

'You're proving my point. Dangerous things get you killed.'

'You're missing mine. Zahra may not have been killed for political reasons.'

Rachel eased the car off the expressway and into the city traffic. She found a parking garage near the base of the Toronto International Film Festival, a location that inhabited a city block, home to the Film Reference Library's collection. They were back in the rain before she answered Nate.

'We might find coronation footage here, we might not. But think about it. The coronation, the letters – they're political events. No matter how you slice this case, the answer comes up the same. It just happens that recent politics make for a more plausible explanation of Zahra's death than anything else.'

She used her Maple Leafs umbrella to cover them both. Fleet-footed, they dodged passersby on their way up the street. Rachel paused to admire the lighted entrance of the Bell Lightbox. This was the right place for steel and glass, in the midst of the city's skyscrapers and under the shadow of the CN Tower. Only once had Rachel's father, police superintendent Don Getty, taken Rachel and Zach up to the observation deck, watching his children dart about, daring each other to skip across the glass floor. The afternoon had been ruined when Zach had slipped, falling onto his elbows. He'd looked at Rachel in delight.

'Come check this out, Ray! It's much scarier if you lie down on the floor.'

Don Getty had been embarrassed by Zach's antics. He'd yanked Zach back onto his feet, shoving the boy into the lineup for the elevator.

'We just got here, Da!' Zach had cried in protest.

Don Getty's right hand had gripped Zach's shoulder from the back. Rachel had quickly moved between them.

'We're ready to go, right, Zach? We've had enough. I'm getting kind of hungry anyway.'

She had latched her father's arm around her own shoulders, maneuvering Zach out of Don Getty's way.

She thought of that moment whenever she looked at the tower, of the fear and dread it evoked in her memory. Though Zach had been sullen on the car ride home, Rachel had kept up a steady flow of chatter, knowing what was coming the minute they crossed the threshold.

'Rachel?' Nate's voice interrupted her thoughts. 'Let's at least check it out. Let's find out what interested Zahra in the coronation.'

He led the way to the reference desk, Rachel at his heels.

Jeremy Engstrom, the librarian, was a man in his sixties, trim and bright-eyed, with a convivial manner as he recognized Nathan Clare. They chatted amiably about common interests and mutual friends, Engstrom delighted to inform Nate that films based on Nate's books were available at the library. He urged Nate to consider the possibility of a reading and film screening. Nate's answer was modest and pleased. He didn't like to be in the public eye, he'd told Rachel. But with Canada's shifting political identity, he sensed he needed to be. The discourse was civil on the surface. The recent election had caused old antagonisms to resurface: anti-immigrant, anti-refugee, disdainful of the claims of indigenous peoples, lurching toward a politics of fear. Everything Nate's father had stood against from his earliest days on the national stage.

Rachel liked this side of Nate, liked his quiet conviction. She had the feeling he could change things without raising his voice or shaking a fist, his courtesy a means as well as an end.

Rachel showed Engstrom her ID, then realized she didn't know what to ask. Nate stepped in for her.

'We're wondering how far back your archives go. We're looking for footage of the coronation of Reza Pahlavi in 1968. Do you have news archives? Or documentaries, perhaps?'

Engstrom looked surprised.

'You're the third person this year to ask me that question.'

Rachel perked up.

'Who were the other two?'

Engstrom shuffled behind his desk. He brought his computer screen to life with a few taps of his fingers.

'One was the filmmaker Zahra Sobhani.' He looked grave. 'I'm sure you've heard the sad news.' His eyes scanned the screen. 'Is that why you're here? It's why that reporter came, Vicky D'Souza. They both wanted to see the coronation, neither explained why.' He shrugged. 'I gave them the same answer. You can access the best documentary on YouTube. It's made by the BBC, there's no need to borrow the library's copy. There are also, I should point out, numerous amateur videos of the coronation on the same website.'

Nate looked thoughtful.

'Then why did Zahra come to you? Even a basic search on the internet would have told her as much.'

'I'm sure I don't know. Not precisely, that is. Ms. Sobhani said she'd viewed the footage available through public sources and was looking for something else, something the BBC didn't have. Footage of the Shah's arrival at the coronation. I told the same thing to the reporter.'

Nate leaned his elbows on the reference desk.

'There's no footage of his arrival? Did you check?'

Engstrom swiveled the screen of his computer around. It listed the date and title of the BBC film, along with the film credits.

'I have to admit, my interest was piqued. I watched it myself. I also viewed the videos online. Ms. Sobhani was right. You can watch the entire coronation except for the Shah's arrival. I found it curious but not particularly interesting.'

Rachel had the sense Nate and Jeremy Engstrom could happily chat about film all day, if she didn't bring them back to the matter at hand.

'So you couldn't help her. She must have been disappointed.'

Pursing his lips, Engstrom tapped at his computer again.

'I didn't say that. I said *we* didn't have anything else. I did a database search for Ms. Sobhani. There's an older film at the reference library on Yonge Street. I told her to try there, though I couldn't guarantee she would find what she wanted.'

'The film's name?'

Engstrom wrote it on a piece of paper. He passed it to Nate with an arch smile.

'It's somewhat florid, I'm afraid. It's called *The Lion of Persia*. I suppose it's meant as an homage to the Shah.'

'Did you tell Vicky D'Souza the same thing?'

'I did. She went directly to Yonge Street from here. I'm afraid you're out of luck. The library closes at five.'

It was just after 5:00 P.M.

Rachel nodded at the screen.

'Is the documentary checked out?'

Engstrom frowned. 'Yes. And it's long overdue. I can't tell you which patron has it.'

If the film was overdue, Rachel didn't think Vicky D'Souza had borrowed it. Perhaps it was still in Zahra's possession. But not in Toronto, or Najafi would have told them as much. Maybe she could try to buy the film online, or request it through an inter-library loan. But she didn't know what she was looking for, even if she found footage of the Shah's arrival.

She had another thought.

'Mr. Engstrom, did Ms. Sobhani happen to mention she was looking for some letters?'

Engstrom's eyes gleamed.

'Curiouser and curiouser,' he said. 'No, she didn't. Vicky D'Souza asked me that as well. Do tell me about the letters.'

Rachel didn't think that was wise.

'I'm afraid I don't know myself. But thank you, you've been very helpful.'

She noticed his wistful expression as they left.

Not for the first time she reflected on people's ability to lose sight of human tragedy when presented with a puzzle to solve. She didn't judge Engstrom for it. Compartmentalizing was a necessary element of police work. And a librarian's job frequently involved a similar hunt for clues. She had the feeling Engstrom was good at his job, and he'd clearly taken a shine to Nate. He could be a valuable asset in the future. She went back to the desk, thanked him with more gusto, and passed her card to him.

Nate was at her heels.

He spoke to Engstrom over her shoulder, his warm breath brushing her neck, chasing a tiny shiver down her spine.

'Jeremy, this library has screening rooms, doesn't it? I know you're closing soon, but do you think we could stay a bit longer?'

The librarian was happy to oblige. To do a favor for Nathan Clare was to shore up the influence that was key to building the library's reputation. What a story he would have to share with the library's board of trustees.

'Of course. Were you thinking of viewing something in particular?'

Nate's fingers dug into Rachel's shoulder, conveying his sense of excitement.

'Would you be kind enough to show us the coronation video?'

To Rachel, he said, 'Let's ask Vicky D'Souza to join us here.' He lowered his voice. 'And maybe it's time for another call to Esa.'

17

The Prison Yard

They've taken my clothes, I'm in for another beating. My eyes and face are swollen, four of my teeth are gone. But none of my bones are broken, that's on today's agenda. It's cold outside, below freezing. A brute of a guard chains me to the wall. 'This is what we do to foreigners,' he says. No point in debating the ethics of citizenship with a man who's holding a club. My kidneys won't survive the philosophy. But that's it, he goes away. He turns the lights in the courtyard off. And I realize. I might be beaten to death, or I might freeze to death by morning. My lips are blue, my skin becomes chilled, but in the courtyard, I see the sky.

18

I know you don't want to trust me, I don't give my name, I don't say who I am – what reason do you have to trust me? This is how the regime turns us against each other, how it turns our green feathers yellow. They tell us we're enemies, we're the ones who made the mistake that sabotaged the country. Or perhaps, as with the election, they never learned to count – it's true, they didn't count the green birds of June, they didn't measure the span of our wings.

Another of their ironies: they offered their support to the people of Egypt, the people who brought a demagogue to his knees. But our tyrant builds a fortress, speaks his mind – reigns supreme.

I would never betray you to them.

Touka says you won't betray us either.

So open your eyes, Inspector Khattak.

Read the writing on the wall.

19

Taraneh was waiting for him at the entrance to the dovecote. A thin strip of dawn wrapped the tower in a layer of gauze, subfusing its outline in a lusterless gold. Khattak had hoped to visit one of Esfahan's *burj-e kabuthars*, or pigeon houses, before his departure from Iran. The Hezar Jarib was the largest of a group, centered in Mardavij Square, its bulbous tower shaded by elms.

The square was quiet as Khattak followed Taraneh inside, the caretaker nowhere to be seen. Khattak noticed the smell. The interior was honeycombed with pigeon roosts, the dovecote musty with the scent of dried guano, neither pleasant nor overpowering. Khattak shaded his eyes, looking up at a circular gallery.

Light filtered through the opening of the tower, a coral glow upon the arches that framed the gallery, eight in all. From the angle below, they loomed up like tombstones.

Khattak thought he saw a shadow cross the gallery.

'Over here.'

It was Taraneh's voice, light and mischievous.

Khattak felt a sudden spurt of anger. The circumstances of Zahra's murder were too grave for him to indulge in the careless games of youth. He didn't know these people, he didn't trust them. He'd had a restless night's sleep worrying about the flash drive and letters in the courtyard. Just before catching his taxi to Mardavij Square, he'd checked on the items. And was stunned to discover a new letter had joined the others behind the brick.

Someone was watching him, but if it was the smoking man,

he'd have taken the letters and the drive, just as he'd taken Khattak's disposable phone.

Khattak asked the taxi to drop him several blocks away from the square, and he walked the rest of the distance on foot, stopping first at an internet café. A message let him know Nate wanted him to call, but didn't tell him why.

He was beginning to think it would be an excellent idea to publicize his friendship with Nathan Clare. He bought another phone at a store several doors down from the internet café and slipped it into a pouch he was wearing on a string around his neck. The drive was in the pouch, along with his passport.

He had no idea if any of these gestures were sufficient, or if he was chasing phantoms.

The letters were disturbing. He recognized something in them, a snatch of memory, a code he could decipher if the memory returned.

Taraneh claimed to know nothing about the letters.

And there was a gravity to the tone of the letters that didn't fit with his impression of Taraneh, which was possibly a blind.

He looked up through honeycombed roosts that glinted like coins of fire. The lonely coo of a pigeon echoed from the top. A spiral staircase led him to the gallery, the air sallow and cool. He inhaled the scent of gypsum and lime. A stripe of gold dazzled his vision. When it cleared, he saw shadows materialize in the tombstone arches that faced him.

Taraneh, Nasreen, and two young men.

He glanced involuntarily at the staircase.

'Don't be afraid, Inspector Khattak, we're on the same side. Why do you think we gave you the drive?'

The young man in the center spoke to Khattak in fluent English, with the faint overlay of a Persian accent. In the waxy light that filtered through the dovecote, his face was pale and smooth, his eyes wide-set and clever. He wore a Sonic Youth T-shirt and a pair of strategically ripped black jeans. When he raised his hand to his springy hair, Khattak caught sight of a band on his wrist. A plastic green band, the magic bracelet.

Supporters of the Green Movement had begun to wear it after the 2009 election. It was imprinted with English and Farsi slogans.

Freedom. Democracy. Hope.

Some of the bands read, 'Where is my vote?'

'Who are you?' Khattak asked. 'How do you know my name?'

'We have a mutual friend. She mentioned you were in the country, she said you'd help us find out what happened to Zahra Khanom.'

He used the respectful form of address for Zahra Sobhani. The mutual friend had to be Touka Swan, but Khattak needed to be sure. He sensed a stillness in the others, a nervous, hopeful attention. He had a sudden, swamping sense he could do nothing but disappoint the hopes of these young people.

'Your friend's name?'

'Touka Swan. I'm Ali Golshani. This is my brother, Darius. He's a film student, he was a student of Zahra's.'

Ali's voice caught on the name. Embarrassed, he blinked away his tears.

Khattak turned his attention to the other young man lurking under an arch.

'Step out where I can see you, please.'

Darius peered out from the gloom, letting the light brush his face. Khattak kept his own expression impassive, trying not to show his reaction to the serpentine scar that colored Darius's face. It puckered the skin under his right eye, snaked across his cheek, and disappeared into the neckline of his shirt. His solemn young face was mournful.

'You've met Taraneh and Nasreen, Taraneh gave you the drive. What did you think of it?' Ali asked.

'Did it come from Touka?'

'No. We have someone inside Evin who made us a copy.'

'Why not give it directly to Touka? She's the one who wanted evidence.'

Ali moved closer to his brother.

'You don't sound as helpful as Touka said you would be. You seem detached. But wasn't Zahra a Canadian citizen? And don't you catch criminals for a living?'

'Forget it, Ali. What did you expect?'

The bitter words came from Nasreen. Her white scarf had fallen all the way back, her rich, dark hair parted to one side. A delicate hand touched a necklace at her throat that caught the streaming light.

'He doesn't know us, why should he trust us?'

Khattak pointed to the band on Ali's wrist.

'Is it safe for you to wear that?'

'Is anything any of us have done safe?' Ali gestured at his brother's scar. 'Probably not. Do you have the drive with you? Did you see anything on it?'

The moment of decision had come.

If Khattak's Iranian idyll were to end, it would be the result of a considered choice.

Rachel and Nate had confirmed Touka Swan worked for the Canadian government. And if Touka had infiltrated this group of young people, it meant she trusted them. If he chose to help them, he would have to accept there was no point in second-guessing them. But still he felt afraid.

He removed the drive from its pouch and held it out to Ali Golshani, who pocketed it, his brows raised.

'There's nothing on it?'

Khattak weighed his words.

'Touka told me she was looking for something that would implicate Barsam Radan in Zahra's death. It's not possible to form a clear picture of who's in the crowd and who isn't, but what is clear is that even if Radan is the one who arrested Zahra, that's not a clear connection to her death.'

Taraneh clapped her hands, the sound echoing through the chamber of the pigeon house.

'You *are* a real detective,' she said. 'Very impressive. Anything else?'

'Don't listen to my cousin,' Ali said. 'Taraneh doesn't understand what's at stake. This isn't a game. The regime can't keep murdering its dissidents.'

A sob sounded from the far end of the gallery. Concerned, Khattak flicked a glance at Nasreen, risking the pull of her eyes. She shielded her face with her scarf, moving to a door at the end of the gallery that led to a walkway outside. The others let her go.

'I'm sorry,' Ali said. The apology was for Nasreen. 'I shouldn't have been so frank. Nasreen's brother is being held at Kahrizak prison. They've had no word for fifteen months. For all we know, Saneh is dead.'

Khattak circled the gallery until he was at the door, pulling it closed. Nasreen didn't need to hear his next question. As notorious as Evin was, Kahrizak's recent reputation was worse. The brutalization of young men and women at Kahrizak had caused a scandal, the prison shut down after the election. When the regime had secured its grip, Kahrizak had reopened.

'Why do you think he's dead? What was he charged with?'

He didn't know if the question mattered. He was speaking about a criminal justice system that had rotted through from the inside.

'They haven't charged him. He was held at Evin at first, then released, then picked up again. Then released. Then finally taken to Kahrizak. Since then we've heard nothing. No one will tell us anything, no matter whom we ask. His situation is like Roxana's.'

The grief in his voice welled up.

'Do you know Roxana?' The connection flagged Khattak's attention.

It was Darius who answered him, his long fingers stroking over his disfiguring scar.

'Yes. We worked together. We're all supporters of the Greens – the children of writers and artists and unionists. Our parents were once dissidents, now it seems to be our turn.'

He said it with a note of disbelief in his voice: How was it possible Zahra had been killed so easily, with so little accountability?

Khattak's missing memory resurfaced, the mystery of the letters unraveled.

The children of writers.

The writer's child.

We are bound together, chained.

His secret correspondent was writing about the Chain Murders, a series of assassinations that spanned the 1990s. Dozens of prominent intellectuals had been murdered, either openly or in secret, the murders coming to light in the brief period of freedom known as the Tehran Spring.

In 1997, Mohammad Khatami, a dark horse reformist candidate, had been elected president by a landslide popular vote. He'd run on a platform that promised the people greater freedom. Under his administration, restrictions on the press had eased. Dozens of new publications were launched, and a series of exposés on political crimes was published – the most riveting of these on the Chain Murders.

In the fall of 1998, six of Iran's most respected writers and academics had been assassinated in a string of mysterious attacks. The press had uncovered a connection to similar attacks dating back to the earliest days of the revolution. In response to a public outcry, a committee formed to investigate the murders held the Ministry of Intelligence and Security responsible.

The victims of the Chain Murders had been founders of the Iranian Writers' Association – a group of intellectuals who espoused independent thought, and whose critique of the regime was subtly and subversively apparent in their writings.

Khattak looked at Darius, his voice cool and steady.

'Is Zahra's death connected to the Chain Murders? Is that why Touka needs my help?'

Darius looked shocked.

'What? Why would you think that?'

'You just said your parents were dissidents. That would place them in the generation of the Chain Murders.'

Khattak withdrew the letters from his pouch. He gave one each to Taraneh and Darius, and the remaining two to Ali Golshani, whom he sensed was the group's leader. He spared a thought for Nasreen. If her brother was in Kahrizak, better she know nothing about these letters.

The group read the letters and exchanged them.

'We didn't write these to you,' Ali said.

'Someone who knew me did, someone who knows where I'm staying. A young man named Ali dropped them off.'

Ali's answer was firm. 'It wasn't me. Touka told us to meet you, we have no reason to engage in intrigues. We were planning to tell you everything in order to enlist your help.'

'It was a coincidence,' Darius said with great earnestness. 'Ali is a blogger, I make short films, our parents were academics. Taraneh's mother is a lawyer, Nasreen and Saneh were students. But yes, our parents were dissidents.'

Khattak noted the past tense. Had Nasreen and Saneh graduated? Before he could ask, Ali held up the second letter.

'I think you may be onto something, Inspector. Take a look at this.'

He read the last line of the letter to the others.

'"Find out what Zahra wanted with the letters." I think I know the letters in question, they were quite famous.'

Nasreen re-entered the gallery from the walkway. A cleansing rush of air cut across the odor of the dovecote.

'What are you talking about?' she asked.

Ali ignored her. 'I think Zahra Khanom may have been looking for the correspondence between Prime Minister Mossadegh and

Dariush Forouhar. They were personal letters that Forouhar was said to treasure. I thought they were destroyed years ago.'

Khattak knew the story of the CIA coup that had toppled Mohammad Mossadegh in 1953, an episode of little distinction that had sabotaged Iran's prospects for democracy. A principled champion of democracy, Mossadegh had represented an independent, nationalist position. His government had rejected alignment with either the United States or the Soviet Union, at a time when the United States had sought an ally deferential to its interests, invoking the specter of a Communist takeover. When Mossadegh was accordingly deposed, the Shah of Iran had been propped up in his place – setting the stage over time for Khomeini's revolution.

Like many prominent dissidents, Mossadegh had lived out his life under house arrest. His legacy as a proponent of democracy was still greatly respected inside Iran.

But Forouhar was a name Khattak didn't recognize.

'I'm afraid I don't understand,' he said.

'The Chain Murders, Inspector Khattak.' Ali's answer was quiet. 'Dariush Forouhar was the first of six people murdered in that chain. The Mossadegh letters vanished the same day.'

A cough in the background startled Khattak. He swung around, expecting to see the man from the restaurant rooftop.

A figure emerged from the shadows. It was a young man wearing aviator glasses. His long hair fell to his shoulders, an unlit cigarette poised between his lips. He wore several heavy chains around his neck and five or six green bands on each of his wrists. The sleeves of his Versace shirt were rolled up, the neck unbuttoned down to his waist. He was bulging with over-developed muscles. He eyed Taraneh with an intimate smile.

'This is Omid Arabshahi,' Ali said. 'He wanted to hang back until he was sure you were who Touka said you were.'

Omid Arabshahi made a cavalier gesture. Khattak could tell

he was the member of the group with the strongest disregard for authority, the one who would take the most risks.

'So you're Inspector Khattak,' he said. He spit out the cigarette, speaking English with a drawl. 'Now that we've met, we can get on with finding out why Zahra Khanom was murdered.'

'And why is that?' Esa asked.

'Because I'm the tech expert. I'm the one who can help you with the drive.'

Khattak hesitated. There was a moment on the security footage he needed to see slowed down, close-up. And if he was right about it, it was possible there was more to Zahra's death than the assassination of a critic of the government. Would the regime have risked killing her at this pivotal moment in relations between Canada and Iran? There had to be another reason.

'Have you already seen the footage?'

'Of course,' Omid said.

'And?'

'Radan is there. Like you said, it doesn't mean anything.'

'Anything else?'

'You're the detective,' Omid answered with a shrug. 'We don't even know what we're looking for, do you?'

'I think so. But I don't think it's safe to meet at my guesthouse.'

Ali had a laptop bag strung across his shoulder. Now he unlatched the straps and handed Khattak a book. It was a tourist guide to the sights of Esfahan. The Hezar Jarib dovecote was marked with a note.

'If you're being followed, you'll need that when you leave. If you come to the meeting tonight, Omid will help you with the drive.'

'Who's going to be there?' Khattak asked.

Ali's reply was a little self-conscious.

'All of us. The Green Birds of June. We're the children of the writers.'

Ali had now used two phrases from the letters: the writers'

children and the Green Birds of June. The first reference was clear. The second could mean anyone who was a member of the Green Movement. The stolen election had been held in June.

'Is this a name you use publicly?'

'No. No protest movement can work openly in Iran.'

'Do you have access to unmonitored communications?'

'Perhaps. Why?'

'I need to send some information to my partner in Canada. And I'd also like to send her a copy of these letters.'

Ali made no move to return the letters to Khattak. He divided them between himself and Darius. He passed the drive of the security footage to Omid.

'Omid can photograph them and send them to anyone you wish without being traced.'

'How?'

Omid slid the letters and the drive inside his shirt and buttoned it up.

'It's nothing all that advanced. I'm surprised you haven't heard of Telegram. It's an app that lets you send and receive encrypted messages, which is handy in Iran. Come to the meeting and I'll show you.'

Khattak gave him Rachel's anonymous email address, and asked Omid to forward the footage from Evin. He saluted Khattak, whistling as he descended the staircase. Darius waited five minutes to follow him.

Ali nodded at Nasreen.

'Now you.'

'What about the meeting place? You haven't told him.' Her voice was low and hoarse. She was staring at Khattak, but her expression remained the same: inward-seeing and fixed, frozen at the mention of Zahra Sobhani.

'Go ahead,' Taraneh said, her impatience beginning to show. 'I'll tell him.'

Ali linked his arm through Nasreen's.

'Come on,' he said. 'The caretaker will be back soon.'

She seemed to snap back into herself. She pressed her fingers hard into her neck, blotting out the charm on her necklace. Khattak couldn't tell what it was.

He knew he should have looked away, out of politeness if nothing else, but he couldn't. Her tragedy was so magnetic, it electrified the air around her with the force of a dying star.

She followed Ali down the stairs and disappeared.

Taraneh leaned close to Khattak, her perfume filling his nostrils.

'She's too young for you,' she said, half-teasing.

'So are you,' he replied firmly. He stepped back, retreating under an arch. 'Are you sure you and Nasreen should be involved in the Green Birds?'

Taraneh's flirtatious manner went flat.

'Whether you help us or not won't change anything. We're committed to the movement, Zahra was our friend. She managed to get some of us released.'

'You?' Khattak asked, surprised.

Taraneh flushed.

'Not me, Nasreen. Nasreen and Saneh Ardalan are Kurds. They've been treated more harshly than other members of the Greens.'

Khattak felt his stomach drop. He found he didn't want to think about what might have happened to Nasreen behind the gates of Evin.

'You said they were students, what did you mean? Why aren't they now?'

Taraneh's rearrangement of her scarf betrayed her discomfort with the subject.

'That's not for me to say, we don't share each other's secrets.'

She ducked her head against Khattak, her mood changing on a whim, suddenly playful. She whispered a street address and a time into his ear, then descended gaily down the staircase.

'If you help us, we'll consider you've joined us,' she called up. 'You'll be an honorary member.'

Khattak knew better than to answer.

He explored the dovecote on his own for several minutes, impressed by the purposefulness of the structure. During the Safavid empire, the dovecotes had been used to collect guano to fertilize crops. The smell that lingered mixed with the lighter notes of Taraneh's perfume.

He absorbed the moment, the place. The rose-pink light streaming from the crosshatched opening, the looming tomb-like arches, the red-gold pigeon nooks like a serried cliff rising upward. He followed the path Nasreen had taken to the walkway, looking down on Mardavij Square.

At the base of the pigeon tower stood a thin man shrouded in shadow. The orange tip of a cigarette cast a glow on the lower half of his face. He was fourteen meters below and a short distance away, but Khattak recognized something in his posture. It was the man from the roof. He felt an immediate pang of fear – he *was* being followed, and his activities were being monitored.

Soon the man was on the walkway beside Khattak, his cigarette extinguished, the scent of smoldering bark clinging to the clothes he wore, a spring jacket over an open-necked shirt and dark slacks. He had a face Khattak thought would be difficult to place, his smile sharp, his features congested. His hair was combed over his forehead, his half-closed eyes reminding Khattak of Ahmadinejad, the politician who'd claimed victory in the stolen election of 2009.

The man gestured at Khattak's guidebook.

'You are a tourist?' he asked in English. His Persian accent was rich and beautiful. He spoke in a voice that would not have disgraced a tenor of the opera.

The man knew exactly who he was, Khattak thought. These were just preliminaries.

'Yes,' he replied. 'I'm a visitor to your country. Esfahan is a beautiful city.'

'May I see your book?'

It would have been customary for the man to introduce himself with a flurry of courteous inquiries as to the state of Khattak's health, while urging upon him a list of attractions a visitor should not miss.

Instead, the man reached out a hand for Khattak's book.

He wasn't a covert agent, Esa thought. He had the patina of arrogance of someone with absolute power. Still, Esa expected greater discretion from the Ministry of Intelligence.

Esa handed the book over, grateful Ali had had the foresight to give it to him. And he realized the Green Birds' activities meant they would always be planning for these contingencies.

The man made a show of flipping through its pages. Esa noted the way his eyes scanned the book for signs of hidden information.

'What do you plan to see next?'

'What would you recommend, Agha…'

The man's eyes narrowed. He wasn't pleased by Khattak's familiarity with Persian forms of address.

'Larijani,' the man said. 'I am Mr. Larijani. And you?'

'Muhammad Khattak.' Esa gave his official name, hoping to ward off any background search Larijani might undertake. The name of every male in his family was prefaced with 'Muhammad.' His middle name, Esa, was on his birth certificate.

'Afghani?'

This time Larijani seemed genuinely caught off guard. There were seven hundred thousand Afghan refugees and laborers in Iran. They worked in abysmal conditions for minimal wages and were considered compatriots in the Iranian labor movement.

It told Khattak a great deal that Larijani was familiar with the origins of his Pashtun name, common to Afghanistan and the northwest frontier of Pakistan. But he didn't think a discussion of the arbitrary lines drawn by empire was what Larijani had in mind. He would be thinking Esa was a spy.

'Something like that,' he said politely.

'How long have you been in Iran?'

To deflect him, Khattak went over the details of his pilgrimage visa, recounting sites he'd visited in Mashhad and Qom.

If Larijani wasn't already aware of these details, he would make it his mission to confirm them. And that would buy Khattak some time.

The prayer call of the *azaan* echoed up to the dovecote.

'You came to the *burj-e kabuthar* alone?' Larijani asked.

His questions had acquired a tone of impertinence.

'Quite alone,' Khattak answered honestly. 'It's a restful place. The wonders of its geometry are like nothing I've ever seen. The Safavids were extraordinary builders.'

'So it's geometry that interests you.'

The words were scornful. Khattak could imagine this man saying something similar to a detained journalist or filmmaker. *You claim to make 'art.' Your art is an insult, a perversion of what is natural and good. Your art corrupts the values of the nation.*

He wondered if Mohsen Makhmalbaf could make a film like *A Moment of Innocence* in the present climate. He thought it doubtful.

'If you like geometry, Mr. Khattak, might I suggest you accompany me to the local mosque? You will be interested in its mihrab.'

Larijani waved a hand at the far end of Mardavij Square, where an unexceptional dome reposed inside a garden of poplars.

Khattak couldn't think of a way to refuse.

He scanned the streets that led away from the dovecote. From his vantage point, he could see no one lurking at the base of the tower, no cars or van nearby suggesting Larijani intended to take him somewhere other than the mosque.

To be certain, he said, 'A walk would be refreshing.'

He let Larijani lead the way along the tree-lined boulevard, engaging in small talk as they walked. Khattak deflected the personal questions the other man asked. He spoke of the sights he had seen, the weather he'd experienced, the stunning copy of the Quran held at the Astan-e Quds library in Mashhad.

'You're comfortable praying at a Shia mosque?' Larijani asked with marked disbelief. 'Behind a Shia imam?'

If he wasn't, Khattak thought, he wouldn't have requested a visa to sites of pilgrimage in a Shia-majority country. But this time he sensed Larijani's curiosity was apolitical.

'May God accept our prayers and our differences. I hope to find myself welcome.'

Esa felt a pang of sympathy at Larijani's baffled expression. There was an arrogance of privilege associated with membership in a majority tradition, as with Khattak's undefined upbringing in Canada. Perhaps in Iran, where the situation was reversed, Esa should have felt discomfort or alienation.

But in the Canadian mosques of his childhood, sectarian divides had been remote. Sunnis and Shias differed significantly only on the question of the legitimate succession to the caliphate, after the Prophet Muhammad's death. The word *Sunni* derived from Sunnah – the tradition and teachings of Muhammad. Sunnis considered themselves Ahl al-Sunnah, or People of the Tradition. In this, there was no difference from Shias, who shared the same tradition.

The word *Shia* derived from Shiat Ali, or the Party of Ali, whom Shias considered Muhammad's rightful successor. Ali was Muhammad's cousin, and one of his closest companions. He had married Muhammad's beloved daughter Fatima. In both branches of Islam, Muhammad, Ali and Fatima, and their sons, Hassan and Hossein, were greatly revered figures. Hossein's assassination at the battle of Karbala was the defining element of Shia identity, the battle itself a paradigmatic event.

Though Esa had been raised without denominational specificity, gatherings that retold the martyrdom of Hossein were part of Khattak's earliest and deepest memories. The stories formed part of his identity. Then the influence of Wahhabism had crept in, spread by the influx of Saudi-funded indoctrination. Wahhabism as a variant of Sunni Islam had arisen from the Arabian desert in the mid-1800s, finding prominence and influence through a strategic alliance with the House of Saud. Its stringent recasting of a pluralist Islamic tradition had denounced Shia teachings as entirely heretical. And the friendly and familiar communities Esa had mixed in had divided into smaller and smaller sub-groups.

Esa had despaired of the divisiveness of judging the different paths to God. And Shariati, the sociologist, had written about this as well, in his beautiful book *On Selection and Election.*

Larijani recalled his attention.

'Of course, Mr. Khattak. Our mosques are open to everyone, we don't discriminate.'

He meant it, Khattak could see. It made him appreciate the complexities of human nature anew.

There was a contradiction between Larijani's open invitation to Khattak and the persecution of minorities within Iran. While these included Kurds, Turks, and Afghans, Baha'is faced the most serious persecution, deprived of access to higher education and participation in the political process. What accounted for it, Esa could guess at, as so often difference led to prejudice and injustice. And there was a dynamic he'd encountered in at least some small segment of every community he visited: a sense of tribal superiority. Baha'is were persecuted on religious grounds. Kurds, Afghans, and others because they were held inferior to ethnic Persians. And in the particular case of Kurds, because their loyalty to the state was always deemed suspect.

In Larijani's mind, the warm welcome to the mosque could

easily co-exist beside this disenfranchisement of Iran's own minorities. It was a curious dichotomy.

'Beh farmi,' he said to Esa, at the entrance of the mosque. It was the customary greeting of invitation.

'Beh farmi,' Esa replied in Farsi before realizing his fluency in Farsi was a secret he should have kept.

'You speak Farsi?' Larijani asked.

If Esa admitted it, it would confirm Larijani's belief he was a spy.

He held up the guidebook Ali Golshani had given him.

'This has been helpful.' He smiled a disarming smile. 'I'm not sure about my accent. I give most Farsi words the Urdu pronunciation, since the vocabulary is so similar.'

'You are fluent in English,' Larijani observed.

'As are you,' Khattak said pleasantly. 'Higher education in the Indian subcontinent is conducted in English.'

'You sound like an American to me.'

Khattak said nothing to this. He followed Larijani into the mosque, his senses on high alert. If Larijani suspected him of being a citizen of the West, he would dig deeper into Khattak's background. And Esa wondered how much effort it would take to uncover the details of his Canadian passport, where his full name was listed.

He was so preoccupied by his companion's actions that, for the first time, he failed to take in the sights or to observe the mihrab Larijani had described.

They'd missed the congregational prayer.

Khattak prayed on his own. Larijani had rattled him, and he needed a moment to retrench – to remind himself what faith meant when he was surrounded by the ravages of the regime. His faith had provided him with the ethical framework for his life: everything the Islamic Republic stood for was antithetical to it.

He nodded at strangers who came and went, engaged in

their own pursuits. He knew there were minor differences in his performance of the prayer that would attract attention, but his experience at the pilgrimage sites had been one of curiosity and welcome. He thought of the warmth of the people he'd encountered during his travels, and contrasted it with the dyspeptic temper of the regime.

There were an estimated one million Sunnis in Tehran alone who were not permitted to build schools or places of worship, or to disseminate their own religious teachings. And though this treatment of non-Shia minorities was unjust, the fate of ethnic and religious minorities in many Sunni-majority countries was exponentially worse. He had only to think of the violence against Shia processionals in Pakistan, or the increasingly disturbing attacks against Pakistan's Christian and Hindu minorities. The country's Hazara population, who were largely Shia, suffered extensive persecution by the Taliban, that was typically met with indifference by the state.

Everything was twisted, Esa thought. Distorted into something brutal and ugly. As with the Iranian regime, whose grip on its population was a house of cards poised to fall.

A house of lies.

'*Ya rab,*' he prayed. 'Deliver us all.'

In that moment when his thoughts had turned despairing, Esa realized Larijani had left.

Come to think of it, he couldn't be sure Larijani had bothered to pray.

He wasn't waiting at the mihrab with the disinterested aplomb of a tour guide.

There were three or four men in the mosque, none of them together. Esa lingered under the mihrab, scouting the empty upper gallery with his eyes.

He took out his phone and snapped a few photographs. He pressed several notes into the mosque's donation box, then found his way outside to the garden. Minarets pierced the clouds like torn veils, pools of light splashing over fountains in the courtyard.

Mardavij Square was waking up, families strolling together under the trees.

And Larijani was gone.

20

Interrogation

'Why were you held at Evin?' They don't like jokes, so I don't tell them they should know better than me. I cough up a little blood, making sure to wheeze. I've been trying to analyze a question: Does my condition earn me any sympathy? Or are they ready to finish the job? 'Respiratory infection,' Ahmed said. He was in the cell with me, a pre-med student who warmed my corpse and saved my fingers and toes. I told the others my tricks, what to do, how to fight when it's their turn, but Piss-Pants doesn't get the humor. He's pale with terror, so we keep him at the back, and someone volunteers to take his turn. He's a good boy, only fifteen. His older brother took him to Mousavi's rally. They split up when the Basiji arrived, he doesn't know where his brother ended up. He whimpers his brother's name at night, but I tell him to swallow his weakness. 'If your brother's safe, keep him safe.'

I can't help feeling sorry for Piss-Pants, though the one I should feel sorry for is myself.

21

'This is the coolest thing that's ever happened to me.'

Vicky D'Souza gazed up at Nathan Clare with undisguised admiration. The reporter was pint-sized, using tottering black boots to give herself the illusion of height. Her spring coat was a shade of merlot that matched her lipstick, a contrast to her dark skin and shiny teeth. She wore wing-tipped glasses that rested low enough on her nose to draw attention to a beauty mark above her mouth that Rachel suspected was courtesy of a L'Oréal eyebrow pencil. It was smudged around the edges by the rain.

She was brimming with energy, speaking in quick, clipped sentences that explained why she was more often off-screen than on.

'Are those glasses real?' Rachel asked suspiciously. She felt like a giant beside Vicky.

'Yeah, why? Do they make me look older? Sexier?'

'Do you want to be considered sexy in your job?'

'Not especially, but it's important to know what kind of impression you make on others.'

Rachel half expected Vicky to slap gum around her mouth, so determined was her Lois Lane impression of plucky young reporter.

Nathan offered to take her coat, and she beamed at him.

'Amazing, right? I haven't broken a story in over a year, and here I am hot on the heels of Nathan Clare.' She snapped a quick picture of Nate with her phone, catching him with his mouth open.

She'd leapt at the offer to join Rachel and Nate at the screening room, hoisting herself onto one of three tiny stools stationed before an oversized monitor. Nate chose to stand. Rachel lumbered onto the stool beside Vicky, cursing the gods who believed library patrons were four feet tall and ten inches wide. She could feel her thighs straining to stay on the stool. She straightened her back, hoping Nate hadn't noticed. Meanwhile, Vicky was perched as daintily as a seabird on an ice floe.

'So what gives?' Vicky prompted, beaming at Nate.

Rachel thought it best to let Nate ask the questions. It was harder to say no to a celebrity, assuming that Nate counted as one.

Nate pressed a button on the DVD player hidden on a shelf beneath the monitor.

Rachel winced as a lurching opera score sounded over the posh tones of the BBC narrator. She'd already watched the coronation video twice. Now Rachel was watching Vicky's reaction, no longer dazed by the opulence of the Shah's regalia of state, or the profligacy of the royal consort's sapphires.

As soon as the documentary began to play, Vicky swiveled round on her stool. She hit the button on the remote to pause the film, fixing her attention on Rachel.

'You want to talk about Zahra Sobhani. Am I a police witness?' She took out a Hello Kitty notepad with a matching pencil. 'Do you mind if I take notes?'

'Put that away,' Rachel said. She'd just had a quick lesson in not judging a book by its cover. Vicky D'Souza was nowhere near as flighty as the persona she inhabited. Behind the wing-tip frames, her eyes were as sharp as drill bits.

'This is unofficial. We talked to Max Najafi, and he told us you were digging into Zahra Sobhani's death. We want to know why.'

'Why did you talk to Max Najafi?' Vicky didn't put the notebook away. Instead she chewed on her eraser. 'What does Zahra's death have to do with Community Policing? If anything, this is a diplomatic matter.' She fastened on Nate, her whole expression brightening. 'Is that why you're involved? Is the government relying on your reputation as an envoy?'

Nate slouched against Rachel, waiting as two patrons left the screening room and moved off to one side.

'I hope not,' he said. 'My interest in this matter is personal.'

Rachel elbowed him in the ribs.

'What?' Vicky asked, before Nate could. 'Hold on a sec – where's Inspector Khattak? He's not with you? Why are you two together?'

Rachel snapped Vicky's notebook out of her hand, holding it up like a prize. She hadn't anticipated how this might play out.

'How about this?' she said. 'You agree to keep our conversation off the record, and Nate will give you an exclusive interview on his thoughts about Zahra Sobhani's death. He knew her.'

Nate's eyes blinked behind his glasses, at an outcome he hadn't anticipated. It served him right. He was one of the leading minds in the country, yet confronted face-to-face, he responded like a bumbling uncle.

Vicky D'Souza snatched the notebook back, her enthusiasm unabated.

'Deal. But you have to tell me everything. Like *everything*, nothing held back. Where's the inspector, what angle you're working, all of it.'

Rachel's smile was noncommittal. She gave Vicky an edited version of events, ending with the Mossadegh letters and the coronation footage. She nodded at the screen behind Vicky's head. When Vicky turned to look at the screen, Rachel mouthed the words *be careful* at Nate.

'We've looked at all the available footage of the coronation we could find, and it turns out Zahra was right. The Shah's arrival at his coronation wasn't filmed. We couldn't find any photographs either. We don't know why it's important, but we were hoping you could help us.'

Vicky wrinkled her nose.

'I used the CBC archives to do some research.' She counted off on her fingers, the nails painted a luscious red. A black lightning bolt was etched over the polish on each of her index fingers. 'One, the letters disappeared the day Dariush Forouhar was murdered. Everyone assumed agents of the regime destroyed them. What you may not know is that Forouhar's wife was murdered along with Forouhar. A book of poems she'd written and Forouhar's diary were also taken.'

Vicky gave them a quick summary of the Chain Murders. Rachel listened, appalled. She knew human rights abuses took place with alarming regularity around the world. Activists and journalists were particularly vulnerable when it came to authoritarian regimes, but the blatancy of the Chain Murders came as a shock to Rachel.

'The diary was probably taken so the assassins could track down other members of the Iranian Writers' Association. But we don't know why the Mossadegh letters were destroyed.'

'Is that item number two?' Rachel asked.

'Not yet. Like I said, the Mossadegh letters were personal. Mossadegh is a figure of some importance. Many of the Green Movement posters feature Mossadegh and Mir Hossein Mousavi side by side, linking the Green Movement to Mossadegh's democratic ideals. There's no connection between Mossadegh and the coronation of the Shah: Mossadegh died in 1967. The coronation took place in 1968.'

'So why the arrival footage?' Rachel asked. 'Did Zahra think someone who attended the coronation might have his hands on the letters?'

Nate placed a hand on Rachel's shoulder. She felt the warmth of his touch through her shirt and looked up, but he wasn't paying attention.

'No,' he said. 'Forouhar's assassins would have burned the letters, Mossadegh's words were too powerful. He was Iran's first serious liberal democrat. He passed sweeping electoral reforms, he limited the powers of the monarchy. His nationalization of the oil industry provoked a crisis with Great Britain that led to his downfall. He was too popular for the monarchy to have him killed, so he was placed under house arrest until his death. The letters to Forouhar may have been personal, but they were also a national treasure. They're a loss to the historical record.'

This was the kind of thing Rachel expected Nate to pull from his head. She patted the hand on her shoulder in a gesture of approval. Nate responded by squeezing her fingers, suddenly alert to where he'd left his hand. Rachel didn't shrug it off.

Vicky cleared her throat, Rachel snapped back to attention.

'This isn't the only footage of the coronation. And contrary to expectations, the internet was of more use than the CBC's archives. Take a look at this.'

Vicky switched over to the internet and called up the website of the BBC's Persian news service. A quick descriptor typed into the search engine yielded a two-minute video of the coronation. The sound and picture were relatively clear, the commentator speaking in Farsi. They watched the imperial procession at the palace.

The Crown Prince appeared first, followed by his mother and her six maids of honor. The Shah came next, dressed in military uniform. He preceded the heads of the army, navy, and air force. These were followed by the bearers of the crowns of the Shah and the Empress.

Rachel had studied the imperial crowns in great detail on the internet. Of particular fascination had been a 1968 *National Geographic* article that showcased the coronation. The article had focused on the accoutrements of the Shah: the royal scepter, the imperial sword, the emerald belt – there were no superlatives that could do justice to the wealth on display. But of the Mossadegh letters, there was no mention.

The video ended as the Shah ascended the Naderi Throne, a gem-encrusted throne commissioned during the Qajar dynasty. The Naderi name wasn't a reference to Nader Shah, the raider of India. Rather, the word *nader* meant 'rare' or 'unique.' A lion cavorted on the footrest, while a peacock's tail formed the back of the chair. As a result, the throne was often mistaken for the Peacock Throne of the Mughals, which had long since been looted and dismantled. The Naderi Throne suffered little by comparison; it was just as profuse in gemstones.

'Okay,' Rachel said when the video ended. 'Rich people throwing lavish parties for themselves. What does this have to do with Zahra?'

'I agree,' Nate said. 'This footage has been out in the world for nearly fifty years. What are we looking for?'

'Max said his mother wanted to see the Shah's cap. That's why she was looking for the footage.'

Vicky's answer didn't make anything clearer to Rachel.

'The crown of Reza Shah? It's the centerpiece of the coronation.'

She skipped the video back. The Pahlavi Crown filled the entire screen. Fashioned of gold and silver, the crown was set with a multitude of diamonds. Hundreds of natural pearls were arranged in orderly rows. It was also emblazoned with emeralds, the largest at the crown's apex, a hundred-carat stone blossoming from a plume.

The commentary advised them that the coronation crown, the regalia of state, and the Peacock Throne were kept in a vault of the Central Bank of Iran, treasures that backed the national currency.

Vicky reset the video to the frame of the Golestan Palace, site of the coronation.

'Since when is a crown a cap?' Vicky asked, slipping her notebook and pencil into her bag. 'When Max said *cap*, he meant the Shah's military cap.'

Nate peered down Rachel's shoulder, squinting his eyes at the screen. His breath tickled her ear.

'By all means, have my stool.'

Rachel scooted off before she could fall off. She was flustered by Nate's closeness. She hadn't noticed the Shah's uniform.

'Rachel.' Nate's eyes glinted with discovery. 'The Shah's in uniform, but he isn't wearing a cap. And no one's holding it for him either.'

Vicky punched his elbow.

'That's not all,' she said. 'I couldn't find a single photograph of the Shah wearing his cap during the coronation ceremonies. It's not on the other videos either.'

'What about the video at the reference library? Engstrom said he sent you there. Did you find *The Lion of Persia*?'

'Zahra was the last patron to take it from the library. She didn't return it. But it doesn't really matter, does it? Because we know Zahra was looking for the cap.'

There was no eureka moment for Rachel. She shrugged, unconcerned.

'Seen one, seen them all. The Shah was a dictator, his police terrorized the citizenry. Maybe he didn't wear the cap because he thought he should underplay his legacy.'

'Then why would he be wearing his uniform?' Nate asked. 'And let's remember, the Shah never apologized for the excesses of his police, they were carried out at his direction.'

Vicky nodded happily at Nate's elbow.

'It's true, there's no evidence the Shah wore the cap on the day of the coronation. The real question is why Zahra found the omission important.'

Rachel flicked on the light in the screening room. Vicky looked from Rachel to Nate with the hopeful expression of a puppy.

'I did manage to winkle a few tidbits out of Max. Does the name Vic Mean ring any bells? He said he overheard his mother ask about Vic Mean on the phone.'

Nate's response was wry. 'If you knew, you wouldn't be asking us.'

Vicky flashed him a devil-may-care grin.

'I Googled it like crazy, no luck. But I know someone who might be able to help.'

Rachel waited, her face alert.

'This is old history we're dragging up, right? Well, get a load of this. Before she left for Iran, Zahra met with an archivist at the ROM. The one in charge of records.'

Nate spoke before Rachel could. The ROM was the Royal Ontario Museum, and as such, familiar ground to him.

'Do you mean Charlotte Rafferty?'

'Do you know her?'

'Just by reputation.'

'Max said his mother had an appointment with Charlotte Rafferty. I checked into who she is – that's how I know where she works. She thought Charlotte could help her find Vic Mean.'

'And did she?' Rachel asked. She was getting the sense this case might be about something, after all. Maybe it was a puzzle with a few missing pieces, or maybe it was a chess game.

Vicky slid off her stool. She linked her arm with Rachel's.

'Why don't we go to the ROM and find out?'

Nate smiled at them weakly. 'A reporter, a cop, and a writer,' he began.

Rachel's scowl cut him off. She didn't want Vicky at the ROM. But shutting her out wasn't an option just yet.

22

Bread and Surpluses

One piece of potato, one piece of bread. Fourteen of us in the cell, six are gone, there's a little extra, they forget to subtract the dead. I eat, I chew, I think about my friend Ahmed, who was here for weeks, then mysteriously gone. I chew his share of bread, but I can't ask about him without risking myself or the others. The others want to know how I keep my sense of humor as our numbers continue to dwindle. I'm no longer coughing blood, isn't that reason enough? It's not. So I tell them about a beautiful girl, a girl whose eyes make slaves of kings, whose voice is like a sonnet, whose heart buds like a pomegranate with seeds of love and mercy. I forgot. Before all this, I was a storyteller like Darius. My cellmates love my stories, they make dirty remarks like pigs. 'Shut up,' I say. 'I'm talking about my sister.'

23

The meeting place Taraneh had whispered to Khattak was a house in the Armenian quarter, southwest of the city center. Khattak employed an English-speaking guide to take him on a tour of New Jolfa. He'd spent part of the day at his guesthouse, distracted by a new set of worries.

He'd passed the risk of the letters and the security footage on to a group of young people with far more to lose. By any measure, his actions were not in compliance with the terms of his visa, or with his status as a citizen of Canada.

You sound like an American, Larijani had warned him.

And it *was* a warning. Coupled with the theft of his phone, he knew he was right to be on his guard. As he embarked on his day tour with his guide, he kept an eye out for a tail.

His guide, Bahman, was a middle-aged man who seemed to know less about the sights than Khattak had discovered through his guide-book. They visited a number of churches in the Armenian quarter, before ending up at All Saviors Cathedral, also known as the Church of Saint Joseph of Arimathea. The Kelisa-ye Vank was the focal point of Iran's Armenian church. The Christian community had been thriving at one time, its religious freedom guaranteed by Shah Abbas I, who attended Epiphany at the church and transported significant Christian relics from other parts of his realm to enhance the cathedral's stature.

Bahman dozed on a bench in the churchyard while Khattak inspected the cathedral's anomalous depiction of the Old and

New Testaments. The saga of Abel fanned across the eastern dome, elsewhere the story of Hagar and Ismail was paired with the Nativity. A scene of the Ten Commandments was painted opposite the cathedral's entrance, while a beautifully restored Last Judgment framed the door.

Families mingled in the alcoves, tourists like himself, or Esfahani Armenians whose lineage dated to Shah Abbas's transport of the village of Jolfa on Iran's northern border to New Jolfa on the outskirts of Esfahan. It was a thriving place with an atmosphere of liberal exchange.

When enough time had passed, Khattak invited his guide to dinner at the Khan Gostar restaurant behind the cathedral. They ate a meal of traditional Persian food, watching shadows streak across the cathedral as the sun sank in an amber ball.

It was a peaceful scene that echoed the pattern of Esa's days, reminding him of Iran's contrasts. A vibrant people, steeped in the traditions of an ancient civilization, were eager to engage with the rest of the world. Their daily concerns were similar to Khattak's. Families gathered in parks, young people met in cafés to share their gossip about the day's events – everything was familiar. Just last week, he'd witnessed a painted bride in a fulsome dress posing for her pictures in a park, her mother giving directions to a harried-looking photographer, while the groom stood by, smiling and sweating.

But there was another Iran as well. The country's human rights record had consistently been rated one of the world's worst: a repressive ruling elite maintained the forms of due process without a corresponding legitimacy. An unjust judicial system was deeply politicized, the organs of the state rife with corruption, the forces of law and order militarized. The state's enemies were reformists, intellectuals, students, teachers, lawyers, journalists, union leaders, women's rights groups, artists, filmmakers, and musicians. The prison system was designed to stamp out any impetus for change.

If life was lived in accordance with the regime's rules, this other Iran might pass unnoticed, like a subterranean river running through a channel of denial. Head scarves could slip back on heads, young people could meet on ski slopes, families could watch Western television programs at home. And the green wave that had swept the country in 2009 would recede, the ordinariness of a life without autonomy resumed. But perhaps even this ordinariness, this attempt to continue in the face of repression, was a daily reminder of resistance. A well-known Iranian scholar had described this as 'the art of presence.'

Khattak checked his watch. It was time for his meeting with the Green Birds of June.

He exchanged the ritual pleasantries of offering to pay for the meal with his guide, a performance in which both parties knew their roles. Once the demands of *taruf* had been satisfied, he assured Bahman he would be fine to return to his guesthouse alone.

As a precaution, he indicated to Bahman he was thinking of returning to Tehran within the next few days, his visit to Iran at an end. If Larijani were to stop Bahman to quiz him about Khattak's movements, the message would serve to divert him.

But as he said it, he realized it was also true.

He was anxious to leave, constrained without Rachel at his side, unwilling to attract attention to the work of a group of dissidents whose movement had been crushed.

If the regime had not hesitated to order Zahra's death at such minimal provocation, he feared for Taraneh and Nasreen, and for the confident young men he'd met that morning.

Digging into Zahra's death in Iran was nothing like carrying out a homicide investigation in Toronto. He was on his own, he was carrying the weight of his past mistakes, he was outside his natural authority, and he admitted to himself he was afraid.

How much more he admired Zahra Sobhani as a result.

He would do this for Zahra, he thought. As much as he

thought was sensible and safe, and when he thought he was stepping over the line, he'd get back on a plane to Canada and tell himself he'd done enough.

It took Khattak several tries to find the house. It was at the end of a warren of streets with no number on the door. He passed it twice. On his third try, Ali Golshani pulled him into the doorway.

A finger to his lips, he led Khattak across a deserted courtyard, up a set of narrow stairs to a rooftop with a five-foot concrete wall. There were no lights, the roof was cloaked in black. Several young men huddled over their laptops, sprawled on rugs they had dragged to the roof. Light flickered from their laptop screens and cell phones.

'It's all right,' Ali said. 'Nothing will happen to you here.'

Khattak wasn't listening, shocked by what else was on the roof, shocked he'd been invited to this place. A collection of satellite dishes was situated below the wall in the corners of the rooftop, their mounting brackets loosely bolted, their masts positioned in different directions.

He relaxed all at once, his body no longer communicating its tension.

These young men wouldn't have allowed him onto this roof if they intended to betray him to agents of the regime. The satellite dishes were far more dangerous to the Green Birds than to Khattak. They should have been much more worried than they were. He wondered if the distance from the stolen election had made the young men complacent about their safety.

They had gathered around a broadcast of the BBC's reputable Persian news service. If the state media was Orwellian in its double-speak, the BBC Persia was its corrective. Launched six months before the stolen election, it delivered Persian-language news to a hundred million Farsi speakers in Afghanistan, Uzbekistan, Tajikistan, and Iran. It had distinguished itself with coverage of the protests that arose after the funeral of the leading reformist cleric, Ayatollah Montazeri, who'd become a virtual prisoner in his own home. Accused of working to thwart the interests of the regime, BBC Persia was banned inside the country.

Ali ushered Khattak to a chair. He snapped his fingers, and one of the young men on the roof slipped downstairs to fetch tea. Omid was at the center of the group, Darius at his shoulder. Nasreen was absent. The first thing Khattak had done was look for her.

When Khattak had accepted a glass of tea and taken a sugar cube to sweeten it, Ali dismissed the others without introducing him.

'The fewer of us who know who you are, the better. We think it's best if we keep what we're up to between the Hotbird Six.'

'I thought you called yourselves "the Green Birds of June".'

Khattak sipped his tea, following the discussion on Omid's laptop. It was the re-broadcast of a conversation between a BBC reporter and the Iranian journalist Akbar Ganji. Ganji had broken the story of the Chain Murders with a blockbuster exposé, quoting senior officials inside the Ministry of Intelligence. The agents implicated in the murders had been given pseudonyms, but everyone inside Iran knew whom to hold accountable. For his sins, Ganji had spent six years in solitary confinement, his long ordeal concluded by a hunger fast. He was currently in exile.

Khattak thought of Ganji's maxim.

Wherever the regime is present, the opposition must also be present.

Khattak wondered if the broadcast was for his benefit.

Ali slapped Omid on the back.

'It's the girls who like these poetic names.' He jerked his head at a satellite dish in the corner. 'We named ourselves after BBC Persia's original satellite, the Hotbird 6.'

Khattak reviewed the members of the group to himself.

'There are five of you.'

Ali's humor fell away. 'Saneh is the sixth, he's Nasreen's twin.'

Omid interrupted. 'The BBC Persia switched to other satellites because the authorities were jamming the Hotbird. For a while, the BBC could only run its test card. But now the station has switched back to the Hotbird, we decided we were playing with fire, which is too bad. It was the perfect name.'

He seemed unconcerned by the activities he was describing. Intercepted communications. Underground newsgathering and transmission. Any of these activities could fall under the rubric of propaganda against the system. The penalties, if they were caught, would be severe. And if Khattak led Larijani to these young men or to Nasreen – he didn't want to think about the consequences.

Khattak studied Omid. He might have been twenty-five or twenty-six, though the bulging muscles, greased-back hair, and general air of dissipation made him seem older. Grooves ran from the corners of his nose to his mouth, emphasizing his sardonic style of speech.

Ali and Darius seemed more like university students. Quiet, well spoken, thoughtful, their wavy hair groomed, their faces reflections of each other; young intellectuals testing out theories of democracy and statecraft by joining the underground resistance.

He wondered if their families knew of the risks they were taking.

'A man named Larijani followed me today,' he warned them.

Omid let out a short bark of laughter.

'He's a *lebas-shaksis*, a plainclothes man. He gets all the shit jobs. I'd be careful, but I wouldn't get paranoid, Larijani just wants to get paid.'

'What happens if someone connects us?' Esa asked. He gestured at the satellite dishes. 'What if Larijani gets word about this?'

'The dishes aren't bolted down. If we get a few minutes'

warning, we can shift them over to the neighbor's roof to a shed. It would be a shame if they dragged the satellite dishes down to the street. In Tehran, they crushed them with tanks.' Ali sounded wistful.

'Yeah,' Omid chimed in. 'Because this isn't the only thing we like to watch.'

The young men grinned at each other, a faint blush coloring Darius's cheeks.

Khattak didn't think it was wise to linger on the roof. Larijani could be waiting in the shadows. He should find out about the footage and get out. And he would tell the others to disperse from here as well.

'Did you review the footage on the flash drive?' he asked Omid.

'Darius cleaned it up, he's the film student. But I have it here.' Omid opened a file on his screen, handing his laptop to Khattak.

Esa watched the security footage from the tower again. The images and sound were clearer this time. He jumped ahead to the moment when Zahra rubbed her hand against her neck. Again the movements jumbled together in a blur, other hands reaching for Zahra as she was hooded and detained.

He stopped the film at the critical moment.

'There,' he said. 'Something happens there, something I can't see.'

Darius leaned forward. 'I think I see what you mean.'

'Can you enlarge that section?'

'Give me a few minutes.'

The laptop changed hands again.

'Where do you see Radan?' Khattak asked.

Ali answered. 'He comes from inside the gatehouse at the end. He's the one wearing the suit, the others are in uniform.'

'And you told this to Touka Swan?'

'She saw it for herself.'

Darius called them over. He perched the laptop on the wall, an intermittent light against the mild purple waves that flooded the roof. Khattak and the others joined him. Darius used a freeze-frame function to move the footage a little at a time.

The hand Zahra pressed to her neck encountered other hands, hands that fell away as Zahra was handcuffed and marched away.

For the brief moment the hands touched, it was possible to see Zahra had passed something to her accomplice, something whose square edge was black and gold.

'There!' Ali shouted.

'What is it, do you know?'

It was Darius who answered Esa, a note of wonder in his voice.

'I know because I have one. Actually, I have a few of them. It's a compact flash.'

Esa frowned. 'I'm sorry, I don't know what that is.'

Omid removed his laptop from the wall, cradling it in his forearms. He reviewed the footage for himself.

'You're right,' he said to Darius. 'It's the compact flash from a DSLR camera like the one Zahra took to Evin.'

Now Khattak understood.

Zahra's photographs weren't lost. She'd passed them to someone in the crowd.

Someone the guards had ignored.

They couldn't tell who it was from the footage.

They were at a dead end.

'You were friends of Zahra, you said. But none of you were in Tehran that day, none of you accompanied her to the prison. Why is that?'

At the change in Khattak's tone, Omid pushed his shoulders back. Though he loomed over Khattak, he seemed defensive.

'We have to think of our families. We put them through enough during the election.'

Darius added more, holding up his hands as if he were framing a scene. His long, gentle face was filled with an abstracted urgency, the recent past renewing itself in his words as he spoke.

'We weren't worried about what might happen at a demonstration. We didn't ask if the other protesters were students, or if they were agents of the regime hoping we'd take the bait.'

He went on to describe the days of the election as a fever dream, the faces in the crowd like a waving field of wheat, something to be planted, something to be reaped. He spoke of a sense of jubilation, of personal invincibility. And then he spoke of community, his eyes wet.

Omid interrupted him.

'Tehran was like a war zone. Our families didn't know if we'd been arrested or shot, or buried in the night like the carcasses of dogs. But they couldn't stop us from going out again.'

'We thought everything would change,' Darius said. 'The Green Movement was like a wave.'

Khattak gestured at the roof. He was deeply moved by their description of the protests. He was beginning to imagine the films a young man like Darius would make. But he could also feel the hollowness of their hope.

'And this is what's left? Satellite dishes on a rooftop? What is your actual work?'

It came out sounding harsher than he'd meant.

'There's not many of us left.' Ali braced his elbows on the wall. 'We learned some lessons from the Arab Spring. Libya, Egypt, Syria.' He spoke with an air of detachment, laying out the facts like the journalist he'd been. 'The army moves against the people, the country falls apart, the population is displaced or violently suppressed. Walls go up around the world, saying, "Don't come here, you're not wanted." So in Iran, we chose stability over freedom. But that doesn't mean we've given up.'

Then Khattak was right to worry. 'Then what are you actually doing?'

Ali looked over at Omid, perhaps to ask his permission. After a weighty moment of decision, Omid gave the barest nod.

'We've built a network of others like ourselves. That's why we have someone inside Evin. And he's not the only one, there are many others. Whenever an organization is shut down – a human rights group, a defense lawyer's office, a student protest – we do what we can to further their work. We connect people, we pay informants – we get behind closed doors. And we keep track of our fellow protesters. Every now and again we hack into the regime's propaganda services with information on political prisoners. We keep their voices alive.'

Darius looked at Khattak searchingly.

'We want the regime to know that we're watching, so they don't disappear our friends.'

Khattak's reply was grave. 'They killed Zahra Khanom anyway.'

Darius looked stricken. 'We didn't say we have any power. Their resources are so much greater than ours – they have a dozen hackers for every one of ours. It doesn't mean we shouldn't try.'

Khattak studied each of their faces. He heard the quiet force of their words.

They were representative of a generation who would use music to express their defiance like the rapper Shahin Najafi, or make films to surpass the meditations of Kiarostami. The Iran of social scientists, religious reformists, and civil society activists who'd articulated a strategy of institution-building and engagement, of constitutionality above all, and a democratic future at the end of a long road.

A green road.

The confrontation was simply delayed.

'Tell me about Zahra,' he said at last. 'Tell me how I can help.'

A signal passed between Omid and the others.

'Zahra wanted answers about conditions inside Evin. She asked about Ward 209. She wanted to know about connections between the prosecutor's office and the prison's interrogators. She wanted Roxana out of the country.'

'Those seem like sound reasons for a politically motivated murder.' Khattak said it gently, wanting to bring them around to a truth they would have to accept in time.

'If that's what she wanted, why was she taking photographs at Evin? She wasn't foolish, there had to be a reason.'

Khattak realized he was right. And he wondered if that reason had been orchestrated to place Zahra in a position where she was most vulnerable. Someone could have wanted Zahra at Evin that day – but to get her there, Radan would have needed an accomplice. He wouldn't have been able to persuade her on his own, Zahra would never have trusted him. Which left Khattak with the question, what had Zahra been offered to induce her to dare the prison?

'If it wasn't one of you she passed the flash card to, do you have any idea who it could have been? It would help to see the photographs on her camera.'

'I can ask around,' Ali said. 'Zahra had other contacts. Will you stay in Esfahan a day or two more? Come to the *zurkhaneh* wrestling pit on Tuesday and sit at the back. One of us will meet you there.'

It was the least Khattak could do.

'Don't send Taraneh or Nasreen,' he advised, remembering Larijani. 'Think of the kind of trouble that's possible.'

Omid flashed him an incredulous look.

'Is that how you do it where you're from? Who do you think pioneered the One Million Signatures campaign?' He snorted. 'An Iranian *woman* won the Nobel Peace Prize, it wasn't one of our distinguished mullahs.'

'I'm not discounting that,' Esa said. 'I have as much respect for Shirin Ebadi as I do for Zahra. I'm worried the consequences will be worse for your friends than for you.'

Omid shrugged this off.

'Then you don't know Kahrizak like we do. Girls aren't the only ones who get raped.'

Khattak braced himself against this knowledge.

'Is Saneh Ardalan still alive?'

'We don't know. You can't imagine how little they care about us. If the leaders of the Green Movement are under house arrest, what do you imagine our lives are worth?'

Darius swept his hands together as if he was brushing chalk dust from them.

'Nothing,' he told them. 'They don't even count in the balance.'

As Khattak looked at Darius, he thought of a report he'd read of another of the regime's victims, and of the quiet dignity of a father's elegy for his son. His tribute was still fresh in Khattak's mind.

He wanted to be a filmmaker. He was the kind of boy, believe me, who would have been another Asghar Farhadi. But I knew if my son studied art in this country, he would either starve to death or end up in prison.

The young man had been shot and killed at a demonstration. The government had offered compensation for his death – the family had refused to accept.

We could never betray our son. We give him to the Iranian nation. And we ask the artists to remember him.

Listening to the rhythms of Darius's speech, Khattak recognized an artist prepared to sacrifice himself, not for the nation but for an idea.

This is a path of long and grave suffering.

'All right,' he said. 'I'll be there. But don't take any unnecessary risks.'

Perhaps as a concession to Khattak, Omid offered, 'It's a men's exercise class. They don't allow women to attend, so there's no reason for you to worry.'

Khattak wondered if he was disappointed not to be seeing Nasreen.

Omid asked for his cell phone.

'This is yours?'

'Yes. I have a disposable one I've been using to call my partner. This is my personal phone.'

'You won't need the other one.' Omid made a few quick adjustments to Khattak's phone. 'I've downloaded the Telegram app to your phone. You'll be able to send and receive encrypted messages that are timed to self-destruct. You can do the same thing with phone calls, delete the records. You can also send media, but for now I'll do that for you if it's necessary. You don't need to keep buying SIM cards.'

'The service hasn't been banned?'

Omid shrugged. 'Not yet. It could happen at any time, depending on events.'

Khattak thanked him, unable to shake the shadow of his fear.

Omid smiled. 'You're an honorary member,' he said. 'You could be the sixth.'

24

The American Prisoner

'Do you know Jason Rezaian?' It's the first question any of us gets asked. I feel sorry for Jason, but I'm also jealous. So many people are working to have him released. He'll have phone calls to his mother, rations of rice and kebab, someone will cut his hair and shave his beard. He'll have a table, some books, a pen and paper. I bet the guards ask questions about Anthony Bourdain. His room must be ten times the size of mine. There's no gun to his head, no one asks where he's from, no one calls him a traitor peshmerga. No one hangs him from a hook or beats him with a cable, no one breaks his teeth or batters his genitals. And when the Swiss liaison reports on whether Evin's guards are adhering to the Geneva Conventions, he'll leave behind a piece of soap and a Toblerone bar, enacting a chocolate diplomacy. Jason Rezaian isn't a Kurd. To him, they won't say, 'Tell us what you've done, tell us who our enemies are.'

But I don't know what the hell I'm talking about because I haven't been to the Suite.

25

A case without a case, and technically, Rachel was her own boss until Khattak returned. She hadn't been doing much of late, closing cases, reviewing potential trouble spots, making note of groups they should meet with to further the work of Community Policing. And just a bit of personal stuff on the side – looking for a piano teacher, hoping to relight a spark that had never really had a chance to catch. The piano at Max Najafi's house had reminded her. Nate's ease with the piano had been a luxury Rachel couldn't have afforded in Don Getty's home. But she'd thought she'd always known how to listen, how to hear what the music was saying.

Her mother playing Shostakovich's Romance in C Major.

Hope springing eternal, youth and loveliness, a girl's first kiss.

Her mother racing through the introduction of the *Carnival of the Animals.*

Her father using his fists on Zachary.

And when one of those moods of introspection would bring Rachel and her mother close together, 'Tristesse,' always 'Tristesse.' Rachel hadn't liked it then, she didn't like its somber perfection now. Sometimes Zach had hidden under the piano.

A young Rachel had had a penchant for *The Nutcracker.* In a good mood, her mother would play the 'Waltz of the Flowers' or the 'Grand Pas de Deux,' but these were pieces served better by an orchestra than an out-of-tune piano.

They had listened to a recording of the music on an endless loop, the music transforming the damp space of the basement into a concert hall with velvet seats and a magical stage, a subtle commotion of violins and reeds.

Lillian had never taken Rachel to see the National Ballet.

When she'd finally attended a performance on her own, it had felt as though her heart was no longer stagnant, the music hastening her – delicate as the strings of a harp, bright as the notes of a trumpet – untethered, fleet-footed, vast with her imaginings.

It was why she was playing it now.

Zach was coming over, their last uneasy conversation resulting in a shared project that Rachel hoped they could navigate together.

Anyone would have thought she was crazy.

She was finally out on her own, out of Don Getty's house, distant from the tangled emotions that tied her to her mother, her life a field of spring, redolent with promise.

And now she was taking on her brother, closing down the possibilities of her personal space, of whatever romantic inclinations she may have possessed because she wanted to assure Zach that now he came first, now there was no one else. Not Esa Khattak, not Nathan Clare. And definitely not Don or Lillian Getty.

Zach knocked on the open door, and Rachel reminded herself to play it cool.

She grinned at her brother, waving the paintbrush in her hand.

'Is this what you had in mind?'

She was dressed in a tattered hockey jersey. Her yoga pants had lost their clinging elasticity and were moored drunkenly below her hips. Her hair was piled in a straggly knot on top of her head.

Zach's room was empty, a ladder in one corner, painting gear strewn over drop cloths that covered the floor.

He looked exactly like Rachel. Maybe an inch taller, his face leaner, with the same sparky brown eyes, the same reluctant smile that fought back at the corners, the same square-shouldered frame. He was wearing eyeliner, something Rachel never did. And he was carrying a giant duffel bag. She wondered if it contained the sum total of his possessions.

'You can leave that in the laundry room, if you want.'

Zach slouched over to his sister. He'd developed the habit of pressing a snuffling kind of kiss into her hair, snagging one of his earrings in the process.

One ear had studs. The other had a dangling lightning bolt that reminded Rachel of Vicky D'Souza's fingernails. He shrugged his bag onto the floor, and folded his lanky limbs onto her leather couch.

'You sure you're cool with this?'

It took every ounce of Rachel's self-possession not to betray her quivering excitement.

'I am entirely cool,' she said, flattening her voice on purpose. 'I am as cool as a big sister can possibly be.'

'Shut up,' was Zach's answer.

An awkward grin broke over his face, the first one Rachel had seen in a while. The anger that had simmered between them had faded. They were ready to tease each other again.

Rachel dropped the paintbrush, busying herself in the kitchen. 'You want a drink?'

'Do you have beer?'

Rachel liked the occasional beer, but she'd emptied her fridge in honor of Zach's arrival. He was over the legal drinking age, she just had a healthy respect for alcohol, given their family history.

The 'Waltz of the Flowers' continued to play in the background.

She passed him a Canada Dry.

'Sorry, I'm out.'

They sat and talked for a few minutes, catching up on each

other's news. When Rachel told Zach about Nate's involvement in her latest case, his eyes grew round and wide.

'No shit,' he said.

'No swearing,' she answered. 'And yeah, it's true. People like him, they tell him things they probably wouldn't tell me.'

She was remembering Max Najafi's intense interest in Nate's performance at the piano.

'He's like your Watson.' Zach smirked. 'With a corncob pipe and whatnot.'

'You're thinking of Frosty the Snowman,' Rachel said drily. 'And yeah, he's exactly like my Watson.'

Zach finished his drink and reached for his paintbrush. Rachel had told him his room in her condo was his, he could do anything he wanted to it.

After she'd made the offer, she'd had a sudden vision of Zach painting the whole room black, shuttering its windows and creating a collage of zombies in various stages of decay. But Zach was still under the influence of his Viennese art experience. He'd decided to paint a large mural on one wall, a tree spiraling out from a smaller tree, each of the leaves picked out like the tiles of a gold mosaic, gold leaf on oil, the bedroom wall for his canvas.

Rachel's job was to help him seal the wall with primer.

She'd left the windows in the condo open. A mild breeze drifted through the room as they worked. Zach's room had a view of the park. He took a vivid interest in the maples and alders coming into leaf. He'd always paid close attention to the natural world, a form of escape from their father.

'Ray,' he said. 'How come you're still on your own? Why don't you have someone?'

Rachel swept a swathe of dull gray paint up the wall with her brush.

'My hours are irregular. Most guys don't like that.'

'But some must be willing to put up with it,' he persisted. 'You're not exactly hideous.'

'Gee, thanks.' Rachel cracked a smile. 'I'll be sure to put that on my online profile. "Works with cops. Isn't exactly hideous".'

Zach grunted a laugh. 'I'm just saying. What about this guy Nate? He seems cool.'

Zach had met Nate at one of Rachel's hockey games.

'A bit nerdy but a possibility. He seemed into you, I thought.'

He was painting with more technique than Rachel, his strokes aligned and steady.

'You figure? What makes you think that?'

Now Rachel wished she'd worn her hair down so she could shield her face. But her brother didn't notice the red blotches on her skin.

'He came to your game, didn't he? And from what I remember, it was freezing that day.'

The day of the all-stars game. The game her mother had promised to come to but hadn't shown up for.

'He's a friend of the boss.'

'But *you're* working with him now,' Zach said with the insular familiarity of a brother who'd always been part of her life, and felt he could freely comment.

'That doesn't mean anything.' She reached down to scoop more paint from the tray, wondering why Zach couldn't have let her use a roller. She had the shoulders for a roller, but Zach said painting with a roller lacked artistry.

Artists were not the most practical of people.

'You want pizza for dinner?'

'I was thinking sushi.'

They had come to the middle of the wall, and now brother and sister had no choice but to look each other in the eye.

'It's not because of me, is it? Mum said you haven't dated much, I thought maybe me being gone – it was holding you back. Now I'm here, I'm probably cramping your style.'

Rachel held her breath. Zach cared about her, he wanted her to be happy. She managed a rusty chuckle.

'Trust me, I have no style to cramp, and that has nothing to do with you.'

It would have overwhelmed Zach if she'd said, *I'd rather have you here than anyone else in the world. I'd trade anything for you, I'd do anything for you. I'm trying not to breathe too hard in case it scares you away. I want us to talk. About these last seven years, about everything in between. Everything you did, everyone who helped you, everyone you've come to love.*

'I appreciate it, Zach. Don't worry. If someone decides it's worth his while to take me on, we can work out a system.' And then changing the subject from herself: 'What about you? This thing with Ashleigh over for good?'

Zach took his paintbrush and swiped just the tip of Rachel's nose with it. A droplet fell on her tongue, and she coughed.

'Hey!'

'Subtle,' he responded. He wasn't as dejected as at their last meeting. 'I think so. I guess it was time. You can go a little crazy in Europe, but when you're back home facing the cold light of day, things start to look different.'

Rachel wiped the paint off her nose with the back of her sleeve.

They took their brushes to the laundry room sink and began to wash them in a companionable silence. Rachel wondered if she dared to say a little more.

'Will you be okay?'

Zach flicked a little water in Rachel's face. She spluttered. She'd forgotten this about brothers – the physical teasing, the delight they took in immature pranks. A knot inside her chest began to ease. She splashed him back. They giggled as if they were ten years younger.

'Plenty of fish, Ray.' Zach patted himself down with a towel. 'Anyway, I realized something.'

'Oh yeah? What's that?'

'I don't like girls who spell their names "Ashleigh." I was out of her league, right from the start. She was slumming around with us, she didn't know how to paint. Everything she knew was something she'd cribbed from the internet.'

Ouch, Rachel thought. Ashleigh had probably wanted to enjoy a dizzy summer in Vienna with Zach. Now Zach was judging her with all the harshness of disappointed youth.

She pondered the most tactful thing she could say without alienating her brother.

'She must have wanted you to like her, then maybe it got harder to pretend she was someone she wasn't. I'm glad you parted on good terms, though.'

She'd never had the chance to knock this lesson into her brother's head, but Don Getty had taught him anyway. When a woman was done with you, you didn't bully or belittle her, stalk her friends, call her names, or use violence. You expressed gratitude for the time you'd been given, then opened your hands and let her go.

Police work meant Rachel was frequently seeing the worst of people.

She was glad Zach wasn't in that category.

'I'm proud of you, Ray,' he said to her. 'I know I said it was your fault, me leaving, but what did I know? I was a kid. I thought all cops were like Da.'

Rachel's throat seized up. Her hand fastened on to her paintbrush like a claw. Zach's brown eyes didn't waver from hers. His voice was shaky but determined.

'I know what the news says about your cases, but you're the bravest person I know. The things you do matter.' He sounded younger suddenly, uncertain. 'Don't they?'

Rachel swallowed. 'I think they do. It matters to me that Zahra Sobhani was murdered. I want to know why. I want to do what I can to help.'

'So what happens next? What are you hoping to find at the ROM? I could come with you,' he suggested.

Rachel was surprised. 'You want to help with the case?'

Zach's aversion to policing had been the dividing line between Rachel and her brother.

'I could hang around the museum, there's a new design exhibit I could check out.'

Rachel laughed.

'After the dinosaur exhibit, you mean.'

Zach looked sheepish. 'What's wrong with that?'

A powerful wave of love squeezed Rachel's heart. She had often taken Zach to the ROM to see the dinosaurs, memory's harbor, a place of consolation, free of their father's violence.

'That sounds good. Maybe you could do something for me while you're there. See if there's anything in the collection that might have been of interest to Zahra.'

She told him about the coronation of the Shah. She was wondering if Zahra might have had another reason to find herself at the museum.

'She had guts,' Zach said. 'To take on a regime like that.'

'You know about it?'

'Students in other parts of the world interest me. I'm lucky, you know?'

They left their brushes to dry in the sink. Rachel picked up the phone to order sushi.

She was crushed by her brother's admission.

Whatever the fate of supporters of the Green Movement, by no scale of measurement had Zachary been lucky.

When they'd finished their dinner and Zach had crashed on one of the couches, Rachel settled into work at her table. Her gaze took in the pools of mud in the marshy park, branches snapping back from the weight of snow, tender shoots scraping the air like fingers.

Her laptop came on with a whir, a notice in her email, along with instructions about a service called Telegram.

She opened the top message from an unknown recipient,

accompanied by an outsize attachment. She clicked on the file, ignoring her computer's warning of the absence of a security certificate.

It took a moment for the file to download.

Rachel boiled milk on the stove, making cocoa for herself and Zach.

By the time it was ready, the file flashed up on her screen.

It was the transfer of a video. She watched it in silence, sipping at her drink.

When she recognized Zahra Sobhani's face, she understood what she was seeing. It was the day of Zahra's detention at Evin, the last time Zahra had been seen alive.

Rachel paid careful attention to the actions in the foreground, to the angle of the video, to the car just out of view, to the windswept chadors and head scarves, to the few men among the huddle of women – and then to the rapid denouement: guards, a struggle, a tall, imposing man with harsh, ursine features in a suit that fit him like a skin. And Zahra's hands. On the camera, at her neck, reaching to someone in the crowd.

Though instructions from Khattak would have been helpful, she didn't think it was Khattak who'd sent her the file. It must have been someone he was working with in Iran, who knew how to transmit the video safely.

She wondered what to do with the file. She could sit on it until Khattak was safely out of the country, or she could turn it over to Max Najafi. For a moment she toyed with the idea of sharing the video with Vicky before dismissing the possibility.

The video might prove too much of a temptation.

It was career-making, career-defining.

And she could drag Khattak into a greater mess by trusting Vicky with his safety. Suppose she released the video while Khattak was still in Iran.

Rachel looked over at Zach. He was grinning at his text messages, his rangy body relaxed, his ear piercings reminding her of a young Zach dressed as a pirate on Halloween.

Now wasn't the time to tell Max, she decided.

She'd sent Vicky and Nate to track down *The Lion of Persia*. If they were able to find a copy of the film, she might learn more about the Shah's military cap.

And then she'd have something concrete to discuss with Max because she couldn't go back to see him without offering him something in exchange.

He'd been lost in his thoughts, contemplating Nate at the piano, the unfinished composition veering from its scripted course to something dark and exquisite.

Had Max watched the music or the man?

And Rachel realized she was searching for a weakness, the way she would with a suspect.

26

The Story of Piss-Pants

Piss-Pants is dead. They claim many of us commit suicide, either in prison, or on the way to the hospital. But Piss-Pants really did commit suicide – like a pact he made with the devil he was bound to follow through. Someone helped him, while one of the others, the son of a cleric, recited prayers. I didn't try to stop them, I was weak. I won't be able to stand until my kidneys heal, otherwise I would have told him, it feels like this now – like the world is full of nothing but suffering and pain – but it will pass, and I would know, it happened to me as well. He was sobbing like a child, he said he wanted to die. He didn't want it to happen again, it's the same in every group. They take the youngest to the cell next door, then you hear the grunting and the screams. They shove the youngest back into your cell, naked and bloody, in a state of shock. Piss-Pants was dribbling saliva, his eyes unable to focus. 'Kill me, kill me, kill me,' he said. Someone gave him a belt. The son of the cleric was the one who saw it through, the one who held his hand and looked deep into his eyes until he'd stopped breathing. When I think about the Islamic Republic, I'll remember this son of a cleric and his prayers. He was the second youngest, the one they raped next, the fucking pedophiles.

That's the holy Republic.

27

Nate sat alone at a writing desk placed before a stretch of windows that paneled the lake into even sections like a triptych. In the first panel, a wall of sea foam; in the second, an arbitrary shifting of blues; in the final, a complement of sailboats dashed upon blue-gray waves.

Blue, gray, white.

The ages of a man.

He was thinking of three women.

The first was Zahra Sobhani, whom he'd known at a remove, gracious, brilliant, committed to a cause. She'd spoken at the film festival about the Iran of her youth, the Iran of her memories and dreams, and of her hopes for its future. She hadn't spoken of Roxana.

He cast his thoughts back to the music room in Max Najafi's house, where a cluster of family photographs had lined one wall of the hallway. He found he couldn't remember the faces, distracted by the splendor of the Bösendorfer. When he'd played it, the memory of Zahra's life seemed to be contained in its full, round voice.

Zahra Sobhani had been something of a cipher.

She'd worked the festival circuit like the professional she was, and if in the midst of the celebration of her work, she'd thought of Roxana, no momentary abstraction had betrayed it.

The second woman to trouble Nate's thoughts was Sergeant Rachel Getty, a woman whose many talents had left a lasting impression. He hadn't known her long, and he couldn't say his knowledge had depth, yet they'd shared things that accelerated closeness, deepening it without requiring explanation. He was beginning to feel Esa's absence was not an obstacle to knowing Rachel better.

She was sturdy, practical, eminently sensible, her pleasant face sharpened by perception. There was an unexpected softness to her as well, when speaking of her brother, when she'd questioned Max – when she'd once tried to convince him Esa's life was immediately at risk.

If Zahra Sobhani had kept her feelings contained, Rachel was clear and direct. There'd been a moment in the reference library when he'd thought Rachel had looked at him, not as an affable partner but as a man with depths of his own.

When he'd touched her shoulder, he'd seen attraction in Rachel's eyes, and then just as quickly, a flash of hesitation and self-doubt.

He doubted she saw herself as the men around her saw her: strong, capable, determined.

She didn't recognize the fascination she'd inspired in Vicky D'Souza.

Vicky wasn't the third woman on his mind.

Thinking of the mournful pleading in Max Najafi's eyes turned Nate's thoughts to the woman in question.

You could get my mother back from Iran. There must be someone you know.

He did know someone. He didn't know how much pull she would have, but if there was one thing Nate knew about Laine, she would know the right people. And she would know how to influence them.

He was working on a new book and, in a quirk peculiar to himself, wrote the first draft in longhand before it was consigned to his study with his other manuscripts. They were filed in what his sister Audrey called his 'Cabinet of Curiosities.' All save the first draft of *Apologia*. That one he'd burned. It had laid bare the raw dissolution of self that had accompanied the end of his affair with Laine. Like a manuscript page reduced to embers, or a skeleton leached in lye.

A man made less a man and more a stranger to himself.

He'd stopped talking to Laine, and he didn't want to speak to her now.

There were others who could help him without exacting a pound of flesh, whereas Laine would carve him out at the heart.

He'd be foolish to knock on her door, when Esa had forgiven him the consequences of the affair. Nate had testified against Esa at Laine's word. He'd blindly believed any man would be susceptible to Laine's miraculous beauty, her sacramental enchantment.

Too late he'd learned her fascination for him wasn't the stuff of miracles or legends.

It was a deadly entente.

And in the games Laine had played to intrigue Esa Khattak, Nate had found himself the sacrificial lamb on the altar.

Later, he and Esa had made it up, their friendship too deep to run aground. They had talked of everything and everyone, bridging that rupture of time and loss.

Except they had never spoken of Laine.

Esa hadn't needed to, and Nate had never found the courage.

His book *Apologia* was meant to fill in that silence.

Nate looked out at the flanks of Lake Ontario, gathered to the shore by an unseen hand and released in small diminishments.

He wanted to draw the waves to himself, wanted to draw back the years to a time he'd never known Laine.

He thought of Rachel's eyes, her pragmatic, casual strength.

And hoped this time he'd be stronger.

The pavements were dry. There was no construction on the streets around the ROM. Rachel found a parking spot beside a two-hour meter off Queen's Park, an easy walk to the ROM's front entrance.

She stood beside Zach, feeling a lift of pleasure at the hungry light of morning, the breath of spring on the air and the secret joy of her brother's shoulder bumping along beside hers. He was staring at the ROM's giant glass façade with the star-struck wonder of a child.

An American architect had won the international competition to design the ROM's gravity-defying extension. Daniel Libeskind's design featured five intersecting crystal-edged blocks meant to represent prisms, a tribute to the ROM's mineralogy galleries. To Rachel, it seemed as though the pavement had been heaved up by a luminous slanting glass that cut through the heart of the city. At night the ROM sparkled like a Tiffany diamond.

She paid for the tickets, waving her brother off with a smile. They'd agreed to meet at the cafeteria in an hour. Rachel had opened a bank account for Zach. She could have given him money in a lump sum, but she thought the monthly deposit a wiser arrangement until she could get a better sense of the young man Zach had become. She was housing him, feeding him – she didn't want to undercut his hardwon independence. She knew he had a difficult road ahead pursuing a career as an artist. She wanted him to have the grit to stay on that road.

Zach gave her a thumbs-up at the sign for the dinosaur exhibit. A child's enthusiasm had turned into an amateur passion. He mouthed the name of the new exhibit with exaggerated movements that made Rachel laugh.

Wendiceratops pinhornensis.

'Named after a woman, Ray,' he called out across the atrium.

Heads turned to look at Rachel. Blushing, she pulled up her collar, crossing the spectacular atrium that showcased the museum's dual themes of nature and culture. You could find a dinosaur exhibit at the ROM alongside an Indian sand painting, or a commemoration of a First Nations artist's life, speaking to a moment in history.

Rachel crossed the main space of the Crystal, headed to the staff offices. Charlotte Rafferty had sounded suspicious on the phone, like a woman with too much to do, or a woman who believed every interaction with the police was destined to be a bad one.

It took a few wrong turns before she found Charlotte's office on the second floor. The cramped office had a low ceiling and a narrow window that jutted over Queen's Park. Every available bit of space in the office was piled high with metal-edged storage boxes and long, cardboard cylinders. The withered leaves of a dried-out fern escaped down one side of a cabinet. A gold-trimmed mug of Klimt's *The Kiss* hovered at the edge of the desk. Rachel slid it closer to the center, her hands brushing a giant personal calendar strafed with neon pink reminders. A pine-scented air freshener failed to mask an odor of damp animal fur.

The office connected to a second office through a door. A dry-erase board hung to one side of this door, marked with a series of appointments. Rachel tried to read it, but Charlotte Rafferty stood unhelpfully in the way.

Rachel had assumed that an archivist or records manager would be the ROM's equivalent of a librarian. Charlotte Rafferty's deportment dovetailed neatly with her assumption.

She was a red-haired woman in her late forties, her hair worn in a knot that listed to one side of her neck, a pencil holding it in place. Her face was narrow and pinched behind wire-rimmed glasses perched low enough on her nose to be in danger of falling off. She was wearing a white silk blouse over a black skirt, a cameo brooch pinned at her throat.

She didn't offer Rachel a seat. Rachel took one anyway, urging Charlotte to take her own overstuffed chair.

'I really don't have time for this,' she told Rachel in a querulous voice.

'I did make an appointment, Ms. Rafferty.'

When Charlotte finally sat down and crossed her legs, Rachel was able to read the calendar on the wall.

'What is it you think I can help you with?'

'I'm inquiring into the death of Zahra Sobhani. Her son says she recently made an appointment to meet with you. I'd like to know what that was about.'

'Recently?' Charlotte sounded dubious. 'I don't remember.'

'I can see her name on your calendar, Ms. Rafferty.'

Charlotte read the calendar on the wall, her fingers unlatching from her brooch.

'Do you mean the filmmaker?'

Rachel sat up straight.

'Yes. Do you remember why she asked for the meeting?'

'I don't. I don't know what she would want at the ROM.'

'Had she asked if the ROM might carry a documentary called *The Lion of Persia*? Or did she ask for any other records you may have had of the Shah of Iran's coronation in 1968?'

Charlotte tapped her fingers on the edge of her gold-rimmed mug. Her bracelet caught on the mug's handle and tipped it over. Thankfully, it was empty.

'The Shah of Iran?' she echoed. 'The ROM doesn't house anything like that in its archives. You must be thinking of the Film Reference Library.'

There was a sudden gleam in the eyes behind the wire-rimmed glasses.

Rachel began to wonder if the whole thing – fuzzy librarian, fuzzy memory – wasn't a performance of some kind.

'Maybe,' she said. 'But then why did Ms. Sobhani make an appointment to see you?' She nodded at the overflowing appointment book. 'Perhaps you made a note of your discussion.'

She reached out a hand to the book.

Charlotte jerked it out of Rachel's reach.

'You shouldn't be prying into my personal affairs, you need a warrant for that.'

Rachel looked at her with interest. With the sharp snap of her voice, Charlotte had just dropped ten years. And Rachel noticed beneath her pencil skirt, she was wearing an expensive pair of designer boots with four-inch heels. A Prada purse and matching briefcase were parked on the cabinet behind her head.

'I was going to pass it to you,' Rachel said mildly. 'So you could check for yourself. Would you be so kind?'

Charlotte flapped her hands.

'I don't take minutes of my meetings in my agenda. I wouldn't have time.'

'It must have been important if Zahra made an appointment.' And this time when Charlotte didn't answer, Rachel said, 'You do realize Ms. Sobhani was murdered? A terrible crime was committed against her, so please try to remember.'

Charlotte deflected the question again.

'Shouldn't this be a diplomatic matter? The ROM has several patrons in government circles, I wonder if I should ask for advice.'

'If you can't remember why you met with Zahra, why would you need advice?'

But Rachel knew the answer. Charlotte Rafferty wasn't skittish or absent-minded. She was hiding something. She'd mentioned her government contacts like a threat.

'Go ahead and call them. In fact, you can do it from our offices. Why don't you grab your things? We're at College Street, it won't take up too much of your time.'

Rachel came to her feet. She removed her phone from her pocket and snapped a close-up photograph of the calendar on the wall. She didn't know what the woman was trying to hide, but it wouldn't have taken much forethought to wipe off the reminder of Zahra's appointment.

Most of the appointments were block-printed in tiny, legible writing. The appointment with Zahra at the beginning of the month – on a Friday afternoon at four o'clock – was written across the calendar square in a messy hand, the letters smeared.

Zahra S. 4:00 P.M. Urgent.

'What was so urgent? Why don't you want to tell me?' Rachel remembered another piece of information passed to her by Vicky. 'Does the name Vic Mean ring any bells? Did Zahra ask you to help her find him?' Her thoughts flashed to the brash young reporter. 'Or her, if Vic Mean is a woman?'

Charlotte was staring at her calendar, mesmerized.

'Yes, all right,' she said. 'There's no need to take me to the station. Zahra came here to ask about Vic Mean.' Charlotte shook her head, the knot at the nape of her neck swinging free, red curls unfurling down her back. 'But we don't have anyone on our payroll by that name, you can ask around. Everyone will tell you the same thing.'

Rachel was suspicious of this sudden cooperation.

'Did she tell you why she was looking for Vic Mean?'

'She was ridiculously tight-lipped.' Charlotte glared at the memory. 'She wouldn't tell me why she wanted to know. I would have liked to help, that's part of my job here – finding things others can't find, but I do need some direction.'

Charlotte Rafferty had just described Rachel's experience questioning her without a trace of self-awareness.

'Why wouldn't you want to tell me that?'

Charlotte shrugged. She turned to look out the window at Queen's Park.

'We've become a surveillance state,' she said with prim authority. 'Zahra's business was her own. I don't see why I should disclose it to the police.'

There was a knock on the connecting door. A young Asian man dressed in a tailored suit interrupted them with a quick nod. He wore a gem gallery pin on one of his lapels.

'You're late for the conference call,' he said.

Rachel checked her watch. Charlotte Rafferty had allotted their appointment fifteen minutes. She didn't see any buttons glowing on the phone on Charlotte's desk. She wondered if this was a prearranged interruption.

'And you are?' she asked.

Charlotte answered for him. 'Franklin is my assistant. And he doesn't have time to waste.' She nodded at the connecting door.

Franklin turned on his heel with a finicky movement, grimacing at Rachel. When his back was to Charlotte, he mouthed four words quite distinctly.

The devil wears Prada.

Charlotte didn't hear. She picked up her phone, Rachel took that as her cue to leave.

On her way back to the atrium, she pondered how little she'd learned from the interview, puzzling over Charlotte's hostility.

What did she know about Zahra Sobhani?

Who was Vic Mean, and why had Zahra been looking for him? Why had Zahra thought that Charlotte Rafferty might know him?

A quick search on her phone turned up nothing on the name. When she typed in Victor Mean, she found dozens of names available through different professional websites. She would have to narrow these down, searching either for a direct connection to Zahra or to the coronation of the Shah. But it could be done.

She whiled away the rest of the hour in the cafeteria in the atrium, eliminating the first dozen names and moving down the list.

By the time Zach had joined her, she was halfway through.

They ordered lunch and ate their meal as Zach talked about the new design exhibit. He was thinking of exploring a new direction in his art. The city landscapes had given way to his Viennese phase – the new design exhibit seemed to suggest a return to simple forms and clarified lines, like the tree within a tree on the wall in Rachel's condo.

'Was Rafferty any help?'

'Quite the opposite,' Rachel said. 'She made it clear I was wasting her time.'

'So this was a dead end? Can I still have dessert?'

'Whatever you like,' Rachel said with a smile.

When Zach talked about art, he sounded like he'd lived a thousand lifetimes. When he talked about anything else, he seemed like a half-grown kid.

He ordered them slices of maple pecan cheesecake.

'Maybe the ROM can speak for itself,' Zach said after his first bite. 'If she came to Charlotte looking for something, that something might be at the ROM.'

'But Charlotte said the ROM has nothing on the Shah's coronation.'

'Huh.' Zach took another huge bite of his dessert. Rachel had a feeling it wouldn't be long before he moved on to her portion. She ate faster. 'That's funny. Because there are two exhibits that she may have been interested in.'

Rachel set down her fork. Why hadn't she thought of that for herself?

'Which ones?'

Zach reached for Rachel's plate.

'Sorry, one is a gallery. The Wirth Gallery of the Middle East. I think artifacts and documents from Iran are included in the collection.'

'And the other?'

Zach cleared Rachel's plate before answering.

'The other is a photography exhibit about the Silk Road. It makes a stop in Esfahan. Isn't that where your boss is now?'

Rachel's face went slack.

'How long has the exhibit been running?'

Zach pulled a brochure out of his back pocket. He unfolded its pages, his fingers tracing the lines as he read.

'It's a first for the ROM,' he said. 'It opened two months ago.'

He passed the brochure to Rachel.

She read the description carefully. She was looking for the name of the exhibit's curator. Or the featured photographers.

But the name Vic Mean appeared nowhere on the list.

That didn't mean it wasn't there.

'Come on,' she said. 'We still have our tickets. I think you could be onto something.'

Zach looked pleased with himself.

When she'd paid the bill, he led her up the intertwining staircases to the second floor. Here they wandered down a light-filled aisle to the gallery on the Middle East. Rachel stopped him at the door. She pointed to the plaque beside a set of glass doors that described the nature of the exhibits.

'Nothing past 1900. It ends seventy years too soon.'

They circled back to the Silk Road exhibit, drenched in light from the atrium.

'What are we looking for?' Zach asked.

'Try the name Vic or Victor Mean. Or anything to do with the Shah.'

They took different paths through the photographs, pausing to read the credit panels. Rachel had been expecting black-and-white photography. Instead, the panels showcased a world in color – fabrics, textiles, costumes, rivers, mountains, deserts, markets, train stations, seaports, harbors, and people from every walk of life. They were photographs of the modern phase of cities that had been essential stops for commerce along the Silk Road.

Rachel transited swiftly through China and the five 'Stans' before ending up in Iran, skipping the southern routes through India and Afghanistan. She learned of Esfahan's importance as a city on the Silk Road during the reign of Shah Abbas I, but she could see little to interest Zahra. She found no connection to the coronation of the Shah.

In her second perambulation, she encountered Zach again. He was scrutinizing photographs of life at the Caspian Sea, north of

Tehran. One of the photographs captured a scene at a seaport. A group of capable-looking men with thick, springy hair and handsome, woolly mustaches were gathered at a dock, laughing and smoking.

Zach pointed a paint-stained fingertip at a mid-sized yacht in the background.

The photographer had caught the yacht broadside.

Its name was stenciled below the pilothouse.

Rachel couldn't read the elegant Farsi script.

But she could read the English beneath it.

Zahra.

And floating above the name like a tiny balloon, the image of a film reel.

A flurry of excitement whipped along her nerve endings.

She checked the panel for additional clues.

The photograph had been taken by a Polish photographer in the early 1970s. It was from the collection of a man named Mehran Najafi.

Rachel thought she could guess who that was.

28

Interrogation

'Confess, confess, confess, confess. Call your whore of a mother, your whore of a sister, tell her you're fine, tell her to stop looking for you, or you won't like what happens next.' 'Where shall I say I am that no one can find me, no one can reach me?' 'Tell them you've gone to the mountains.' I flash them the smile of a corpse as their blows land. 'I have no mother, I have no sister. I'm alone in the world, a ribbon of smoke over the land, a child of paradise and terror.' They're so busy with their boots, they don't hear Roxana's song.

Respite

Alone in the cell now. Alone with the shit and the bloodstains. I don't know if anyone makes it out of Kahrizak. Twice when I was released from Evin, I thought it was possible the world would take me back. I could move and breathe and think like a human being, free of torture and pain. The fist that hammered the door wasn't for me, but it was, it always was. Some made it out of Evin, others disappeared. There's a secret graveyard, but the executions aren't secret. They hang you from a crane after Friday prayers, and you begin to think, Is this all God is – an executioner with a noose in his hands? And you wonder if you blame the God of paradise for the savagery of the Republic. Ahmed is gone, Piss-Pants is gone, the son of the cleric is gone, the thirty-nine in the container are gone, the nineteen from the cell are gone – and I'm left. Alone with the shit and the bloodstains.

Interrogation

'Tell us what you know about Zahra Sobhani, she was a traitor, like you.' Blow. 'She was a filmmaker, like me. I was her student.' Blow. 'That's all she wanted, to tell the stories of this beautiful nation, Iran.' Blow. Scent of cologne. 'She was a foreigner, like you. She didn't belong to Iran, neither do you, Kurd. Or are you Baha'i, even worse?' Blow. 'I'm a son of Iran, she's a daughter of Iran.' Blow. 'So you did know her, you worked with her, you conspired against the Republic.' Blow. Blow. Blow. 'Please, I can't –' 'She's dead, did you know that? Your precious filmmaker is dead, the whore of Iran is dead, did you know?'

No, God, no –

Zahra, I didn't know.

29

It was a bitingly clear Tuesday morning. Khattak finished his breakfast and bade Nasih farewell. He had asked Nasih to turn away gifts or letters that arrived for him, fearing for Nasih's safety. Whatever happened with the Green Birds, he didn't want Nasih to pay the price.

'Tell them I'm not here, I've left for Tehran.'

He held Nasih's gaze for a moment longer than necessary, until he could be sure that Nasih understood. A slight frown of worry on his amiable face, Nasih nodded his answer.

Khattak took a taxi to the gymnasium.

The weight he'd carried in the weeks leading up to his visit to Iran was beginning to shift. He was no longer as preoccupied with his mistakes. He'd set aside the question of the life he had taken, thinking of the life he might be able to answer for.

Zahra's life.

He was also deeply interested in the puzzle he couldn't unravel.

Who was sending him the letters?

And how did a yacht at the Caspian Sea fit in to the puzzle?

He'd read Rachel's text first thing that morning, a text she'd sent through Telegram, hearing the self-deprecating humor beneath her words.

My brother and me, sir. We're tag-teaming this one. He's the one who found the yacht.

She made no mention of Nate or Sehr Ghilzai.

She'd also filled him in on Charlotte Rafferty's unwillingness to cooperate. They were due another phone call soon, but it was no substitute for an investigation with Rachel by his side.

As he'd done the night before, he had the taxi drop him several blocks from his destination, taking a circuitous route to the gym. Its Persian name was *zurkhaneh*, which translated as 'house of strength.' It had a single opening at the top and a sunken octagonal pit for the *zurkhaneh*'s activities in the center. There were three sections around the pit: one for the audience, one for the athletes who had come to participate, and one for the musicians who conducted the session. The audience's section filled the greater part of the circumference. A drummer was seated in an alcove above the pit, a comfortably overweight man poised with a large traditional drum known as the *zarb*, a microphone above his head. Beneath this alcove, a digital clock announced the time. Fifteen men were doing warm-up exercises in the pit, a video feed of their progress blaring from the wall. One of the men was Omid Arabshahi.

The first thing Khattak noticed was the portrait of Ali, a figure revered in the Sunni and Shia traditions, as the cousin, son-in-law, and successor of Muhammad. A kind face with solemn, dark eyes loomed over the audience from one side of the gym. Beneath it hung an art deco portrait of Ayatollah Khomeini and Supreme Leader Khamenei, two unsmiling heads paired together like the watchful eyes of Big Brother.

The ancient sport of *varzesh-e bastani* practiced within these walls had originally served to train warriors, its roots in the Parthian era, while spiritual elements from the Sufi and Shia traditions had been incorporated over time. The exercises began with calisthenics, moved on to weight training, and culminated in combat practice.

Any male could join the *zurkhaneh* after a suitable period as a member of the audience. Today, the gym was packed with observers. Khattak cast around for a sign of Ali or Darius. The drum sounded, and the exercises began, the master, or *morshed*, reciting the praise of pious religious figures over the heads of the athletes. The athletes jumped in time to the beat of the drum, rotating through a sequence of movements.

A hand touched Khattak's shoulder. Ali slipped onto the bench beside him. Piped-in music rang out in accompaniment with the drum. The religious hymns had switched to a recitation of poems from the *Shah Nameh*, the *Book of Kings*. The young men in the pit took turns whirling in the center, echoing Sufi rites. One lost his footing, sparking a round of laughter.

'Where's Darius?' Esa asked, under cover of the laughter.

'Watching from the other side. I need to talk to you first.'

'What were you able to find out about the flash card?'

'Wait,' Ali said. 'We've sent photographs of the letters to your partner in Toronto. I'm afraid we burned them afterward as the safest thing to do. Have you received any others?'

Khattak pressed subtly against the zipped outer pocket of his jacket.

'I'll take it before I leave and send it on.'

'Were you able to make any sense of them?'

He felt Ali's shrug against his shoulder, the audience packed together. Omid glanced up, grinning as he flexed his massive biceps in the pit. Khattak was impressed by his stamina.

'They're preparing a demonstration for Eid Nowruz, the Iranian new year. That's why we picked today for a meeting. We knew the *zurkhaneh* would be full.'

The Persian new year was ten days away.

Khattak hoped to be out of Iran by then.

'The letters are a record, that's all,' Ali went on. 'A record of what happened after the election, may God praise the Supreme Leader and uplift him.'

Khattak understood this to mean the Green Birds hadn't been able to decode the letters. Otherwise, Ali wouldn't have spoken in platitudes that praised the regime.

'Did you ask the girls?'

'Yes. They didn't know either.'

Ali slipped a hand into Esa's pocket. When he removed his hand, the letter was in it.

'Shall I send this to your partner?'

Esa nodded.

Noise sounded in the *zurkhaneh*'s pit. Weight training had begun. Each of the athletes collected a pair of heavy wooden clubs called *mils*. They raised and lowered the *mils* above their shoulders in a series of maneuvers. The sound of the clubs filled the gymnasium. Omid was adept at the maneuvers. Khattak wouldn't have wanted to face him in the dark.

Ali slipped away. He hadn't answered Esa's question about the flash card, tipping his head to the other side of the pit.

Khattak followed his gaze.

Darius was seated just beneath the drummer's alcove. He made a subtle gesture with his hand. Khattak squeezed out of the audience and headed to the exit. A few minutes later, Darius joined him in the street. They walked a little distance apart. When Darius disappeared inside a well-lit electronics store, Khattak waited several minutes to follow him. The shop was crowded with customers, the latest model televisions displayed from floor to ceiling, the shelves stocked with laptops, a Persian pop song blaring in the background.

Khattak scanned the store for Darius. The young man was waiting at the back, in front of a door marked *Staff.* He was wearing a conspicuous gray T-shirt with a white bull's-eye on it. At the heart of the bull's-eye was a skull with a red X across the mouth. The words *Tehran City* were printed beneath it.

To Khattak, the T-shirt read as the slogan of a dissident.

When Darius led him through the staff door to a darkroom at the back, Khattak asked, 'What are we doing here?' And pointing to his shirt: 'Isn't that dangerous for you to wear?'

Darius's smile transformed his face, splitting the scar in two just above a muscle in his cheek. It lightened his eyes, softening them. Like Ali and Omid, his features were striking.

'It's the name of an Iranian rock band. They sing about girls, fast cars, broken hearts.' He shrugged. 'Iran belongs to the young. They can't stamp us out, even though they want to. And don't worry, I work here. We have a few minutes, my friend is watching the door.'

He opened one of the cabinets at the back of the room, bringing back an envelope labeled *Park Scenes*.

'What's this?' Khattak asked, becoming aware of a chemical smell in the room.

'We spread the word about the flash card. Someone left these photographs at the store. I don't know if it's all of them, but we thought you'd want to see.'

The envelope shifted in Khattak's fingers. He was holding the photographs from Zahra's camera, her last public act of defiance.

He swallowed down the lump in his throat.

'Have you looked at these?' he asked Darius.

The young man ran his fingers along the crew neck of his T-shirt.

'I've seen them. But I don't know what I'm seeing.'

'Radan? He's there?'

'Yes. In some of the photographs.'

Khattak shook out the envelope, spreading the dozen or so photographs along the surface of a table in the darkroom. Darius flicked on a small overhead light above the table.

One by one, Khattak studied the photographs.

Six were of the exterior of Evin prison. These included shots of the watchtower and of the sign *Yazdashtagah Evin*. The next group were photographs of the milling assembly of women, many in dark chadors, some in white. They were taken at close range. Khattak could see the faces of most of the women. Of others, he could see only their chadors. In some cases, the women had been accompanied by the men of their family: an old man with a threadbare turban and a grief-stricken face, a youth with sepulchral eyes, sunk deep within the hollows of his face. Nearby was a middle-aged man whose face was weathered by outdoor labor, defeated by the vagaries of Evin. There was another man farther back in the distance. Khattak couldn't make out his face, he could only tell the man was bearded. He was carrying a case in his hands, perhaps containing paperwork for a prisoner's release.

In the background of each of these photos were the guards. Four uniformed guards and the man in the suit, Barsam Radan.

The disdainful disregard on Radan's face didn't bode well for Zahra – or for any of the women seeking information about missing sons and daughters, locked in Ward 209, if their bodies hadn't disappeared like Zahra's.

'Do you recognize any of these people?' he asked Darius.

There were two photographs left in the series. From the angle of the pictures, he realized Zahra had pointed the camera halfway to the ground. The pictures were waist-level. He could see hands. He was fairly certain one of the hands was Zahra's, as he could just make out a piece of the camera's strap falling across her wrist. It was reaching for the fine-boned hands of another woman, a woman in a manteau, judging from the sleeves that ended at her wrists. He scanned the previous photographs of the women again. They were dressed in chadors or scarves. No one was wearing a manteau.

'No,' Darius answered. 'Apart from Radan, I don't recognize any of them. Most of them are probably at Evin, still looking for their loved ones. Do you think it matters?'

Khattak showed him the two photographs.

'I think this is Zahra's hand. It looks like she knew someone in the crowd. Maybe it's the same person who had the flash card, the person who sent you the photographs. Could you try to find out? It's important. This person may have seen something that would help, something to implicate Radan.'

Darius looked doubtful.

'Wouldn't they tell us if they had? It was their choice to send us the photographs, no one made them do it.'

It was an excellent question.

Why help with Khattak's inquiry but choose to remain in the shadows? Was someone trying to point him to a deeper reason behind Zahra's murder?

He realized he knew very little about Darius or any of the others. Taraneh had said they kept each other's secrets. He wondered if Darius would be more forthcoming.

'How did you get interested in the Green Movement?' he asked.

Darius answered his question with a question.

'How old do you think I am?'

'Twenty-one? Twenty-two?'

Darius touched his scar, its fissures forging fresh trails on his face.

'I'm twenty-nine. I thought the scar made me look older.'

Khattak shook his head. 'You and your brother seem younger to me.'

'Ali is older than I am,' Darius told him. He tried another smile that fractured his scar. 'The election stopped time for us. I was in film school, Ali had found a job at a newspaper. When we joined the protests in support of Mousavi, we didn't know the costs would be so high. We were arrested.' The smile on his face faded, leaving only the scar. 'We were lucky to be released, so many others have vanished.'

'That doesn't sound like luck to me,' Khattak said.

But it could have been.

It was a system of justice where the rules were arbitrary, where decisions over life or death could be made without accountability. Those who raised their voices were given reasons to become silent.

'We're better connected than most people. We paid the price in other ways.'

Darius's hands sorted through the photographs on the table, laying the last two side by side. He and Khattak stood close together under the light from the bulb overhead. Darius's voice dropped low. It whispered over the hum of a printmaker in the corner.

'Ali's newspaper was shut down. He's barred from writing for publication. His colleagues are in jail or under house arrest, so he spends his time reading. He understands the principles of the movement much better than he did when we were arrested. He knows what he wants for the future.'

'And what is that?'

Up close, Darius's scar flickered like a flame over his skin. Khattak took a step back, his sleeve catching on the edge of a photograph. He looked down.

'The same things anyone wants. Accountability for what happened during the election, the freedom to make our own choices.' His hand strayed to his scar. 'I was expelled from my program, and I've been banned from making films, so now what do I do?'

He stabbed his finger at the photograph on the table. He pointed to Zahra's hand. At a glimpse of the white sleeve of her blouse.

The chemical scent of the photo processing solution assailed Khattak's nostrils. He felt a strong desire for fresh air. He could see nothing of note in the photograph. A blank sleeve, a hand reaching for other hands. The clamor and crush of a crowd.

Darius slid one photograph over the other, aligning Zahra's sleeves.

Khattak scrutinized the photographs.

In the first photograph, there was a band of writing on the sleeve.

In the second, the sleeve was bare.

The photographs had been taken seconds apart.

He looked around the darkroom. There was an enlarger on

the opposite counter. He carried the photographs over to it. He placed them under the lens, one at a time, peering through the viewfinder. He could just make out the writing on the sleeve, a neat row of capitals printed in English. ADTVBMJBT.

In the second photograph, the edge of the sleeve was torn off, the writing missing.

In the split second before she'd removed the camera's flash card, Zahra had passed the scrap of writing to someone in the crowd. Or she'd dropped it.

He asked Darius if the string of letters meant anything; the young man shook his head. He pinned Darius with a steady glance.

'Can you send these to my partner in Canada?'

He hadn't mentioned Rachel's name, and he didn't intend to. She was safe in Toronto, and he planned to keep it that way. The name of the recipient on the email address he'd given the students was 'puckface48.' It was so close to an epithet and so entirely in Rachel's style that it made him smile. The Maple Leafs hadn't won the Stanley Cup in decades. Rachel had other accounts for each successive year the Leafs had failed to make the play-offs: 'puckoff47,' 'whatthepuck49.' She'd saved 'puckanddoublepuck50' for 2017. Before Omid had shown him the Telegram app, Khattak had rotated his emails to Rachel through these accounts.

'This is the first time I've seen you smile,' said Darius. 'I thought Esfahan didn't agree with you. I wondered how that was possible.'

Khattak looked at him, surprised.

He hadn't realized Darius was monitoring his actions with such interest. Could Darius have been the one following him, sending him the letters?

'You're writing to a woman,' Darius guessed. 'That lightens a man's spirits.'

Khattak tested his theory.

'Alas for the lack of rose petals in modern communications.'

Darius skipped over his comment. 'She's your lover, this woman?'

A blunt question that flouted the conventions of Iranian etiquette.

Esa's imagination failed to conjure up Rachel's response if she heard the question. The most she'd been able to bring herself to do was to call Esa 'boss' in the offhand manner of two friends at a bar. He couldn't envision her casting him soulful looks, or pretending she needed his help. Rachel's modus operandi ran more along the lines of, 'You're slowing me down, sir, do you mind?'

'She's my partner,' Esa said, his voice weighted with things he wouldn't share.

'I ask because I wonder how you might court a woman, what is it you would do?'

Behind the words was a plea.

'You're not married?' Khattak asked gently.

Twenty-nine was not young to marry in Iran.

Darius spread out his hands.

'I have no profession. I'm on a watch list, and I have this scar.'

Khattak didn't tell him the scar didn't matter. He knew very well that it did. He also wondered why, with the prevalence of plastic surgery among the upper classes of Iran, Darius hadn't taken steps to have it repaired. Was the scar a badge of honor? Was he struggling for legitimacy among his peers? Did it prove his courage in the face of affliction?

Khattak found he couldn't ask.

'What about Taraneh or Nasreen?'

Darius's laugh was bitter.

'Taraneh is like a sister, we were raised together. And Nasreen is focused on Saneh.' He eyed Khattak with a measuring glance. 'Nasreen asks about you, though. Is there anything I should tell her?'

Khattak thought of Rachel, he thought of Sehr, he thought of a woman named Mink. He remembered his wife, Samina, and the life he'd left behind in Toronto. A man dead at his hands, a sister who wouldn't speak to him. Too many uncertainties, no means of absolution.

How could he say, *I've killed a man, will you tell her that? Will it change what she wants from me, how she looks at me?*

'There's nothing to say. I'll be leaving for. my own country soon.'

Darius didn't press him. Politely, he turned away, replacing the photographs in the envelope.

'I'll send these to your partner. And in the meantime, I'll try to find out who left them at the store.'

Khattak gestured at the darkroom.

'It's someone who knows where you work. Someone close by, a member of your group.'

'Nonsense,' Darius replied. 'The person who had the flash card was in Tehran. None of us have left Esfahan, so it couldn't be one of us.'

Khattak didn't share his confidence. Zahra had somehow been persuaded to visit Evin, knowing the risks involved. Who had convinced her of that? Someone she trusted? And he wondered how well Darius knew any of the others, how deeply he'd pried into their personal histories. The only one he could know with certainty was his brother. And he'd seen the care Ali had taken with Darius, heard the tenderness of an older brother for a younger one who'd suffered.

Whose idea had it been to join the demonstrations after the election?

And who was carrying the guilt of that choice now?

'Darius,' he said, softening his tone. 'Please be careful with the photographs. Burn them as soon as you can, don't carry them anywhere.'

A glimmer of something troubling rose in Darius's eyes.

Khattak couldn't describe it. He experienced that sense of oppression again, its echo in the young man's voice.

'You also, Inspector Khattak. A passport can be a mirage. If you don't believe me, ask Zahra. Ask her how safe that Canadian passport made her feel in the end.'

30

The Suite

They brought a sobbing boy into a cell that twenty of us once shared, and they've taken me to the Suite as an upgrade. I told the boy to be strong, and he'd find a way to survive. I didn't believe it, but I told him anyway, what does one act of kindness cost me? Kindness costs nothing, rewards everything, Nasreen says. So now, I find myself in solitary. Fifteen or twenty times a day a guard walks by the window to check if I'm still alive. The cell is six by seven feet, with a ceiling that's eight feet high. If I could stand, I'd be able to touch three sides of the cell at once. As it is, I spend my first night on the floor, reading the words of everyone who passed through before me. You can get through this. Don't give up. No one stays here forever. Ya Hossein, ya Hossein. This cheers me up, but not for the usual reasons. Someone still believes in the dominion of Imam Hossein after everything they've suffered at Kahrizak. That's funny. Or they believe Mir Hossein Mousavi has a magical key that unlocks these doors, and that's even funnier. It's quiet and clean here, so it's a little bit like paradise. I don't know what kind of monsters lurk on the other side of the door, but someone in that pack of wolves cleaned out this cell for me. Maybe it's one of Roxana's devotees – she has many at Evin. Maybe they know Zahra loved me because Roxana loved me like her own brother, like Nasreen loves me – we were always in this fight together. And maybe this means something to the wolves.

Murder and torture are just a job for some, they don't need lofty convictions.

31

The Esfahan City Center was Iran's largest mall, a sprawling complex that encompassed luxury stores, a theater, a museum, and a hotel. It was also a popular, modern tourist destination.

Touka's hip was aching, her leg sore from her march around the mall. Walking prevented further deterioration, the price she paid for mobility. Her limp disarmed suspicion, her gray hair assured disinterest. She'd been a breezy blonde in her day, attractive to men, but those days had ended, a judgment passed on her by others. Though her mind was as sharp, her heart as generous as in her youth, it didn't seem to signify.

Khattak hadn't dismissed her. He'd listened to her with interest and treated her with respect. She hoped he'd been able to make something of the video. Just as he'd seen beyond her limp, she'd seen beyond his tricky reputation – a reputation she'd tried to use against him, only to be shamed by his dignified response. A pawn in someone else's game, Esa had managed to acquit himself well, tougher than his thoughtful demeanor suggested. He used his natural courtesy as effectively as Touka managed her limp.

She waved him over, her face lit up by the glow of the Apple store's windows.

'What have you learned?' she asked him.

He told her, slotting the facts neatly into a frame. She found the timeline as intriguing as he did. Zahra's inquiries in Toronto, her trip to Iran, her meeting with a representative of the Supreme Leader. Her visit to Evin prison with her camera, the letters on her sleeve. And her disappearance and murder.

He told Touka about the car. She promised to take another look at the video to see if she could track down a plate.

'Do the letters on her sleeve mean anything to you?' Khattak asked. 'Are they a code?'

'Not one I know of. I'll send them to your partner, one less communication from you.'

Khattak told her about the Telegram app and his discussions with the Green Birds. This was more than Touka had hoped for from Khattak's initial reluctance. The fact that he'd seized the initiative and come up with results were elements of his personal attraction for her.

'What can you tell me about a man named Larijani? He followed me to the Hezar Jarib and insisted on taking me to the mosque.'

Touka leaned forward with interest.

'He's a low-level functionary. If you do something to trigger his interest, he'll take it to the next level, and that's when I would worry. Although –' she paused. Esa waited her out. 'Is it coincidence that Larijani was assigned to follow you? I've heard rumors about him.'

'What kind of rumors?'

'That he's one of Radan's men. The kind who carries out his errands.'

That put a new complexion on things, he thought. It made Larijani a more serious adversary.

'What if Larijani connects me to the Green Birds, and takes that to Radan? What would happen to them?'

His concern sounded genuine. Touka wondered at the thoughts behind the disciplined face. Taraneh and Nasreen were attractive young women, but Khattak didn't seem like the type to get distracted. Perhaps there was something in Nasreen's moody sorrow to compel him, as it had compelled many men to try and help her – the effortless pull of a beautiful woman's need.

She knew of men who'd responded to that need before getting burned by Nasreen's single-minded focus on her brother.

Touka resisted the urge to warn Esa. She had no idea if his thoughts had turned in that direction, or if he felt anything more than the natural concern for a group of young people steering their way through deep waters. He should want to be out of this. That he hadn't yet asked made Touka respect him more.

'They have powerful connections if they run into trouble. Allegiances are often divided among the ruling elite. The heirs of the 1979 revolution aren't necessarily enemies of the Greens – look at Mousavi and Karroubi, former revolutionaries. More importantly, the Green Birds have very little contact with me, which is just as well, otherwise they'd be accused of treason and hanged.'

She attempted caution and reassurance in the same breath.

'What about you – are you safe?'

Touka liked the way Khattak's green eyes warmed up as he asked the question.

'I have an exit plan, don't worry. If we were in Tehran, it would be a different matter. As we're here –'

She didn't want to tell Khattak his idyllic days in Esfahan were coming to an end. To pursue the investigation further, he'd have to leave for Tehran. Instead, she brought up the message he'd sent her about the photograph at the ROM, the reason for their meeting at the mall.

'I've been digging into the yacht. It was owned by Mehran Najafi, so it's a safe bet the yacht is named after Zahra.'

Khattak's eyes stayed on hers.

'Mehran is Zahra's ex-husband. He's the father of Max and Roxana.'

She gave Khattak a moment to digest this.

'Where is he now?'

'That's what I'm trying to find out. He travels a great deal in country. I think it would help if you visited Roxana's family. Her mother might have that information.'

'How does that work with the family under house arrest? Is there a guard on the house?'

'One of the Green Birds will take you.'

'I don't think Larijani has dropped me, and I don't want to put them at risk. As regrettable as Zahra's death is, I don't think it's worth him connecting us.'

That was it, Touka realized. That was what she liked about Khattak. He wanted to help, but he weighed this against considerations he believed were of equal worth.

She eased out of her seat, her hip twinging at the movement. She rubbed at the spot with a surreptitious gesture. Khattak came to his feet and offered her his arm. She smiled her thanks at him, leaning into his strength for a moment.

She wondered if he would ask about her hip, people usually didn't. Khattak surprised her again.

'Is it the result of an injury? Are you in any pain?'

She shook her head. 'It's a muscular condition I was born with. It doesn't impede me, I just need time to adjust.'

She thought she could be forgiven for basking in a handsome man's attention, but she didn't want his pity. And it didn't seem like Khattak had any to offer.

'What do you think of Iran?' he asked, his tone conversational.

They strolled through the mall, Khattak accommodating her pace.

'It's layered, isn't it? There's so much natural beauty, so much architectural brilliance – so much cultural complexity. It fascinates me. What the world thinks of Iran seems ludicrous when you deal with people in your daily interactions.'

'There are other things beneath the surface.'

He told her about the letters from his secret correspondent. Touka listened with avid interest.

'The human rights situation is egregious, I agree. And these kids endanger themselves by acting on behalf of political prisoners, and by spying on the regime. But on the other hand – 60 percent of university students are women. The literacy rate is 85 percent. People don't think about these things when they think about Iran. Did you see that gorgeous bridge in Tehran – the new one, Tabiat?'

Khattak nodded.

'It was designed by a twenty-six-year-old woman. What does that tell you?'

'It's a country of contradictions.'

'You seem very much at home here,' Touka observed. And he did. She wondered if that was just his fluency in the language. She was beginning to think it was deeper, something in Khattak's bones, in how he carried himself through life.

'My parents' country of origin borders Iran. I suppose there's a great deal I recognize, much I'm able to embrace.'

Touka thought he was the kind of man who would find his place anywhere because of how he interpreted the world. For Khattak, unlike Touka, whose job required it, the world was more than a system of barriers – it was something to lay claim to, a place of common ground. He had an openness to the world, a welcoming in, rather than a fortification of fear against the unfamiliar.

'Was there anything else?' she asked him. Khattak paused beside the gleaming windows of a men's store. Touka examined the available choices with interest. Tailored suits, sports coats of the variety that murmured of exclusive parties and dignified hotel lobbies, shirts with starched collars and cuffs. The onyx cuff links inscribed with Persian script were a nice touch; she wondered what they said. The store's name? Or some absurdly romantic love poetry? She could imagine the entire ensemble on Khattak: shirt, cuff links, blazer. And that silky black hair brushed neatly to one side, just above those winged eyebrows.

She'd been in Iran too long, she thought with grim humor. She needed the after-hours company of a man, and she needed to stop ogling Esa Khattak in public.

'Is there a database of some kind I could access? Somewhere I could find out about Zahra's life in Iran before she moved to Canada? I'd like to know more about the yacht, more about her ex-husband. Why did the marriage break up? How did the photograph end up in the exhibit at the ROM?'

This was the perfect moment to tell him he needed to return to Tehran. She didn't think he was ready to hear it.

'Zahra was born in Tehran, and now she's died there. You could find that information in Tehran, but not without attracting the attention of much bigger fish than Larijani.' Radan's name lingered in the air, unspoken. She waited a moment. 'Or you could ask Roxana's mother, Maryam Ghorbani.'

They moved down the concourse where an enormous glass-walled shop with floors tiled in sparkling quartz offered up a display of the country's most famous export: Persian carpets. The carpets hung from shining gold rods, arranged by geographical region. The explosion of color and pattern gratified and overwhelmed at once.

'What can you tell me about Najafi?'

Khattak stood before a vintage Qashqai Yalameh tribal rug, cleverly lit from below to showcase a painterly palette of purples and blues. The rug had to be worth thousands of dollars.

'He was an exporter. He had the reputation of being a handler. He could get goods where they needed to go without questions being asked. He was well-connected.'

'Was?' Khattak picked up on the significance of Touka's word choice.

'No one knows where he is now. And no one knows what's happened to Roxana.'

Khattak's reply was grave.

'Perhaps by backing the Greens, Roxana did something

even the best-placed connections couldn't save her from.'

It was Touka's turn to ask him what he meant.

'You can't trace Mehran Najafi. Maybe the regime has him.'

32

Interrogation

He's grunting behind me. He stinks of heroin and sweat. 'Do you know what we did to Zahra? The same things we do to you. The mother of a whore, she liked it.'

Zahra, Zahra Khanom. I would die a thousand times to see you safe.

33

Rachel answered the call from Nate on the first ring, cramming her phone against her ear as she hauled a bagful of garbage from her condo to the disposal chute on her floor.

'Any luck with the coronation video?' she asked.

'Quite a bit more than I expected. Vicky has a friend who works at Vortex Records. He managed to dig up a bootleg copy of the film.'

'Did you watch it?'

'We both did.' He sounded sheepish. 'She was actually very helpful.'

Rachel slammed the door of the chute with more force than necessary.

'And what did you find out?'

She was startled by the sound of a helpless cry behind her. Something small and black brushed against her ankles, causing Rachel to stumble over her own feet.

'I thought I told you to get lost.' Swearing into the phone, she shooed the black cat away from the chute. 'Sorry, Nate. I didn't mean you – it's this cat that randomly appears on my floor – hang on a sec.'

She knocked on a few doors along the hallway, the black cat following like a puppy at her heels. None of her neighbors answered. Rachel retreated to her condo, but as she opened the door, the black cat shot through the opening like a bullet. It streaked through the hallway and launched itself onto a sofa. Instead of settling onto a cushion, it made a series of comments as it picked its way along the tight space between the sofa's backrest and the wall. Its yellow eyes blinked up at Rachel, content.

The cat could wait. Rachel returned her attention to the phone. She could hear Nate laughing under his breath.

'Sorry about that. You were saying?'

'The bootleg copy was missing some of the footage, but in the part we were able to view, the Shah wasn't wearing his military cap.'

'A dead end, then.'

She was watching the cat with reluctant fascination. It had leapt from the sofa to the windowsill, where it began a leisurely grooming ritual.

'Not quite. Rachel, are you listening?'

'Yes.' She mumbled into the phone. 'I really don't like cats. But go on. There's no video of the cap, but there *was* something else?'

'Vicky's friend told us there are very few copies of *The Lion of Persia* in circulation. A wealthy Iranian bought out the rights.'

Rachel's eyebrows shot up. 'Did you happen to get a name?'

'As a matter of fact I did.' For the first time, Rachel noticed his excitement. 'It was Syed Mehran Najafi.'

Rachel pondered this in silence. She wandered over to the window, where the cat pushed its soft, black head into her palm, purring at the contact.

'This doesn't mean you can stay,' Rachel warned. But she headed to her kitchen, where she filled a small white saucer with milk. 'I'm feeding the cat,' she told Nate.

'Rachel,' he said, exasperated. 'Forget the cat. Do you realize what this means?'

'Mm.' She was petting the little cat, who had come to investigate the saucer, its fluffed-up tail brushing against her legs. 'It means we've connected both Zahra and her ex to the video. What we don't know is why. Did Vicky have any theories?'

'Not really. She thinks the answer may lie in the part of the video that was missing.'

'Maybe.' She realized Nate deserved a more enthusiastic response for his efforts. 'Thank you for tracking it down, oh, and Nate – let's leave Vicky out of things from now on. It doesn't look like there's anything else she can give us.'

There was a brief silence. The cat lapped daintily at the saucer. Rachel reached down to scratch it behind the ears.

'I'm afraid that won't be possible,' Nate said, at last.

'Why not?'

'Because she's sitting right here.'

34

The Suite

Joojeh has begun to talk to me, he's as desperately bored as I am. He pretends to be a villain when the others are around, when we're alone, he offers conversation with my bread and surplus. A few days in a row, he's brought me blocks of cheese and tiny little packets of honey. He tells me he admires the peshmerga, the ones at war with ISIS. 'Even your women fight,' he says. I shrug one shoulder, the other is dislocated. 'I'm Iranian,' I say. 'I'm not with the peshmerga.' Joojeh smiles. 'You should be, they fight like Rambo.' He hoists an imaginary machine gun across his chest like Sylvester Stallone. I show him my useless arm, he feels bad. I pass out when he shoves it back into place.

35

It was Vicky's turn to demand Rachel's attention on the phone.

In return for the information provided by her contact, she insisted on a full accounting of Rachel's discoveries at the ROM. Rachel tried to put her off, Vicky refused to yield.

'Listen,' she said. 'We had a deal. You asked for my help, and I gave it. You can't back out on me now.'

Rachel scowled at her phone. 'This is a sensitive police investigation, we don't want it to turn into an international incident.'

Vicky clicked her tongue in disapproval.

'No wonder people don't trust the police. Let me remind you of two things, Sergeant Getty. One, you still don't have what you need from the video, whereas I might have other ways of finding it.'

Rachel considered this. 'What's the second thing?'

Very sweetly, Vicky replied, 'There's nothing to stop me from filing a story now – I have plenty of material. If you want me to keep quiet, you'll have to keep your word.'

Rachel's voice became rough. 'Are you threatening a police officer?'

Though Vicky's answer was determined, Rachel could hear the uncertainty beneath her words.

'I'm just standing up for myself. I've played fair with you, Rachel. And I'm not a complete novice – I know what I'm doing. There will be a point when you realize you need me, but what if you've already burned that bridge?'

Rachel wasn't convinced. She found Vicky's cooperation suspicious.

'Why would you keep things under wraps? What reason do I have to trust you?'

'What reason do you have to doubt me? If I accept your terms, there's a much bigger story just around the bend. And anyway –' Now her voice dropped a little. Rachel seized on it at once.

'And anyway, what?'

Vicky sounded rueful. 'I really *like* Inspector Khattak.'

Rachel had seen his effect on women. That was something she could believe.

Grudgingly, and not at all sure of the wisdom of doing so, Rachel brought Vicky up to speed. When she'd finished with the call, she realized she needed to catch up with Khattak. One of his contacts had mailed her a set of photographs. They needed to be assessed, and if possible, shared with someone in a position of authority. She decided Nate and Vicky could dig into the background of Najafi. His name had now cropped up too often to be ignored. Touka Swan had also sent her a message. Mehran was the father of Max and Roxana. And according to Touka, he hadn't been seen in some time. That was something Vicky and Nate could work on. Rachel needed to talk to Max without delay.

But when she called his house, she was told he was in session at a studio on Queen Street. She found it odd he wouldn't have delayed the session, but the sharp-tongued girl on the other end of the phone informed Rachel musicians had flown in from all around the world to record with Max. The sessions couldn't be canceled without inconvenience and expense to everyone involved.

When Rachel asked what was being recorded, the girl on the phone hung up. Rachel was left with a few different options. Meet up with Nate and Vicky, follow Najafi to the studio, or pass the photos on to Sehr Ghilzai. She settled on viewing the photographs at home, a cup of coffee at her elbow. The cat had finished its milk and demanded to be let out. Rachel wasn't sorry to see it go, though she could still feel the imprint of the little cat's head in her hand. She hadn't wanted Zach to see it. She and Zach had had a cat of their own once. Their mother had told them their father had drowned it in a creek – something Rachel no longer believed.

Now Zach was out with friends. She wondered briefly if one of those friends was Ashleigh, the pretty brunette Zach claimed to have outgrown. It was better than heartache, she thought. She'd had a peek at his room, and the gold-leaf tree was beginning to take shape, a glimmer of promise against a backdrop of sea-green oils.

She pulled up the photos on her screen, opening a separate tab to compare them to images of Evin on the web. The photographs were as depressing as she'd imagined, the watchtower, the spiked wall, the despairing assembly of women gathered before the gate.

She zoomed in on a car that appeared in one corner of a photograph. She could make out a shadow in the driver's seat, but whether it was a man or a woman was impossible to tell. The man in the suit was Radan. He had a long, low side part that reminded her of Newt Gingrich. His skin was the texture of paraffin wax, the tilt of the eyes making her think of a Tajik or Uzbek. Maybe his job was weighing on him.

A little digging produced a report on the Ministry of Intelligence. Rachel made a quick study of Radan's background. It wasn't hard to read between the lines. His swift rise through the ranks could be attributed to his taste for authoritarian methods, and his wanton disregard of judicial process, a strange irony; Radan had once held the post of Prosecutor-General.

He was considered one of the Ministry's most effective interrogators. When a prisoner needed to be broken, 'the Great Fire' was the one they sent.

Rachel sipped at her cooling coffee, lost in thought.

Radan was at Evin to apprehend Zahra and attend her interrogation.

But he was normally stationed at the Ministry in Tehran. So if he'd been on hand to arrest Zahra, it couldn't have been coincidence, he would have known Zahra's plans.

Rachel pondered this. Zahra would have had a minder since the moment she arrived in Iran, it would have been easy to stay abreast of her plans. Her minder would only have needed to pick up the phone to inform Radan that Zahra was on her way to Evin.

And Radan would be there waiting.

But Zahra would have known this. So why had she put herself at risk by going to the prison and taking photographs? How would photographs of the exterior of the prison have helped her secure Roxana's release? That was a question she needed to answer because the answer was linked to the reasons for Zahra's death.

A fresh thought struck Rachel. She set her mug on the table with a thud.

What if Zahra had been tracking Radan's movements, instead of the other way around? Perhaps she'd gone to Evin because she'd known Radan would be there. The representative of the Supreme Leader may have told her as much.

Frustrated, Rachel sifted through the photographs.

Almost as a reflex, she sent the photographs to Sehr Ghilzai with the header PRIVATE AND CONFIDENTIAL. For extra measure, she typed in, FOR YOUR EYES ONLY.

There was a second email from the same source. It directed her to study the contrast between two nearly identical photographs of Zahra. The sender had added a blunt explanation.

Letters on her sleeve. ADTVBMJBT.

The string of letters reminded Rachel of the Film Reference Library. The letters were like the call numbers on a film recording or an audio file. She made a note to check that out.

She searched her pockets for the business card she'd taken from Jeremy Engstrom, and sent a quick query to his email address.

She was trying to make sense out of things that didn't fit together and was getting nowhere in the process.

She wasn't used to working without Khattak at her side.

It was dark by the time Rachel arrived at Max Najafi's studio, a venture he must have sunk a great deal of money into. It was in the West Queen West area, situated between the Argyle Lofts and Trinity Bellwoods Park, close to tennis courts at the south end of the park. The studio was housed inside a restored Victorian building, a former bakery whose units had been converted. Rachel read the list of patisseries and galleries until she found the studio – Caspian Recordings.

There was a pause when she announced herself, then someone buzzed her up. The studio was on the third floor, and Rachel took the stairs, glad of the chance for exercise. When she reached the doors of the studio, she took in the name artfully applied to the glass – *Caspian Recordings* was written in an English script styled to look like Persian. The small reception area with its Eames chair and modular glass desk was unstaffed.

Rachel proceeded to the music room. Here, several musicians were gathered in a largely empty space where three tall windows looked out over the park. Maples, ash trees, red oaks, and lindens populated a park intersected by trails. The trees were beginning to bud over the gently rolling green. The musicians played in a circle that made the most of the view.

Four men and three women, most of them young, were gathered in a space that accommodated a piano, a violin, two guitars, a *tombak* drum, and other stringed instruments Rachel couldn't identify. Situated at intervals, microphones amplified the musicians' efforts. The girl in the black dress, whom Rachel had first noticed at Max Najafi's house, wore a skintight pair of jeans and a clinging, cowl-necked sweater. She stood before a vocalist's microphone.

A Kermanshah carpet in ivory covered the knotted pine floor. A second door on the opposite side of the entrance led to a sound engineer's booth, where a man with a mustache snapped his fingers in time to a sound only he could hear.

Max Najafi was at the piano, one of the women was playing the violin, while the other musicians provided a subtle background to their duet. The girl at the microphone broke off in mid-syllable.

'Max,' she said. 'She's here.'

No one troubled to introduce her, and she herself was more interested in Max Najafi's reaction. He was dressed head to toe in black, a silver chain around his neck, a cheap plastic band on his wrist. He'd left his hair untended. It sprang up from his skull like a pompadour, the curls richly textured and shining. There was a strength in his face that suggested the music had reinforced his courage.

He spoke to the others in Farsi. One of the women took his place at the piano. He nodded to Rachel to follow him to the reception hall, closing the door behind them. Rachel could still hear the music, the fullness of its sorrow wrapping around the delicate finality of the piano. And the violin like an afterthought, expanding and falling in a measured swoop of grace notes.

She sat down with Max on a patterned green sofa in the reception area.

'You wrote that for your mother,' she guessed.

Max shook his head. 'It was for the second film. For the follow-up on the students at Evin.' He attempted a smile. 'You hear the grief in it, that's why you think it's for my mother. Do you have some news for me?'

Rachel thought about the photographs on her laptop. Sharing them wouldn't be a kindness. She also didn't know if that was her choice to make.

'I have a few questions, for the moment. I thought it would be helpful for us to trace your mother's movements. I spoke to Vicky D'Souza, who told me your mother had gone to see Charlotte Rafferty at the ROM. Do you know why?'

Max's fingers moved in his lap. He wasn't conscious of it, Rachel realized. He was following the melody played by the pianist, the music instinctual to him.

'The ROM?' he asked, puzzled. 'I thought Charlotte Rafferty was at an auction house.'

This was news to Rachel.

'What made you think that?'

'I heard my mother on the phone. She was talking about a lot – "Our lot," she kept saying.'

'Do you know which lot? Did it have something to do with the Shah's coronation?'

The foggiest outline of an idea rose in Rachel's mind. Could Zahra have been trying to purchase the Shah's military cap? But Charlotte didn't work at an auction house, she worked in Records Management. Was that the perfect place to track down the history of the cap? Charlotte had denied knowing anything about Zahra's interests – what if she had some reason of her own for withholding the truth?

Max Najafi seemed bewildered by Rachel's questions.

'What interest could my mother have had in the Shah's coronation? Our work is contemporary. We're concerned with the present struggle in our country, not the past. No, wait – hold on. Maybe I didn't understand.'

Rachel held her breath.

'The lot,' he repeated, a horrible comprehension taking hold. 'Maybe she meant Lot 209, Ward 209. She may have been keeping up with the Greens and didn't want to involve me.'

'What's Ward 209?'

Max didn't answer at once. He was listening to the last strains of the violin, a concurrence echoed by the piano's diminuendo.

'It's the detention wing of Evin. Roxana was transferred to Ward 209.'

But what could the ROM's archivist have to do with Evin's detention wing? And what of other unexplained questions: the whereabouts of Mehran Najafi, the photograph in the Silk Road exhibit, the Shah's arrival at his coronation. The name Vic Mean, the letters on Zahra's sleeve, the Forouhar letters, the letters sent to Khattak in Esfahan.

As Rachel saw it, two figures were at the heart of Zahra's murder: Roxana Najafi and her father, Mehran. And on both these figures, Rachel possessed very little information.

Her sense of frustration bubbled up again. She would be more useful to Khattak's inquiry if she could get to Tehran and dig into these questions.

Max was staring at her, expectant.

She told him about the photograph of the yacht.

'It was from your father's collection. What can you tell me about that? And about your father?'

Max responded as if he wished to say several things at once, the words tripping over each other in his haste.

'He was a bit of a charlatan, my father. I suppose you have to be in his profession, importing-exporting. And he traveled all the time, most often to places like Persepolis and Neyshabur. He never said exactly what he was trading, my mother claimed it was caviar. For a time, the business made us very comfortable. My father managed to find favor with whoever swept to power. Maybe it was the caviar, Iranians have a taste for it.'

His laugh was bitter. The *tombak* in the next room sounded a hollow beat. The musicians had taken up a different song.

'Where are Persepolis and Neyshabur?' Rachel asked after a pause.

'Inside Iran. Neyshabur is the birthplace of the legendary poet Omar Khayyam. Persepolis isn't far from the city of Shiraz. It's one of Iran's most famous attractions – a city of Achaemenid

Persia that's been preserved as a World Heritage Site.'

Rachel nodded at this. It was interesting, but didn't seem relevant.

'When was the last time you saw him?'

'Six months ago. My mother and I went to Iran to see Roxana. We hoped my father would act on her behalf, but he said there was nothing he could do, it was a particularly busy time for him. He was tied up on the Caspian, closing a deal with the Russians. He had a special contact named Mordashov. We saw my father several times during that visit, his answer was always the same. Since then, he hasn't called, he hasn't written, as if Roxana and I don't exist.'

Wouldn't Roxana's father have sweated out her fate in Ward 209? Wouldn't any father? But the thought of Rachel's own father was an immediate check on her assumptions.

'Why did you and your mother have to ask for his help? What about Roxana's mother? Didn't she get involved?'

'Roxana's mother is a simple woman, she wouldn't know where to go for help.'

'What kind of terms were your parents on?'

The corners of Max's mouth lifted in the parody of a smile.

'Even after the divorce, my parents remained close. My father called my mother regularly until the business with Roxana. Then things went sour. My mother called him just before she made her last trip there, desperate to have him do something for Roxana. Something he told her the last time they were together must have given her hope.'

Rachel wondered what it could be.

'Did she see him once she reached Tehran?'

'I don't know.' The thought was a new one for Max. 'And when they talked, I don't know what they talked about. I'll tell you one thing, though. If he ever felt his responsibility as a father, he would send my mother home. He would call me, he would share my grief.'

He was right. It was strange that Mehran hadn't called his son at the news of Zahra's death, especially if the parents had remained on good terms. Which left Rachel at a bit of a loss as to what to pursue next.

'Do you have any idea how that photograph ended up in the Silk Road exhibit?'

The vocalist from Max's band appeared at the door. She tapped at a delicate wrist, displaying a diamond-studded watch. There was a trace of possessiveness in her expression.

'Your girlfriend?' Rachel asked.

'Paristesh is a colleague. She also worked for my mother. We are distantly related.'

Judging from the young woman's expression, she would close the distance given the chance. Max seemed oblivious to her interest.

'I'm coming, Pari,' he said. The young woman didn't leave, so he went on to answer. 'My mother knew about the exhibit and convinced my father to lend the ROM photographs from his collection. He was knowledgeable about Persian art, though his real passion was antiquities. Perhaps that's what my mother discussed with Charlotte. A partnership with the ROM.'

Paristesh spoke up, a note of surprise in her voice.

'If you're talking about the ROM, Zahra Khanom's contact wasn't Charlotte Rafferty. She was speaking to someone named Lin.'

Rachel stood up. She gave a brief explanation of her visit.

'How do you know this?' she asked.

Paristesh spoke in the rich tones of a trained vocalist. Her plain face was accentuated with makeup, edging her over the border to a youthful prettiness.

'I kept her appointments.'

Rachel tried not to betray her excitement at the words. She should have undertaken a thorough search of Zahra's belongings after her first interview with Max. She remembered now that she'd wanted to search for Zahra's diary or her notes on the new film.

'Did she have an appointment book?'

Paristesh looked at Max for permission. He nodded.

'Yes, it's here, in my desk.'

Paristesh fished out a small silver key on a chain from under her sweater. She glanced at Max, who didn't notice, with a blush. She arranged herself in the Eames chair, moving neatly and quickly to unlock the desk drawer. Rachel could see it was kept in order. Paristesh extracted a black date book she passed to Rachel.

Rachel flicked back through the date book several months, working her way forward. Paristesh pointed helpfully to the first appointment with Charlotte Rafferty. Rachel moved ahead, week by week, to Zahra's departure for Tehran.

Nowhere did she find the name Lin.

There were, however, a series of appointment times listed beside the initials *FY*. And in one case, a location and a time, Winfield Park at 2:30 P.M. This came two days after the last appointment with FY. No other names or initials had been recorded in that period. But beside the last appointment with FY, Zahra had written two words and heavily underlined them.

The Yellows.

Rachel turned to Paristesh.

'There's no Lin listed here, no mention of the ROM.'

Paristesh's answer was impatient.

'Most of the time, she didn't note down places, just names and times. But Lin's right there.' She pointed to the diary. Her eyes widened in dismay. 'I'm sorry, I should have realized. Lin is Franklin Yang. He's Charlotte Rafferty's assistant.'

And that might explain the scrawl on Charlotte's calendar, and Franklin Yang's well-timed interruption. He must have wanted to talk to Rachel.

'What about "the Yellows?"' Rachel asked. 'Does that mean

anything to you? Does it signify a connection to the Green Movement – the Greens?'

Max and Paristesh looked at each other. Neither seemed to know.

Rachel asked Paristesh one more question.

'This appointment at Winfield Park. Do you know what that was about?'

Paristesh locked the desk drawer and slipped the key back under her sweater.

'I'm afraid I don't. I can look around her papers and let you know if I find anything.'

Such a search should be undertaken by Rachel and no one else. She didn't know who to report to on this with Khattak so far away. She settled for suggesting she'd work with Paristesh to sort the papers later in the week. She asked again about the coronation and the Shah's cap. Paristesh folded her hands. Zahra had never discussed the purpose of the appointments with her, she hadn't asked Paristesh to find her video footage of the coronation, she'd never mentioned the military cap. Nor had Zahra mentioned her ex-husband's name.

With her non-answers, Paristesh conveyed an impression of Zahra as a woman with a great deal on her mind in her last weeks in Toronto. Beyond that, she couldn't help.

Rachel thanked them both for their time.

Max laid a hand on her forearm. She noticed the green, plastic band on his wrist was inscribed with three words.

Freedom for Iran.

'Sergeant,' he said. 'When I've finished the piece for my mother, I'd like you to hear it. And if you'd be kind enough, bring Mr. Clare back with you. He did something that helped me understand it.'

From the other room, the strains of the violin rose again.

'When the violin forgives the past, it begins to sing,' he said.

'Rumi?' Rachel guessed.

'Hafiz,' he answered. 'If you have Hafiz and the Qur'an, you have everything.'

This, too, sounded like a quotation.

Rachel didn't wonder at it. As she'd found with Zach, artists and musicians belonged to their own world.

An undiscovered country.

36

Khattak waited for Maryam Ghorbani at the gravestones of her brothers in the Golestan-e Shohada, the Rose Garden of the Martyrs. Seven thousand graves marked Esfahan's share of the casualties of the protracted Iran-Iraq war, begun a year after Khomeini's revolution.

Iran's neighbors had feared the revolution would inspire their own populations to rebel against their ruling tyrannies. On the pretext of border skirmishes, and backed by Saudi Arabia and other Arab allies, Iraq had launched its invasion of Iran in 1980. Internally, the invasion had served another purpose. It had provided Khomeini with the opportunity to consolidate power in the face of increasing internal dissatisfaction and dissent. Instead of answering the people's demand for social and economic justice, he had mobilized the country behind the war effort. The graves of the war's martyrs were scattered all over the country.

And in Esfahan, the Rose Garden of the Martyrs was one of the few places Roxana's mother was permitted to visit. She made a daily pilgrimage to the tombs of her brothers, killed in the fighting to recapture the border town of Khorramshahr from the Iraqi army – a battle that had passed from history into folklore, aligning God, state, and martyrdom in the national mythos.

Khattak had kept up a vigil for most of the morning, wandering the gravestones like a tourist, occasionally nodding his head at families who'd come to mourn the dead in this labyrinth of ghosts. Placards hung above the graves. Each one hosted a picture of a martyr on one side and an image of Khomeini on the other, tying the dead to the legacy of the republic, a legacy reinforced by the Iranian flags planted at the graves.

Potted roses dotted the gravestones under romantic billboards. Some scenes idealized the war, others portrayed a comradely affection, a fallen soldier cradled by another.

Khattak meandered through the rows, reflecting on a war that had squandered the promise of a generation. The war had lasted eight years, claiming a million lives. Arabic graffiti could still be spotted among the ruins of Khorramshahr.

We have come to Khorramshahr to stay.

Many of the Iranians Esa had met spoke of the defense of Khorramshahr with pride, but when it came to the reciprocal trespass into Iraq, their eyes had slid away from his.

We were proud to defend our country from attack, but when we crossed the border, we didn't know what we were fighting for anymore. To invade another country wasn't who we thought we were.

Nothing had been gained by the war. A million dead on both sides for a cause that amounted to nothing in the end was something Esa couldn't fathom. There were things worth dying for, he believed, but the schemes of old men in turbans or despots in Ba'athist palaces were not among them.

Or he might have been simplifying the Iran-Iraq war and the sacrifice of the dead.

He knew if he asked the families at the graves, they would insist on their martyr's reward for rising to the call of the nation. Those who admitted the war's transgressions would be few: to admit such a thing was to deny the dead had died for anything at all, the idea of a thing more meaningful than the thing itself.

Maryam Ghorbani entered the garden of the martyrs from the north end. She headed to a bench not far from where Khattak stood, touching her hand to the photographs before the graves.

These were photographs of two boys whose somber eyes belied

their extreme youth. They had set their mark upon the earth, the grave opening to receive them like a pool of black blossoms.

Esa felt inexpressibly sad. He remembered the book Taraneh had given him, written by the famous sociologist of religion; Ali Shariati's lyrical essay on the plight of the oppressed had stayed with him. He thought of Shariati's elegy for Muhammad, the messenger of Islam.

His eyelids under the heaviness of death curtained our shining sun.

What did the mothers and sisters and daughters of these martyrs feel when they came to the Golestan-e Shohada after the years had passed? The sight of the woman in her coal-colored chador bringing flowers to the graves of her brothers raised a lump in Khattak's throat. He waited for her to finish scattering the petals for two young boys deprived of their lives. Khorramshahr had known suffering on a scale he couldn't imagine, the city erased by a war without grace. The closest parallel he could think of was Assad's bombardment of Aleppo.

These tyrants, these broken cities, this prodigal waste of life.

He felt a sinking in his bones as he took a place upon the bench, a little distance from the woman who didn't look at him. She was small to begin with, but grief had diminished her further, her careworn face lost within the folds of her chador. She was reciting a series of prayers by numbering the segments of her fingers.

When she finished, her shoulders caved in, hunched before the portraits of her brothers.

Khattak took a breath. He introduced himself in a hushed, respectful tone, as a friend of Zahra Sobhani's, explaining his errand in some detail.

Her head swiveled in his direction. Her bird-bright eyes considered him before she turned back to the gravestones. She straightened her shoulders, the tips of her toes swinging above the ground. She didn't look around. If she was afraid of the regime's minders, he couldn't tell.

'Where are you from? Though your Farsi is polished, I can tell you aren't from Iran. Afghani?' she asked.

He told her the truth. She placed one gnarled hand over the other, scattering crushed petals. The scent of roses infused the air.

'Please,' he said. 'I know you don't have much time. I have a few questions I need to ask. Can you tell me what Zahra was doing in Tehran? Do you know where your husband is, Khanom Ghorbani?'

She took her time replying, unmoved by Khattak's urgency. Perhaps she was wondering whether she could trust him, perhaps she kept her family's secrets to herself, conditioned by the regime's censorship.

'It would be good to know,' she agreed. 'Zahra was very kind. It didn't matter if Mehran had disappointed us, we understood each other. She loved Roxana, just as I love Mahmood.'

Rachel had told him Mahmood was Max Najafi's original name.

'Zahra asked Roxana to desist from her activities. She knew what it was to be harassed by the regime, so did Mehran. I begged Mehran to have Roxana released. When that didn't work, I asked Zahra to convince him.'

As Khattak had conjectured.

'Why wouldn't your husband have done what he could to free Roxana?' He gestured at the cemetery's grounds. 'You're the sister of two martyrs. Doesn't that result in some clemency from the regime? Aren't the people outraged on behalf of your family?'

'What can I tell you, Aghayeh Khattak? We belong to a country that doesn't belong to us.' She pressed the palms of her hands to her eyes. 'You see where my daughter is now, you know what they did to Zahra.'

Khattak couldn't find the words that would speak to her conclusions, so he invoked the traditional acknowledgment of reverence for the Prophet's martyred grandson. It expressed his personal sympathy, and it affirmed his deep-rooted religious and cultural ties to the people of Iran.

'Ya Hossein.'

'Ya Hossein,' she echoed, with a pleased smile, shading her eyes from the sun with her hand. Petals drifted to her lap. With a spark of mischief, she added, 'Ya Mir Hossein Mousavi.'

Which explained to Khattak why the family was under house arrest.

Like many supporters of the Green Movement, Maryam Ghorbani's family had been supporters of the 1979 revolution. The intervening years had shown her the revolution's decay. Some of its most prominent figures had charted a new path as leaders of the Green Movement. Maryam would have come to believe in the moral stature of men like Mousavi and Ayatollah Montazeri, the spiritual leader of the Green Movement. She may have been inspired by the presence of Zahra Rahnavard at the forefront of the movement. This Esa had gleaned from his conversation with Omid Arabshahi, who had spoken of the women's movement with enormous pride.

Khattak re-examined his assumptions yet again. A black chador said nothing about a woman's thoughts or hopes or her engagement with her country's political future. There were voices on all sides of the spectrum. He had misjudged Maryam Ghorbani. She was under house arrest because she'd made a political choice.

Then what of Mehran? Why was Mehran conspicuously absent, when the women of his family had taken a stand?

The regime has suffered a crack.

What was the crack? Where was the crack?

'Mehran was working on a business deal. He seemed to think if it turned out well, he would be able to ask for anything he wanted. Zahra didn't listen. She said Roxana's freedom couldn't wait on his schemes.' The ghost of a smile whispered over Maryam's lips. 'We have been victims of those schemes, so I could understand Zahra's impatience. But now she's dead and Mehran has disappeared. Now no one is left who can fight for Roxana.'

And Khattak couldn't promise he would try. He had no jurisdiction to act in Iran. And if Roxana was associated with his activities, it could seal her fate inside Evin.

'Why was Mehran imprisoned?' he asked at last.

Her answer astounded him.

'He was in and out of prison. The first time was after a visit to Neyshabur – and I don't know the reason for that. But he was only in Ward 209 once. He claimed he'd found Mossadegh's letters to Dariush Forouhar. Mossadegh is no hero to the regime – but why would they have imprisoned Mehran for that? The letters were burned the night the Forouhars were killed. Mehran was released once he recanted.'

But Khattak's hidden correspondent had written: *Find out what Zahra wanted with the letters.*

He was beginning to peel away the edges. The Mossadegh letters mattered. Just as he now knew Roxana was his correspondent. She'd written to him of her father's time in prison.

The how of it didn't matter. What mattered was the why.

Esa called Rachel, reaching her at their offices where she'd gone to run a background check on Mehran. Discoveries were compared, the route of Mehran's travels discussed, and conclusions drawn. Khattak pondered the military cap's importance to Zahra. No matter how he tried, he couldn't draw a line from the Shah's coronation to the Mossadegh letters and the Chain Murders, straight to the rise of the Greens.

'Let's speculate, Rachel, as we have nothing conclusive to go on.'

'I thought you said speculation was the enemy of good police work.'

'I didn't know you'd memorized my homilies,' Khattak answered. 'Please, I'd find it helpful.'

Rachel chuckled under her breath.

'All right, but then I'm really going to go out there, so don't say you weren't warned. I've been thinking about Mehran Najafi's yacht. Max said he was an exporter, caviar in the main. Touka told you he was more of a renegade, doing favors for top dogs. Are you with me so far?'

'Yes.'

'Suppose those trips up the Caspian, the business deals with his contact Mordashov – suppose he had something lucrative to export, some kind of stolen goods. Say it's these letters. Nate told me something about them. Mossadegh's legacy isn't one to mess around with. His letters should be part of the record – some would call them priceless. If they weren't destroyed, as everyone assumed, maybe Mehran found a buyer for the letters, and that's what had him so distracted he couldn't focus on Roxana.'

'Where does Zahra fit into the picture?'

'That's easy. Max said his folks were on good terms. Let's say Mehran put her in the picture. He says, "Hey, don't worry. I've got something cooking, and then we'll deal with Roxana." But Zahra doesn't want to wait. She sees the letters as leverage – maybe there's something in them, something that discredits the regime – don't ask me what, I'm just reaching here. So she sets up this meeting with the Supreme Leader and tells them what she has. She demands access to Roxana, they give in – what she doesn't know is that Radan will be there waiting. They trace the letters back to Mehran – presto, he disappears, never to be heard from again. And now they know they can do what they want with Zahra.'

'Why do they torture her, then?'

Rachel had been getting carried away, enjoying the

outlandishness of her theory. The mention of the circumstances of Zahra's death brought her back to reality with a thud, curbing the excitement in her voice.

'Aside from it being *de rigueur*? To find out what she knew about the letters.'

But Khattak thought they could just as easily have gotten the information from Mehran. When he pointed this out to Rachel, she fell silent.

'Do you find it odd,' he asked her, 'that Zahra had printed letters on her sleeve on the day she visited Evin? Or that she tore them off?'

'You're thinking they were some kind of insurance policy?'

'In a way. She wanted Roxana out, so she made sure she passed her leverage – whatever it was – on to someone else.'

'Any idea who?'

'I think the answer is in those letters.'

'The letters on her sleeve, you mean. Not the Forouhar letters. Not the letters you've been receiving.'

He told her his theory that Roxana was the author of the letters, connecting it to Mehran's time in prison. It was a reasonable conclusion, but for someone who'd just been suggesting an international smuggling conspiracy, she poked holes through his modest proposal with an air of palpable smugness. He grinned at the phone in his hand.

'I don't think the answer's in Canada, sir. I want to come to Iran, and help you dig for the truth. And I want to meet your stalkers and set them straight.'

Khattak tried to picture that meeting and failed. His smile widened. Mistaking the smile, a passing car honked an invitation at him.

'You'd need to come with a tour group of some kind, and getting a visa is difficult, given there are no consular relations between Canada and Iran. You'd have to have your visa processed through the Pakistan embassy in D.C. And you wouldn't know until the last minute if you'd been granted one, which would make for an expensive flight.'

'I have friends in high places,' Rachel said airily. Khattak thought she was surprised he'd given in, but the chances of Rachel getting the visa were slim to none, or he'd have done more to deter her.

'Or you could come home,' she added, sounding wistful.

'Believe me, I'd like to. I think I owe it to my newfound friends to try to get at an answer. If I can't make progress on my end, I'll deal with Touka and book the next flight home.'

'What about this other stuff, sir? This lot Zahra was interested in – our lot, she said. Do you think it means Ward 209?'

An unpleasant recollection forced itself to the forefront of Khattak's thoughts. After the mass arrest of protesters, many had disappeared. Later, a rumor had emerged of the purchase of a secret plot of land inside Tehran's cemetery, Behesht-e Zahra, a graveyard for the missing.

Could this be the 'lot' on Zahra's mind? Not a prison ward but a grave?

Zahra had begun inquiring about the lot after her last known contact with Mehran, who hadn't been heard from in weeks. And then she had sought out Charlotte Rafferty, but what connection could an archivist at a Canadian museum have to a graveyard in Tehran?

He agreed with Rachel's conclusion that this was a case where none of the connections were apparent, even to a seasoned detective. He listened with interest to her tales of Vicky and Nate. Then she asked him about 'the Yellows.'

'Do you think it could mean an offshoot of the Greens?'

Khattak wasn't familiar with the name. He would need to ask the Green Birds if there had been a reference to the Yellows in Roxana's letters. He searched his memory. *Changing our green feathers to yellow.* He'd assumed it meant the fear the regime had stoked with its crackdown. He would ask about this and about the burial plot in Behesht-e Zahra, to find out if it was more than rumor.

'Talk to Franklin Yang. Make that your first priority.'

They discussed the possibility of recovering Zahra's body through Nate's or Sehr's contacts. Khattak gave Rachel his unvarnished views – nothing could be done on that score. He ended the call. The timer was set to delete his record of it.

As much safety as he could hope for, if Larijani was on his trail.

37

Interrogation

'Your sister is here, did you know? She's Radan's little Kurdish slut. She moans for him like a whore. She gets on her knees – she likes it.' I smile, so they break my teeth. 'If she's here, show me, let me see her.' There's a hole in my lower lip, blood everywhere. 'You'll see her when we've finished. You can have a turn, unless you want one of us.' Uproarious laughter.

When it comes to sexual pathology, the Catholic Church has nothing on the mullahs.

I try not to think of Nasreen.

38

When Esa reached his guesthouse in the evening, Ali and Taraneh were waiting for him, dressed casually in jeans and sweaters, Taraneh with a black coat over her clothes and a blue scarf that framed the waves of her hair. They greeted him, falling into step.

'You shouldn't be here,' Esa said. 'You shouldn't risk a connection with me.'

Taraneh smiled at him pertly, but Ali seemed to weigh his words. His face was pale, his eyes searched out the shadows in the street.

'We're in this,' he said. 'It's too late to back out now. Tell us what you've learned.'

Esa recounted his meeting with Maryam. Ali listened, frowning. He came to a decision.

'Come with us. There's something we need to show you.'

'What about Larijani? What if he's watching?'

'We've thought of a reasonable cover. Have you ever seen a *ta'zieh* performed?'

Khattak shook his head. The martyrdom of Hossein at the battle of Karbala was reenacted as a passion play called the *ta'zieh* in the month of Muharrem. It was observed as a period of mourning on the Islamic calendar. Hossein had been killed on the tenth of Muharrem – the date of his death known as Ashura, the Day of Remembrance. The *ta'zieh* was a commemoration of his death that excited a display of public grief akin to the reenactment of the Crucifixion.

An imperfect analogy but the closest Esa could come to articulating its appeal.

Though the *ta'zieh* was a tradition exclusive to Shia Islam, the martyrdom of Hossein was mourned across the Muslim world, bridging all divides, and understood at its heart as an act of profound moral consequence: Hossein's martyrdom represented a stand against tyranny. It had been co-opted by the Green Movement as a strategy of resistance to expose the regime's hypocrisy.

Esa had participated in Shia religious gatherings at friends' homes as a child, but the storytelling that took place during these *jalasehs* or *majlises* was different from the enactment of a passion play. He wondered at the *ta'zieh*'s impact. He preferred to think of himself as being guided by a cool and rational mind, but it was possible he might be affected by the performance.

Then he stopped to consider. The Iranian new year was a week away, a time of celebration. The passion play was reserved for the month of mourning.

'Who would perform a *ta'zieh* now?'

Ali looked uncomfortable, like a man trying to convince himself he'd taken the necessary precautions against arrest.

'We will. We've gotten quite good at it, you'll be impressed. It's our cover story for meeting. We formed an amateur troupe of players to convince anyone who might be watching us we've turned over a new leaf. I don't know if it fools the regime, but it's how we shore up our credentials.'

Esa didn't think the regime would be as sanguine. He nodded at Taraneh.

'Surely women don't participate in the performance?'

'Please don't worry about us,' she said sweetly. 'We'll be assigned our proper role, preparing the *haft-seen* for the new year's celebrations, leaving the men to their rightful place.'

He accepted the rebuke, knowing he'd earned it.

'We're meeting at Omid's house with other members of the

Greens. We use Omid's courtyard as a stage, it's close enough to theater in the round.'

'I thought the *ta'zieh* was banned in the cities.'

'If we're interrupted, we'll call it a village entertainment. You said you needed to know more about Zahra's movements. She met with us several times. When we couldn't meet in person, we used Omid's house as a drop zone.'

'A drop zone?'

Ali shook his head impatiently. 'I don't know the right phrase in English. A place we could leave each other messages. That's what I want to show you.'

Khattak asked them about the Yellows.

'Are they another group of activists like the Green Birds? Does the name mean anything to you?'

Neither of them had heard of the name. They didn't know why Zahra had written the words in her date book – there was no such group that they knew of.

Taraneh spotted a taxi and flagged it down. Khattak held the door for her, Ali followed. Khattak chose a spot in the front seat beside the driver, letting himself be talked into the outing.

Esfahan at night was a traveler's paradise. The domes and towers of Naqsh-e Jahan shone like planets illumined by miniature suns, the park a black band of stars. They disembarked at the south end of Siosepol Bridge, a Safavid construction mounted on a series of pontoons. Its thirty-three arches burned like the embers of a giant's torch, an auroral glow reflected in the river. If a sorcerer had flung open his hand, so might the arches of Siosepol have sprung up.

It was the largest of eleven bridges to span the Zayanderud River.

Its pedestrian walkways were lined with trees that lifted in the breeze like the arms of ballerinas. Khattak and the others were hemmed in against the crush of families enjoying an evening excursion. Notes of almond blossom and lemon drifted through the air, tinged by a hint of camphor. Folk songs thrummed through the buzz of the crowd, groups of men gathered to sing. And the water, lying like a black pelt, carried the sound away.

It was a long walk over the bridge past the teahouse on the southern bank.

'Will I be meeting any of your families?'

Esa was thinking of the flowers he'd failed to take to Maryam Ghorbani, the crumpled rose petals in her hands a reminder of what remained to be done, the rituals of grief he should have personally observed.

'Just the Green Birds,' Ali said. 'We planned it that way.'

Taraneh's eyes flicked to his. Esa thought it better not to ask about Nasreen. Taraneh was still an unknown quantity, he didn't know why she had joined the Greens, or if she was serious about the movement's goals. Life seemed to lie lightly upon Taraneh, ideas darting through her mind like butterflies at a trellis. He imagined her drawn to the excitement of these clandestine meetings. If Zahra had shared her secrets with a member of the Green Birds, he didn't think it would be Taraneh.

Who, then? Omid? Nasreen?

As the players began their rehearsal in the courtyard, Ali urged Esa up the stairs that led to the roof. Here the night was quiet, a circle of deepening blues above their heads, bathed in the glow from the arches of Siosepol. Someone on a neighboring roof was smoking a bittersweet tobacco. Esa felt his heart twist. The scene was imbued with an indelible nostalgia.

He remembered what had brought him to Esfahan.

Omid called Ali back to the courtyard.

'We're stuck on a passage, come help.'

'Wait here,' Ali said to Khattak. 'I'll send someone to show you around.'

Khattak held up his glass. He was captured by the magic of

a night where lights bobbed above rose-scented rooftops. He felt a surge of longing, thinking of his grandfather's house in Peshawar. The family had gathered on the rooftop terrace in the evenings, the television news playing on a muted screen, trays of fruit in the center of a handwoven carpet, while his cousins had served him tea and his sister, Ruksh, had lain with her eyes closed and her head in their grandmother's lap. The coconut oil in her hair had mingled with the scent of jasmine. The faded notes of film songs had floated up to the terrace.

Omid's house reminded him of Peshawar. The room behind Esa was lit with lamps, a gauzy light filtering through the curtains. It was sparsely furnished with low settees, a wooden desk, and embroidered hangings in shades of blue. The wall facing Esa was papered with a thick damask whose floral pattern had peeled away at the edges.

'May I bring you more tea?'

Nasreen didn't use Esa's name or his title or any customary form of address. When she spoke to him, Esa realized he'd expected her to come.

'Have you come to tell me Zahra's secrets?'

He set down his glass on the low stone wall of the roof.

She had materialized from the night, her dress an indigo blue, her scarf a white drift about her neck, its band of swallows obscured by the dusk. A glance at her speaking, dark eyes, her face dim and pale, gave him the very real impression he was looking at a ghost. She put a hand to the curve of her hair, and it passed.

She cleared her throat as if she hadn't spoken in days, her voice a little hoarse.

'I'll show you the wall,' she said.

She flung the doors of the room open.

Khattak followed her into the room, noticing her habit of leaving enough space that a third person could have walked between them. Saneh, the shadow-twin? Missing in Kahrizak or just missed? Both, he thought. Her long white fingers were questing, seeking the empty spaces for her brother.

'There's nothing in this room.' He made the words a query.

Nasreen beckoned him to the wall where the paper had peeled.

'Ali and Omid said to show you, but I don't know if you want to carry this.'

The thin skin beneath her eyes looked bruised. She was bearing the weight of a missing brother, a brother who if returned to her one day would no longer be recognizable as the one who'd left.

'Zahra came here?' He ran a careful hand over the blue-and-gold damask, surprised at its smooth texture. It was tack paper, the damask a printed illusion.

'This room is known to the Greens. They leave each other messages on the wall.'

She stood on tiptoe, reaching up to a peeling corner.

Esa wanted to assist her, but felt himself too close to her.

She rolled down the paper without his help, curling it into a scroll.

She watched him, her fingers playing with the gold charms at her neck.

Esa took stock of the wall. And realized Roxana had written of this.

Read the writing on the wall.

There were messages in Farsi on the wall, as well as cartoons, slogans, and in some instances, the moody drawings of artists sketched in chalks or brisk sweeps of charcoal. Meeting places and times were scribbled over or scratched out. In one corner, a spray of hashtags fanned out, testifying to the reach of social media.

#Iranelection, #stolenelection, #SeaofGreen, #GreenWave, #GreenMovement, #whereismyvote, #Neda, #IamNeda, #22-Khordad, #25Bahman, #FreeJason, #FreeSaneh, #journalism-isnotacrime, #IranFreedom, #StopExecutions, #humanrights, and countless others.

One of the drawings depicted a writer seated before a piece of paper with a pen in one hand. A badge with the word 'journalist' was fixed below the collar of her blouse. A giant pair of scissors gaped open at her neck. When Esa looked at it closely, he realized the eye ring of the scissors formed a pair of shackles around the writer's wrists. If she tried to write, the blades would shear her neck, severing her jugular vein.

'Who drew this?' Esa asked.

A faint smile touched Nasreen's lips.

'No one signs their name, Inspector. The wall is dangerous enough as it is. In your country, the press is unrestricted, isn't it? Journalists are free to hold the government to account.'

Esa thought of the corporatized cable news. Talking heads discussed regions they'd never visited, making dangerous assumptions about peoples and cultures they didn't know, and languages they couldn't access. He contrasted this with the hazards risked by journalists in authoritarian states. Turkey, Iran, and China ranked at the top of a list of countries where a journalist's demand for accountability could lead to detention without trial. Journalists were often disappeared for daring to publish the truth, a list of names that lengthened like a bloodstain.

Nasreen came to stand beside him, the tag ends of her scarf grazing his arm, a flight of birds on his sleeve. He held his breath. He could sense the anarchy of her emotions. The restlessness of her fingers, the tamped-down fury that kept the lines of her face taut, the brittle energy she exuded, enraged by her loss.

He wondered which of the outpourings on the wall was hers.

Each week I go to visit him, I pray not to see Kahrizak again.

We speak in whispers, frightened of the air around us.

The voice of my torturer has faded. Its echo haunts my body.

Their public confessions are like public gang rape.

The writing bled over into other segments of the wallpaper, a forlorn query segregated by itself: *Why do all roads lead to Evin?*

In a large, imperfect Arabic script, someone had written *Allah*.

He couldn't see which of these messages was connected to Zahra.

'Did you know Zahra well?'

Nasreen drew his attention to a scribbled note at eye level.

'This is Zahra's. And this.'

Two words beneath a well-executed drawing in chalk.

Esa scrutinized the words scribbled in a cramped hand, the letters nearly on top of each other. It was a name, or possibly a location – Jeb Tavern, the *J* and the *n* extended in flourishes. He peered closer. No, there was more to it. It was Jebby Taverner, a name then. And decidedly not an Iranian name. Jebby, he thought. Jacob? Jedediah?

Next he examined the drawing, a shaded rectangle on a horizontal axis, inset with parallel lines, one corner at the top shaved off. It looked like a wooden frame except the interior of the frame was sectioned in parallel lines just like the frame itself. It resembled something else.

He searched for a number buried in the drawing: Lot 209. There wasn't one. Maybe Zahra hadn't dared to add it, hoping the drawing would be enough.

'It's a coffin,' he said. 'Why did she draw a coffin? Is it for Roxana?'

Nasreen flinched from the words. She touched the necklace at her throat again, dislodging it from the folds of her scarf. Now Khattak could see what the charms were, three tiny stars strung side by side. She had pressed the imprint of them into her neck.

'If it's anyone's coffin, it's Zahra's. We don't know Roxana is dead.' Her voice became rough. 'We don't know Saneh is.'

'Forgive me, that was thoughtless of me.' Khattak touched her shoulder. She stiffened and moved away.

'Tell me about your brother,' he said. 'Tell me what you know about Zahra.'

'Please,' she said. 'Roll up the paper and seal it.'

Khattak obeyed, taking a quick photograph of the name and sketch and sending it to Rachel with a question mark. He snapped a few additional photographs of the wall. Like his other messages, it was timed to self-destruct. When he'd finished, he joined Nasreen on the terrace. She was leaning against the wall watching the *ta'zieh*. The players had divided into groups on opposite sides of the courtyard. The characters who represented supporters of Hossein wore white robes with emerald turbans. Hossein's enemies were dressed in black with thick red bandannas wrapped around their foreheads. A few of the players had veiled their faces, assuming female roles.

Khattak looked for a third staging area, typically given over to the seat of the usurper, the Caliph Yazid who'd ordered the deaths of Hossein's family. Instead, where the players in black were assembled, a dais had been raised. A young man with an imperious white turban presided over the gathering, an attendant in black to either side. The young man was Omid Arabshahi.

The players in white fell on their knees. Like their turbans, their armbands were emerald green. Darius and Ali were at the center of this group. Classical music played in the background.

An uneasy feeling settled in Khattak's stomach.

This was supposed to be a traditional *ta'zieh*. The players should have formed a line, moving in time to the music's rhythms. And where was Shemr, Hossein's executioner?

Omid rapped his knuckles against a lectern.

'Shall we begin the trial of Hossein?'

There had been no trial. Hossein had been killed in the course of battle. His head had been paraded on a lance.

Darius rose to his feet. He spoke with an unaccustomed formality.

'Most honorable Caliph, Commander of the Faithful, may one among the judges be appointed to represent this descendant of the Prophet?'

A sweep of Darius's hand indicated Ali Golshani had been cast in the role of Hossein.

Instead of a gavel, Omid slammed a blunt-headed ax on the table. With his attention on Darius, Khattak didn't see it materialize. His hands jerked in response.

Nasreen looked over at him.

'It isn't as sharp as theirs,' she said, just as Omid said, 'We've already decided the question of his guilt. Read out his crimes.'

A search beneath Darius's armband yielded a piece of paper. Darius cleared his throat.

'Must the prisoner condemn himself?'

'Read the crimes!' Omid thundered.

His face was so pale Khattak didn't think he was acting. Darius was quick to comply.

'By challenging your leadership, Commander of the Faithful, the upstart Hossein has insulted the holy sanctities. He spreads propaganda against your reign, his followers have colluded against you. They are enemies of the regime.'

Regime, not *caliphate*.

A warning bell rang in Esa's mind.

Ali raised his head. He offered a single sentence, an air of invincibility about him.

'Ma bishomarim.'

We are many.

Behind him, the players in green formed a line. They raised their hands in victory.

Nasreen whispered the words, 'Allahu akbar.'

God is Greatest.

Esa drew a sharp breath. He understood the Green Birds' play. It was the natural evolution of a strategy the Green Movement had pioneered by appropriating the symbols of the regime, an act as clever as it was dangerous.

Allahu akbar was the rallying cry of the supporters of the 1979 Iranian revolution. They had assembled in the hundreds of thousands, roaring in the public square, demonstrating against the Shah of Iran's injustices. In 1979, the revolution had symbolized hope. It had promised social justice – it had promised the people everything. But when the Islamic Republic's tyranny and corruption had succeeded the despotism of the Shah, the Greens had struck back in the revolution's own language.

Allahu akbar had floated from the rooftops of Tehran in the ensuing days and weeks after the stolen election of June 2009, this time to signify the dissent of the opposition at the falseness of the regime's slogans. Posters appeared that paired the leaders of the Green Movement with images of Mossadegh, the most formidable advocate of democracy in Iran's history. *Shah raft* became *Ahmadi raft*: the Shah is gone, Ahmadinejad will be gone. Demonstrators injured at protests displayed their bruises and bloody clothing proudly, in the tradition that repression could only fuel revolution, it couldn't undermine it.

But perhaps the most significant strike of the Greens had been the act of co-opting Ashura, the culminating event of Muharrem, the date of Imam Hossein's death. In 2009, the opposition had proclaimed: this year's Ashura is Green.

And *ta'ziehs* were performed on Ashura.

Khattak gazed down at the performance in the courtyard with a faultless comprehension of its language. The trial of Ali Golshani, the 'self-inflicted interview,' was dressed in the symbols of the martyrdom of Hossein. The regime that claimed to esteem Hossein beyond any other figure was implicated in his murder.

It was bold and brilliant and completely without subtlety.

As the drama unfolded, Hossein was torn from his family without the opportunity to speak in his own defense. Omid, as the Caliph, performed an elaborate charade. He signed declarations, asked questions that offered Hossein the opportunity to incriminate himself, and proclaimed the verdict before deliberations were able to take place.

It was a perfect simulation of the current regime's show trials: defendants were without access to counsel or family, without knowledge of the charges against them, or evidence offered to substantiate the charges, the outcome assured in advance.

He turned his back on the performance. Nasreen hadn't answered his questions. She hadn't spoken of her brother, imprisoned at Kahrizak, or explained her relationship with Zahra. Nor had she offered an explanation of Zahra's message on the papered-over wall, another cause for worry. It would take little effort for a man like Larijani to ransack the house and discover the Green Birds' wall of subversive messages. He was appalled by the risk. Zahra had been tortured and raped – how could the Green Birds believe they were safe when the messages on the wall challenged the regime at every turn?

One message in particular had caught his eye.

Resaneh shomaid.

He translated it as, *You are the messenger, you are the media.*

He pondered its subtleties, its contrast to the *ta'zieh*. The people as a conscious voice for change became the message of change. And the nuances of 'messenger' – a reference to the messenger of God, a touch of the divine in all human creation.

If you belonged to God, how could you be undone by the regime?

Nasreen had stared at the cartoon of the journalist. Was there a connection to Zahra's work as a documentarian?

'Was that Zahra in the cartoon?' he asked.

Her reply was indirect.

'Why does no one think a woman can be a prisoner of conscience?' she mused. 'Take Zahra Rahnavard, for example.'

Zahra Rahnavard – scholar, painter, university chancellor, the author of dozens of books – a key figure in the Green Movement's leadership. She'd opposed the government's anti-women legislation in the penal and family law, arguing on the side of religion's innate progressivism. She had silenced the naysayers and hardliners with her thorough knowledge of the Qur'an.

Her status as Mousavi's wife was secondary to her own accomplishments, but her presence at Mousavi's side had galvanized the Greens. Holding her husband's hand, she'd spoken of gender equality, accusing the regime of failing to fulfill its constitutional and international duties to ensure the rights of women.

Zahra Rahnavard was under house arrest, just like Maryam Ghorbani.

When Khattak left Iran, the struggles of the Green Movement would continue. He could contribute nothing beyond his attempt to unravel Zahra's murder, and for that, he needed answers.

'Will you answer a few questions before I leave?'

Startled, Nasreen's eyes found his. She must have thought him bemused by the rituals of the unfolding *ta'zieh*. He wasn't. He was beginning to feel tired and impatient.

'What was your relationship with Zahra?'

Nasreen, too, had made up her mind. Something in her face shifted. She let out a sigh.

'She was a friend. I brought the case of my brother to her, she promised to help.'

'Did Zahra tell you she'd requested a meeting with the Supreme Leader? Do you know the purpose of that meeting?'

A faint frown colored Nasreen's brow. 'Zahra's only preoccupation: Roxana's release.'

Khattak wasn't certain this was true. He left it aside for the moment.

'Do you know what the sketch on the wall means? Do you recognize the name Taverner?'

'No, I haven't heard it before.'

Her eyes shifted away from his. He suspected her of lying.

'Have any of the others?'

'No, I'm the one Zahra spoke to most.'

She bit her lip. This was something she hadn't meant to tell him.

'Why did she come to Esfahan if she needed to be at Evin?'

'To meet with the Green Birds for her film. To speak to Roxana's mother.'

'Do you think there's a chance Roxana will be released?'

He watched her face for any sign that Zahra had confided something of her progress.

'I have hope,' she said.

But she didn't, he saw. Her face sagged at the question. She was pressing the stars on the chain into her neck again.

'Why do you wear that necklace? What do the stars mean?'

'You don't know?' He shook his head. 'I wear these for Saneh. He's a starred student.'

'I'm not familiar with the term.'

She raised a single star on her fingertip. Her nails were unpainted.

'If you're a student who becomes politically active, you're blacklisted by the regime. You can recant if you sign a document promising to give up your activities. If you have one or two stars and recant, you're allowed to return to your studies.'

'And three stars?'

'They're for Saneh,' she repeated. 'With three stars, the ban is permanent. You can never return to school. We were treated more harshly in any case because we're Kurds, but to Saneh it didn't matter.' Her hoarse voice choked on the words. 'He refused to recant. He argued we were better off than Baha'is, who are blocked from post-secondary education. The ban put us on an equal footing, he said.'

She told him this without self-pity. He asked how long Saneh had been in Kahrizak. He asked why she continued to risk her own safety, given her brother's torturous fate. He used the word deliberately. Her face altered again, it made him think of the letters, the writer's allusion to Rumi. A treasure among the ruins, the bones of her skull fragile inside her scarf.

Darius had told him Nasreen had asked after him. He was interested as well, attracted by an aura of mystery. She avoided his questions, making for the stairs.

A loud hand banged on the door to the house. It sounded twice more with the force of a battering ram.

The players in the courtyard scattered, pulling down the dais and hastily rearranging themselves. Ali motioned to a few to leave from a door at the back. Darius ripped up the piece of paper and swallowed the tiny pieces. He raised the volume on the classical music. An angry voice sounded over it, quarreling with Omid. Just as Khattak had feared, it was Larijani.

Moving swiftly, Esa shut off the lights and closed the screen doors to the second-story room. He made his way down the stairs, his glass trembling in his hand.

Larijani hadn't come alone. There were three men with him, dressed in black, belligerent in their movements like guns already cocked. Larijani scoured the courtyard with his eyes, his lips hitching up in a sneer.

'I know you.' He pointed to Ali and Darius, turning to Omid. 'What are they doing here? What are any of you doing here?'

Khattak intervened.

'Agha Larijani,' he said with utmost politeness. 'I met these young people at the bridge. They invited me to watch a *ta'zieh*.'

Larijani swiveled round, his eyes cataloguing every member of the party. He nodded at his men. They began to move through the house, searching it room by room. Khattak heard Taraneh's voice from the kitchen. She was scolding the intruders. One of the men climbed the stairs to the roof. Khattak tried not to watch his progress.

Larijani ignored Khattak. He jabbed Omid in the chest with a finger.

'There are no *ta'ziehs* at this time of year, don't lie to me.'

Coolly, Omid explained the nature of the rehearsal. He

discussed the rites of the performance in detail, making small, obscure comments about the script. He offered to call the players back together. He'd been prepared for a moment like this. Or it wasn't his first time dealing with the Ministry's agents. He'd known Larijani's reputation, as soon as Khattak had mentioned him.

Khattak was waiting for the sound of footsteps from the roof. A cold sweat had broken out on his back. The palms of his hands were damp. He couldn't emulate Omid's composure.

Larijani changed his tune. Not wanting to lose face, he asked Khattak sourly, 'Were you impressed?'

Rushing over the words, Khattak discussed Shia processionals in Pakistan. Larijani ceased to listen, his attention diverted by the sound of Taraneh's voice. He noticed the sweat glistening on Darius's face.

'Where are your parents?' he demanded.

'Visiting friends.'

'There are women here without chaperones.'

'They're my cousins,' Omid said easily. He still hadn't asked why Larijani had burst into his home. He told the players to rise, Larijani waved them aside.

He pointed to Khattak. 'It's time to consider the date of your departure.'

Khattak bowed his head without comment.

Larijani's men completed their search. One of them held up Omid's laptop. The other two had returned empty-handed. Darius sucked in an audible breath, his scar inflamed on his face.

'You're going to explain this to me.' He jerked his head at Omid. 'And you.' He indicated Darius, nodding at his men. Darius swallowed compulsively.

'As you wish,' Omid agreed, unperturbed.

'Perhaps I should come instead of my brother.' As pale as Khattak, Ali sidestepped the attempt of Larijani's men to fasten on to Darius. 'I worked with Omid on the script.' He shielded his brother behind him, stumbling over the words.

There was a fractional pause before Larijani agreed, 'Yes, you're the journalist.'

He turned a black scowl on Khattak. 'The performance is over. Get back to your hotel.'

It wasn't a suggestion. Khattak looked over at the others. Was there any way he could intervene? Omid caught his eye, shaking his head quickly.

And when he still hesitated, Larijani barked at him, 'I told you to leave!'

Khattak didn't delay again. The players left Darius behind. Khattak followed them, his thoughts with the Green Birds of June.

And struck by fear for Nasreen.

39

The Suite

'Joojeh, I beg you, is my sister here? I'll give you everything I have if you tell me, please say she isn't here.' Joojeh looks over his shoulder, back at the tiny window of the cell. No one's there. He puts a finger to his lips. 'Don't believe them,' he says. 'She isn't here, she's safe.' 'And Zahra?' I ask, my heart in my throat. 'Khanom Sobhani, she's safe?' Joojeh's eyes waver. He looks away and shrugs. 'She's dead,' he says. 'It was quick, and everyone knows.' He motions me away from the door. And hands me a packet of honey.

Zahra

They've taken her to interrogation. A female guard searches Zahra with disgusting familiarity, a hand between her legs. Men who look like animals are grinning as they watch. Zahra's blindfolded, she can't see. She's handcuffed, so they shove her along, and she stumbles. Someone laughs, it's Radan. Her head snaps up, she knows Radan's voice. He shoves her into a chair, pressing his crotch into her face. She leaps away. 'You can't do this,' she says. 'I know what you've done, I've been to see Khamenei.' He reaches across the desk to shut off the camera. He barks orders to his men. They leave him alone with Zahra. 'It doesn't matter,' he says. 'You're too late, you'll be dead by this time tomorrow. And when I'm done with you, I'll move on to

Roxana.' Zahra isn't intimidated. She sits with her back straight and speaks in a fearless voice. 'I demand to see a lawyer.' Radan laughs. 'In this room, I'm lawyer, prosecutor, executioner, judge.' He lowers his zipper. His fist smashes into her skull.

I wake up in a cold sweat. Night after night, I dream this.

40

Khattak stayed awake late, deeply concerned for the others. Had Omid and Ali been released? Would they be? Who could he ask? He wouldn't dare to contact them now. Larijani would be watching.

He remained in his room to avoid arousing Nasih's suspicion. He'd showered as soon as he reached the guesthouse, the moments of peace on Omid's rooftop shattered by Larijani's intrusion. The only step he could take was to send Touka an encrypted query. It yielded no reply.

He let the silence and the scent of the lemon trees settle in his room, the air turning cold as the hours advanced. Leaves skittered across the pavement, pushed along by an aimless wind. Too afraid to sleep, he left his window open, alert to sounds of intrusion.

He was thinking of what he'd learned, and wondering if the ruse of the *ta'zieh* had worked. Larijani had turned up on a night when Khattak was at Omid's house. Either Larijani was tailing Khattak, or the surveillance of the Green Birds was more thorough than they knew.

When dawn arrived, he arose and performed his prayers. In the long supplication at the end, he remembered Zahra Sobhani. He prayed for the release of Saneh and Roxana, and the countless others detained as prisoners. He prayed for the living and the dead, thinking of Omid and Ali.

And he wondered how many similar prayers had gone unanswered in the years since the revolution, how many families' disappointed hopes had dwindled into mourning. The memory of Maryam Ghorbani's bereaved eyes was fresh in his mind. He'd spent some of the night reading about the battle of Khorramshahr and the long-forgotten Iran-Iraq war.

Many of the Green Movement's supporters were children of war heroes who'd fought the invasion at Khorramshahr. A twenty-six-year-old by the name of Mohammad Ali Jahanara had led the townsfolk in defense of their homes, under the Iraqi army's relentless bombardment.

Neda Agha Soltan's killing by the Basiji had evoked Jahanara's memory, equating Saddam Hussein's Ba'athists with the leaders of the Iranian regime.

Tell Jahanara the Ba'athists are in Tehran, firing at our girls.

It was an echo of exquisite force.

And it was painful to Esa that Roxana, whose uncles had died as young men at Khorramshahr, was considered an enemy of the regime. Her protest songs had captured the popular imagination, and the spirit of the movement for change. God knew if she was alive or dead, or if Lot 209 was her burial place.

He ended his prayer and dressed in fresh clothing, making his way to his seat under the quince tree. A handful of ringed plovers were pecking birdseed from a wooden feeder. Their small chirps softened his fears.

Indecision gnawing at him, he called Rachel, keeping his voice low.

She sounded excited and energized, bringing Khattak up to speed on Franklin Yang and Zahra's meeting at Winfield Park.

'I think it means Windfields Park,' Khattak noted. 'It's a nature park in the Bayview area that follows the Wilket Creek. It's on the border of Edwards Gardens. Why did Zahra go there?'

Edwards Gardens was one of the city's loveliest parks, awash in roses and waterfalls, a popular site for wedding parties and nature enthusiasts.

Rachel told him about Max Najafi's studio in Trinity Bellwoods.

'I'm sensing a running theme here. Could they have been scouting locations for their film?' She sounded doubtful.

'Find out,' Khattak advised. 'And let me know if you have any luck with Jeb Taverner or the drawing.'

'Watch yourself, sir. And remember what I said about my travel plans.'

'Rachel –'

He couldn't say he didn't want her to come when he very much did. He was picturing her earnest face and bouncy ponytail with something deeper than fondness. But then he thought of Larijani's arrest of Ali and Omid. They could be disappeared – and so could anyone connected to them. He made this clear to Rachel, though he knew he couldn't override her. She warned him in return, a spike of alarm in her voice at his proximity to danger. He could hear her determination harden. She wouldn't leave him on his own. Discouraging her was futile.

They talked a little longer, Esa checking behind the brick in the courtyard wall. The dark space was empty. If Roxana had been sending him the letters, someone else was her courier. He acknowledged the fact with some reluctance: it was time to return to Tehran. And it was more than time for him to leave Iran.

Rachel was at the door, resolved to accelerate her plans. She didn't like what was happening in Iran. She wanted Khattak home, or she wanted to be there to protect him. Her keys were in her hand, and her cell phone in her pocket when a knock sounded at her door. She hadn't buzzed anyone up, and Zach had his own keys. It was probably one of her neighbors, wondering if she was the owner of the cat. Rachel grimaced at the thought. Even if she wanted to be, she couldn't. Not with Zach moving in. She would make that clear and be on her way. Squinting, she checked the peephole, dismayed to see her mother. She would rather it was a neighbor holding the little black cat.

She glanced back at her condo, hoping she hadn't left it in a mess. A quick look around, the blinds open to the crisp green frontage of the park, the tall trees stretching their limbs to the sky. Everything had been tidied, the coffee tables dusted, knickknacks in their place. The countertops were spotless, the dish rack drained. This was her mother's first visit to Rachel's home, and Rachel hadn't told her Zach was in the process of moving in. He'd brought her the pink tulips that brightened up the kitchen. The door to his room was open, his bag on the floor.

Another glance, this time at her clothes. Her spring jacket was back from the dry cleaners. Her slacks were ironed, and she'd polished her shoes over the sink. Her hair was brushed back into its usual style, her lips reddened by lip balm. She gave off an aura of confidence.

Taking a breath, she opened the door and summoned an easy smile.

'Hey, Mum. I was just on my way to work.'

Her mother's eyes found hers. She hadn't troubled over her appearance. Her parka was too heavy for the weather. Beneath it she wore a dull green dress and court shoes that had gotten scuffed on the still-damp pavements. She was wearing a pair of gold earrings in the shape of small shells. Rachel wondered if Zach had bought them, she knew they weren't from her father.

'I need to speak with you, Rachel. I wouldn't have come if I didn't.'

Rachel relented. There was a note in her mother's voice she wasn't used to hearing.

'All right, Mum. Give me your coat, then.'

She offloaded her work gear on the credenza in the hallway, hanging her mother's coat in the closet, avoiding her own gaze in the mirror. She had framed a lettered quotation of Tennyson's on the wall beside the mirror.

For all is dark where thou art not.

It wasn't a religious observance. It was a grim reminder of

what her life had been like in the years Zach had been missing. Where other people might have put up something inspirational, Rachel chose to remember. She viewed her relationship with her brother as a trust: the framed quotation reminded her not to fail again. She hoped her mother hadn't noticed.

She asked Lillian to sit on one of the leather couches, planning to edge Zach's door closed before her mother could glimpse inside his room.

Lillian shook her head, her lips pressed firmly together. She gestured at the door.

'Is that Zach's room?'

She pushed past Rachel to the other room. The smell of fresh paint filled the air. The room, with its large picture window, was empty of furniture, the floor protected by drop cloths. The laces of one of Zach's sneakers was caught on the zipper of his bag.

Green-gold trees glowed from the center of the wall, their yellow branches wearing their leaves like garments. The mosaics glittered like a secret fire, the pattern of the trees spiraling out from the center. Rachel thought of summer's kiss, she thought of extravagant joy, she wondered that Zach could have learned so much during his time in Vienna. It was the perfect antidote to her framed quotation, a gift of green, a tree of hope.

Her mother didn't share Rachel's joy. She clasped a hand to her heart as if stricken down by the tree.

'Why did he paint this?' she asked.

'Because he's happy,' Rachel said. 'Why shouldn't he be?'

Lillian Getty stumbled. When Rachel saw her face, she let out a cry. She helped her mother to the sofa, bringing a glass of cold water for her to drink. Lillian took a sip at a time, gathering her courage with her color.

'After everything I've done for you – don't do this to me, Rachel.'

Rachel's heart pounded in her ears. The saliva in her mouth ran dry.

'What are you talking about, Mum?'

Lillian Getty lifted her head. Her watery eyes were clear.

'My son. Don't take him from me, Rachel. Don't bring him here, don't divide his heart, don't set him on a path to walk away.'

'Mum.' Rachel's hands were shaking. 'He's out of work. He can't pay rent. What is he supposed to do? Go back to a shelter? How could you want that for him?'

Her mother's eyes cut at her like glass, Rachel shuddered at the look. She had always known she mattered less than Zachary, but she hadn't known this – this resentment that flared from a bottomless source.

'Don't insult me, Rachel. Zachary could come home.'

Rachel had been kneeling beside her mother. Now she raised herself to her full height, incredulous at the thought. There was a painful gap in her mother's acknowledgment of reality.

'Do you honestly think Zach would return to live under Da's roof? What are you imagining – Da's going to welcome him with open arms, and Zach will walk right into them?'

Her mother spoke through stiff lips.

'Things are different now. Your father has changed. He wouldn't … he wouldn't –'

'He wouldn't what, Mum? Bloody him with his fists, lock him in the garage?' She flung a hand at Zach's tree. 'Batter the art right out of him? No,' she said firmly. 'Zach goes back to that house over my dead body.' She eyed her mother with newfound conviction. 'I love you, Mum, but you listen to me. I'll do everything in my power to make sure no one hurts Zachary again. I'll press charges if I have to.'

The certainty in her mother's eyes faded. Her chin began to tremble, and at the sight, shame flooded Rachel's chest, threatening to swamp her. It was familiar to her, she had carried it for years. She blinked furiously, her muscles tight, her hands clenched into fists.

'You can come to my place,' she said. 'As often as you or Zach want, but don't ask me to turn him out. Not when he's asked something of me, not when I know he's safe. Haven't I earned some peace of mind?'

Lillian moved past Rachel blindly, fumbling for her coat in the closet. She clutched the parka to her chest, lurching to the door. When she turned back, her face was wet with tears.

'And what about me, Rachel? Haven't I earned anything? After all these years as Don Getty's wife, haven't I earned my son?'

Shocked, Rachel took a step away from Lillian.

Unspoken between them was the reality of what Lillian had done. She had let her daughter search for Zach for years, while all along, she'd known he was safe. She'd kept her knowledge from the rest of the family, making him believe Rachel had abandoned him.

He hadn't told her as much, but it had to be the reason he refused to accept any further assistance from their mother. And Rachel knew the moment to ask had come. She drew a shaky breath.

'Why did you never tell me the truth, Mum?'

Her mother responded with such evident sorrow, it took Rachel a moment to absorb the sense of her words.

'I believed you would tell your father.'

Her hand was on the doorknob, she was ready to leave.

'Wait,' Rachel gasped. 'What did I do to make you think that? I was just a kid myself.'

Lillian shook her head. She was crying openly, her chest heaving with little hiccups.

'I'm a fool,' she whispered. 'I shouldn't have come to you, Rachel.'

41

There was a knock on the door of the guesthouse that jolted Khattak out of his thoughts. It was followed by an angry exchange in Farsi. A moment later, Nasih appeared in the courtyard, Larijani and one of his men at his heels.

Khattak rose to his feet. His face pale, he asked, 'Is anything the matter?'

Nasih was shoved aside. When Khattak moved to help, Larijani pointed at him in warning, his arm sharp as an arrow.

'Who is this man?' he barked at Nasih in Farsi.

Nasih's face was even paler than Khattak's.

'A guest, Agha. You know I run a respectable business.'

'A guest from where? For how long? What has he been doing at your house? Does he have a computer?'

Nasih fell over himself in his haste to satisfy Larijani's questions. He gave the specifics exactly as he knew them. He mentioned his loan of the laptop, but he didn't bring up the delivery of Khattak's mysterious gifts.

Khattak pretended incomprehension as Larijani turned on him.

'You borrowed this man's laptop. Why?'

'To watch *The Magnificent Century*. It's a fascinating drama.'

Following along, Nasih quickly confirmed this. He kept Khattak's fluency in Farsi to himself.

'Oh, really?' Larijani narrowed his eyes. 'Describe it.'

Khattak thought quickly. He hadn't watched a single episode, but his sisters had mentioned something of its storyline, and two of its central characters.

'I'm a little behind,' he said. He filled in the rest as best as he could from memory.

Larijani dropped it. 'Why aren't you with a tour group? How do you know those dissidents?'

Khattak's heart dropped at the use of the word *dissidents*. It meant the Green Birds were on Larijani's radar. How? Why? And if they were, why hadn't Larijani raided the roof in the Armenian quarter?

'Agha Larijani, I *was* with a tour group. Esfahan was the last stop on the tour. The city is so beautiful, I chose to extend my stay. I haven't been anywhere else.'

He didn't mention Varzaneh. He hoped Nasih wouldn't either – but he knew if pressure were applied, Nasih would have no choice but to confess everything he knew.

'Shall I fetch my itinerary for you to see?'

'No,' Larijani snapped. He motioned to the guard holding on to Nasih. 'You. Get it.'

Hurriedly, Nasih turned over the key to Esa's room with an apologetic grimace.

Esa shook his head – a quick gesture of acknowledgment. He had brought this trouble to Nasih's doorstep. And now it was clear that Nasih had never been spying on him.

He watched Larijani's man barge into his room, and listened to the ruthless sounds of his search.

Larijani dismissed Nasih.

'This simpleton doesn't know anything.'

Khattak spread his hands before him. 'Agha Larijani, what is it you wish to know? Your country is open to tourists, that's why I came for the pilgrimage.'

'Do you take me for a fool? Where are you really from?'

Not knowing what else to do, Khattak answered the man with a volley of remarks in Urdu. He spoke quickly, fluently, not feigning his distress. Uncomprehending, Larijani stared back at him.

His aide returned to the courtyard, Khattak's travel portfolio in his hands. He held up Khattak's Pakistani passport. Larijani snatched it, holding it between his thumbs. He flipped it open to the photograph page where Khattak's name appeared first in English, then in Urdu.

Muhammad Khattak.

Only his Canadian passport bore his full name.

Beneath this was listed the name of Khattak's father.

If Larijani flipped to the next page, it would show Khattak's place of birth as Toronto, Canada, a fact that had gone unremarked when Khattak had applied for his visa. Anxiety tightening his chest, he reached for the portfolio and drew out the itinerary printed for him by the tour group. A dozen postcards he had bought at the shrine at Mashhad spilled from the case, scattering across the courtyard.

Larijani swore at him. He took the itinerary, snapping the passport shut.

Though Khattak was desperate to retrieve it, he busied himself collecting the postcards. He heard the clink of ice cubes in a glass. Nasih had returned to the courtyard, bearing a tray of glasses.

Larijani was reading his itinerary, checking each of the stops on the tour against Khattak's hotel stamps. He passed it back to his aide.

As Nasih offered him a glass of water, he snapped, 'This man has been at your house the entire time? Since he arrived in Esfahan – not at any other residence?'

Nasih raised the tray in a placatory gesture.

'Of course, Agha. I would have told you if it were otherwise.'

Esa took a glass, his fingers slipping on its wet surface. Larijani's man hadn't taken his eyes from Esa's face.

Esa took a sip, more to calm his nerves than for any other reason. He bowed his head at the other man.

'Ya Hossein,' he murmured politely. Out of habit, Nasih and the guard responded with 'Ya Hossein.'

It was a respectful gesture that invoked the cruelty of Imam Hossein's thirst at the battle of Karbala. The guard took a glass and sipped from it.

'Ya Hossein,' he said again, wiping his own brow. His suspicion seemed to ease.

Larijani barked at him, and the guard set his glass back on the tray, a sullen resentment in his eyes.

'How do you know the dissidents?' Larijani asked again.

Khattak had had time to think of an answer.

'I met them at the Siosepol Bridge. Your people are so hospitable – as soon as they heard I was a tourist, they invited me to witness their *ta'zieh*. And they performed it beautifully.'

Was it too much? Or not enough?

Larijani fanned Esa's passport across his hand.

Opening it. Shutting it. Opening it. Shutting it. Fanning it again.

Esa leaned over to the guard to point out a stop on his itinerary.

'After Esfahan, the shrine at Mashhad meant the most to me. Next time I'll bring my family.'

Larijani clenched the passport in his fingers.

'No,' he said. 'You won't. I'll be putting your name on a list. Get on a bus and get out of Iran, before I change my mind.'

He dropped Esa's passport onto Nasih's tray with a casual flick of his wrist. He nodded at his man, who dumped Esa's case at his feet.

Larijani turned on his heel. A second later he turned back.

'Your phone, Mr. Khattak.'

Esa had placed it behind the brick in the courtyard wall. It was no more than two feet from Larijani. Despite the temptation to glance over at it, Esa trained his gaze on Larijani's face.

'I lost it at a restaurant.'

The glasses trembled on Nasih's tray. He knew that Esa had another.

Larijani interrogated his aide. The man shook his head in

reply. He hadn't turned up a cell phone in his search.

'No phone, no computer,' Larijani said with obvious skepticism. 'You travel very light, Mr. Khattak.'

Esa smiled politely. 'I wanted to see this beautiful country – I didn't need distractions.' He tested Larijani. 'And I really don't know how I came to lose my phone.'

Larijani's eyes narrowed. An unpleasant smile appeared on his face, distorting his unremarkable features.

'I hope you've enjoyed your stay,' he said coldly. 'But if I find you here tomorrow, I'm afraid you won't be leaving.'

No more than a moment after Larijani had left, Khattak's phone buzzed behind the brick with the notification specific to the Telegram app. Touka had answered his message.

His face white with fear, Khattak looked straight at Nasih.

'*Ma bishomarim*,' the other man whispered.

He gathered up Esa's glass and left him alone in the courtyard.

42

Franklin Yang had refused to meet Rachel at the ROM. He wanted secrecy, he claimed, and a promise of total discretion. Rachel had proposed Edwards Gardens as a meeting place. The gardens occupied several lush acres in North York, along the well-heeled Bridle Path.

The park was a hodgepodge of delights: crisscrossed walking and cycling trails, fountains and quaintly vaulted bridges, a waterwheel, a series of rock gardens. As part of the estate, the Toronto Botanical Gardens offered garden tours, field trips, and a promising horticultural library. But Rachel had chosen the gardens because of their proximity to Windfields Park – she was hoping the location might loosen Franklin's tongue. She was in a foul mood, her thoughts divided between Esa's safety and her encounter with her mother.

She found Franklin Yang at a waterfall in the park.

He was doing yoga exercises on the bridge. He straightened out of a complicated stretch and came down to meet her by the water. His hair was teased up in a scented pomade, and combed back from his scalp. He was wearing a blue checked shirt that adhered to his lean frame. Rachel pegged him as in his early twenties.

Rachel motioned him to a bench, where he had parked a large leather portfolio. He sat rather close to her, and he smelled as good as he looked, a heady mix of citrus and ginger. Rachel looked down at his feet. His shoes weren't meant for a ramble along a park trail: they were polished loafers with sharp, silver buckles.

'Why didn't you try to speak to me, the day I came to the ROM?'

The question was too blunt. It reflected Rachel's internal turmoil. Franklin stiffened at her tone.

'I don't need any additional trouble.' He pinched his lips together.

'Additional?' Rachel pounced on the word. 'Are you talking about Zahra Sobhani? Your name is listed in her address book, you met several times. And Zahra's assistant told us you were close, she called you Lin.'

'Everyone calls me Lin,' he said with a pout. 'But yes, I'd like to think we were getting close.' He looked at Rachel with an expressive movement of his eyebrows. 'I thought it might be worth my time to cultivate the acquaintance, but it wasn't just that, of course. She needed help, and when Charlotte put up such a stink, I was happy to do what I could.'

His tone suggested he would have been glad to do a great deal more, if it would have helped him get back at his boss.

'How did you help her, Mr. Yang?'

'It was all about the Yellows, wasn't it? She was trying to track them down. Charlotte said the very idea was absurd, but Zahra thought if anyone would know, it would be an archivist at the ROM. Seeing as how we led the project to begin with. Inescapable logic, if you ask me. Not that Charlotte agreed.'

None of this made any sense. Except for the words 'the Yellows' noted in Zahra's date book. Rachel's interest in Franklin sharpened.

'Slow down, Mr. Yang,' she said. 'Start at the beginning. What are the Yellows? And why would an archivist at the ROM be expected to know of them? What do *you* know of them?'

Franklin Yang widened his satiny eyes.

'I thought you knew all about it. You said you did on the phone.' He reached for his portfolio, its handle slipping in his hands.

Belatedly, Rachel softened her tone.

'I knew Zahra was investigating the Yellows, and I know about the coronation video. What I don't understand is how the two connect. I also don't know where to find Vic Mean. I was hoping you might help.' Thinking grimly of her own family, she said, 'I promised Zahra's son I'd bring his mother back from Iran, which is something I won't be able to do unless I have some leverage.'

His fingers dithered over the leather portfolio.

'This won't get back to Charlotte?'

'Not from me. Though I'm interested in why she told us she didn't know anything about Zahra.'

'Charlotte won't lift a finger if she can't see the benefit to herself. Imagine a head of archives who loathes the task of actually consulting the archives.'

'Was it the archives Zahra wanted to search? Because Charlotte told us the ROM has no records on the coronation of the Shah of Iran.'

'That's true, as far as it goes, but I think you've been misled. Zahra wasn't interested in the coronation, she was interested in the Yellows. The Iranian Yellows, to be exact.' He puffed out his chest in the blue checked shirt. 'Which speaks to our expertise.'

She forced herself to ask again calmly.

'What *are* the Iranian Yellows?'

A little surprised, Franklin unzipped the portfolio.

'They're a priceless collection of diamonds – they form part of the Iranian crown jewels.'

And when Rachel looked blank, he added, 'The crown jewels are so phenomenally valuable they back the national currency to this day.'

With a flourish, he pulled a massive volume from his case and dumped it on Rachel's lap.

'Zahra came to us because the ROM pioneered an inventory of the national treasury in 1968. It was led by our chief mineralogist.'

Rachel stared down at the book's shiny gold cover.

Four photographs of fabulous treasures adorned the center of the cover in a narrow strip. The third in the row was the picture of a giant yellow diamond.

At the top of the cover, two names were printed in capitals. MEEN & TUSHINGHAM.

She flipped to the inside cover.

The authors of the gemological study were listed as V. B. Meen and A. D. Tushingham. A closer inspection yielded their full names.

Victor Meen and Arlotte Tushingham.

Rachel's heart began to race. She was finally on the right track.

Rachel pulled up a photograph on her phone, trying to connect the dots. It was the picture of the letters on Zahra's sleeve: ADTVBMJBT. It was safe to assume she'd solved part of the code at least.

Arlotte Douglas Tushingham, Victor Ben Meen. The third man was missing from the book's cover. JBT. Jeb Taverner. She would have to find the connection between this man and the Yellows.

Zahra had worn the letters on her sleeve to prepare against being taken. The letters were a clue to the Yellows. An idea had taken root in Rachel's mind: Zahra's sleeve, the message on the wall at Omid Arabshahi's house, the role Mehran Najafi had played, the reason he'd made no effort to free his daughter. She didn't think he was at a port on the Caspian, enjoying his caviar.

The one part of the puzzle she wasn't able to solve had to do with the Shah's coronation.

'Tell me about the Yellows,' she said. 'Why was Zahra concerned with them?'

Moving his hands expressively, Franklin recounted a tale that was part spy thriller and part *Arabian Nights*. The crown jewels were a dynastic treasure that had traded hands many times during invasions and internecine plots. Though the treasure originated in the Safavid courts of the 1500s, Nader Shah's raid on India's Mughal empire in 1739 constituted the bulk of it: thousands of chests filled with gold and silver coins, and a superlative number of diamonds, gemstones, and pearls. The greatly reduced, contemporary collection had been established by a descendant of the Qajar dynasty, and documented by ambassadors to the royal court. Nasiruddin Shah was the last of the Shahs to enlarge the collection, and the first to establish their display at the Golestan Palace.

'That's where the coronation of the Shah took place,' Rachel said.

Franklin shrugged. He was more concerned with the far distant past.

'He was also the one to take an interest in South African diamond mines.'

'And that's significant, why?'

'It's where the bulk of the Iranian Yellows originate. They're called Cape diamonds. Originally, the term referred to diamonds from the British Cape Colony in South Africa, but now it's synonymous with the color and line patterns of yellow diamonds.'

'Where are the diamonds now?'

Franklin stared at her in surprise.

'Where they've always been. In the custody of the Central Bank. They're housed in a highly secure vault in Tehran. They've been there since 1960.'

'And they've never been anywhere else? In a public museum or on a world tour like the treasures of King Tut?'

Franklin checked his watch with an impatient tut-tut of his own.

'The bank vault is a museum – the entire collection is on display there. The crown jewels have never left the country.'

Which brought Rachel to a dead end. If the diamonds had

been under guard for more than fifty years, it dismantled the theory she'd been developing.

'Wait, I'd forgotten! There *was* an exhibition, well, not a public exhibition like buying a ticket to the ROM and having your pick of the galleries – more along the lines of a private celebration – hail, fellow, well met and all that.'

Rachel struggled to keep herself from grabbing Franklin's shoulders and shaking him until he got to the point.

'When was this?' she asked with forced calm.

'Two months ago?' He said it as if Rachel would confirm the answer. 'It was kind of a big deal, Sergeant Getty. There was a high-level visit from Chinese government officials. A private display was arranged of some of the choice pieces in the collection – the easily transportable ones. The transfer was overseen by representatives of the Central Bank. It was only for one evening. The jewels were returned the same night.'

That didn't mean something hadn't been arranged in advance, Rachel thought with a spike of excitement. A sleight of hand, a quick substitute, a few stones peeled off from the rest.

'How many stones are we talking here, Mr. Yang? Ten? Twelve? Would they be missed in the midst of so much other bounty?'

'Oh no, I didn't mean to mislead you. The Yellows are twenty-three diamonds. But they never left the vault.' He put one hand to his mouth as the other adjusted his portfolio. 'None of the loose stones – and there's an extensive collection of emeralds, as you'll see – were part of the private exhibit. I'm sorry, I really do need to get back.'

Rachel picked up the book on the bench and fell into step beside him, her theory crushed.

'Did you tell all this to Zahra? I mean, did she ask?'

'She did ask, yes. And I told her exactly what I've told you. The Yellows haven't been out of the vault since 1960. I told her to pay no attention to rumors, no matter what the letters may have said.'

Rachel stopped in her tracks.

'What letters?'

Franklin looked at her as though she'd grown another head.

'The Mossadegh letters, tell me you've heard of those. They're the reason Zahra came to see us. Her husband told her about the letters. He said Mossadegh believed the Yellows had been stolen or would be stolen – one or the other.' Franklin gave a little shudder. 'It's an exquisite story if you think about it. Mystery, intrigue, political dynasties. He'd heard a rumor someone was planning to switch out the stones at the royal coronation.'

The coronation. Where it had all begun.

'How do you know they didn't?'

'I told you,' Franklin said patiently. 'The Yellows have never left the vault. They weren't part of the coronation.'

'Did Zahra have the letters? Had she *seen* the letters?'

They had reached the crowded parking lot. Franklin shaded his eyes against the sun.

'No one has seen those letters, they were burned the night they were stolen. Zahra told me as much. You know how these things are. Rumors beget rumors – Zahra didn't believe them. But her husband talked about the rumor, and then at some point, he recanted. Some kind of pressure was put on him, Lord knows why, and that's what sparked Zahra's interest in digging deeper. Now if you don't mind, Sergeant Getty –'

Rachel minded. She minded very much. She wasn't done with Franklin Yang, and she suspected she wasn't done with Charlotte Rafferty either.

She looked around the gardens. They had passed the waterfall and the playful, meandering creek and she hadn't noticed, absorbed by the task of untangling the riddle. They had reached the park's spiral garden, and she found it a perfect metaphor: she was spiraling down to the heart of the truth.

Zahra had learned of the rumor from Mehran. She'd gone to

the ROM to find out about the diamonds, because the ROM had pioneered an inventory of the treasury.

When she asked Franklin if the name 'Jeb Taverner' meant anything to him, he gave an elegant shrug of his shoulders.

'Zahra wanted to speak to Victor and Arlotte, I assume to talk about the Yellows and corroborate the rumors. I couldn't help her with that, they're both deceased. She didn't mention a "Jeb," but to tell you the truth, though I unearthed this ancient tome for her' – he nodded at the cumbersome book – 'I haven't actually read it. Maybe Jeb photographed the collection. Maybe he was part of the family that financed the expedition. You'll have to read it through. Gemstones are much more Charlotte's specialty than mine.'

But Charlotte Rafferty had denied any knowledge of Zahra's activities, just as she'd denied knowing the name Vic Meen, however it may have been spelled.

Frustrated at the drying up of her lines of inquiry, Rachel remembered why she'd chosen the gardens as a meeting place.

'One last thing, Mr. Yang. Do you have any idea why Zahra might have scheduled a meeting at Windfields Park? It was the last meeting on her agenda before she left for Iran.' She waved a hand at a burgeoning willow whose branches trailed over the creek. 'It's just north of here, maybe you've heard of it, maybe you've been there.'

To her surprise, Franklin Yang struck a peevish pose, one hand on a jutting hip.

'That's just the kind of thing Charlotte should have told you. And since she hasn't, promise you'll keep my name out of this. More trouble with Charlotte is honestly the last thing I need.' He favored Rachel with a knowing look. 'It's not a place, Sergeant Getty. Winfield Park is a person. He's a contact of Charlotte's. I sent Zahra to Winfield to ask about the treasure. He's a gemstone cutter, quite well-known in his field.'

Rachel took a moment to absorb this. She needed another

meeting with Charlotte Rafferty. But more than that, she needed to speak to Winfield Park. She took his contact details from Franklin and, as a last resort, held up her phone to Franklin's face.

'Do you recognize this?'

It was the photograph Khattak had sent her of Zahra's sketch.

He frowned. 'I'm afraid I don't. It looks a bit like a coffin, doesn't it?'

Rachel thanked him for his time. Despite the death of her theory, Franklin Yang had proved to be a fount of information. There were new avenues to pursue.

And the book.

She hefted it in her hands.

She was itching to read the book.

43

Nate passed the long drive to Ottawa with his thoughts for company. He'd wanted to ask Rachel to accompany him. They could have stopped for a picnic lunch at Tweed and caught each other up on the banks of Lake Ontario. Just as well the sleeting rain had dashed that idea, for he could imagine what Laine would make of it. She'd think he'd brought Rachel as a form of protection because he couldn't face her on his own. Worse yet, she'd score points at Rachel's expense.

A man could be a fool at least once in his life, he believed; a fool about money, love, friendship, family. Any or all of those. And a writer needed to be, if his books were to traverse the shared experiences of his audience. But more than once or twice would be terribly unwise. He no longer had any illusions about Laine, he wasn't worried about his susceptibility to her. Rachel would have been welcome for her own sake, not as a shield against Laine.

He stopped in Kingston for lunch, finding a brasserie on the lake-front and choosing a meal he didn't taste. Laine had taken his call, accepted his reasons for wanting to see her, and otherwise stayed silent. There were none of the probing, teasing questions he was used to, none of the barbed provocation he'd once found irresistible. Her voice flat, she gave him directions to a café downtown, and the window of an appointment time.

'Don't be late,' she'd told him. 'I have another meeting after yours.'

He fueled up the car, though why he was driving his Aston Martin instead of his more reliable SUV, he couldn't have said.

He hoped it wasn't because some part of him hoped to impress Laine. Walking away had been his choice – no choice really, when the truth about Laine and Esa had come to light. She'd played one friend against the other, damaging both. Now things between himself and Esa had returned to normal, the friendship too cherished to risk again.

He had to play this meeting with Laine right, so he could walk away unscathed.

By the time he pulled off the highway on to the quiet streets of the capital, the rain had eased off, light poking through windows like a handful of broken straws. If this was spring, it was tardy. Despite the presence of new cafés and restaurants, the city looked gloomy and dank, unwelcoming to outsiders, preoccupied with the business at hand, most of the business belonging to banks and civil servants.

He'd wanted to meet Laine at the RCMP's national headquarters on Leikin Drive. She'd refused, choosing an out-of-the-way café in the market instead. Nate parked in an underground lot with a parking attendant. He snagged his silver-headed umbrella from the backseat of his car as a precaution against the rain's return.

He was dressed in black, like a man about to attend a funeral. From his hangdog expression, one would have guessed the funeral was his own. He found his way down Sparks Street, past the banks, art galleries, and souvenir stores, and across the bridge that spanned the Rideau Canal. He passed by the stately charm of the Chateau Laurier's masonry and turrets, and the photography museum curled up in its illustrious shadow.

Dull pink coins of light, reflections of the streetlamps, bobbed over the surface of the black water of the locks. A chilly wind penetrated the warmth of Nate's coat. A fresh flurry of sleet swiped at his glasses.

By the time he reached the café, he was reconsidering his

choice of a parking spot. He hadn't wanted to leave the Aston Martin in the street, now he thought better of his decision. A round-armed woman with a habit of yawning widely led him to the table where Laine had arrived before him.

She didn't stand. He removed his glasses to dry their surface, memory filling in the beautiful lines of her face. A little older, yes, her face more graven with experience, but the long-lashed eyes and dark sweep of hair pulled to one side of a swanlike neck were the same. What was different was the watchfulness in her face. Laine had always been intemperate with her emotions, storming, laughing, seizing, defying.

The Laine who waited for him to hang up his coat and shake off his umbrella without moving from her seat or changing her expression was new. He would have guessed at it as depression, and not something she was putting on as a means of garnering his interest.

He took the seat across from her, wondering if he should have thought to bring her a gift.

Laine loved gifts, the more expensive the better.

But he wasn't her hapless fiancé anymore.

'It's good to see you,' he said for want of anything better, regretting it at once when she answered him with that same eerie calm, her eyes on his face.

'Is it?'

Of course it wasn't. He didn't know why he'd said it, not normally beholden to social niceties. He waited for the sleepy waitress to take their order before explaining his reason for seeing her. In stumbling sentences, he told her about Esa's work in Iran and Rachel's efforts in Toronto, both aimed at uncovering Zahra's activities, and answering the question of whether those activities had led to Zahra's death.

'I thought Esa was on leave,' she said tonelessly. 'And I don't understand how Esa or his partner would have jurisdiction over this matter.'

Nate redirected her. 'What about the RCMP? Is there any involvement on their end?'

The waitress brought their drinks: an Irish coffee for Nathan, a jasmine dragon tea for Laine. She took a sip, studying the porcelain handle of the cup like it was a curiosity.

'None. Zahra Sobhani's murder is a diplomatic matter.'

'So you can't help me,' he said, deflated by the response.

She transferred her gaze to Nate.

'I wouldn't have made you drive four hours if I had nothing to offer.'

His interest quickened. An Édith Piaf song began to play in the background. The passion in the singer's voice squeezed at Nate's heart.

He'd nearly married this woman. Once everything to him, now nothing at all. She seemed to feel it, too, choosing her words carefully.

'There's no formal inquiry into Zahra's death. Our government asked for one and was refused. With the nuclear deal in place, we would have begun the process of normalizing relations between our countries, now that process is stalled.'

Nate sensed she wanted him to pursue the subject.

'What would get it started again?'

'The return of Zahra's body. An admission of responsibility, perhaps a lesser official prosecuted for the crime.' Her mouth formed a misanthropic smile. 'Everyone wants to get back to business. Zahra's death is inconvenient.'

'Her murder, you mean.'

'Her murder,' Laine echoed. She nodded as if satisfied by the correction.

'Do you think the government will make a serious effort? Given that Max Najafi isn't going to let it go. He can't travel to Iran – he's insisting on the return of his mother's body.'

'So you haven't heard,' Laine said. 'They've buried her. They offered Zahra's mother a pension as compensation.' And at Nate's quick look: 'She's refused it, of course, as a matter of principle.'

Something about the way she toyed with the words made Nate realize Laine had agreed to meet him for reasons unrelated to his inquiry. She poured herself a second cup of tea.

'You're still angry with me,' he said.

Laine's body tensed. She shook her head.

'I'm angry at myself. What I did, the game I played – it was despicable. Esa's made it quite clear there's no forgiveness to be had.' Her long lashes swept down. The solemn curve of her mouth stabbed at Nate's self-assurance. He shouldn't have come, he realized.

'Did you come because of Zahra?' she asked. 'I could have told you what you wanted to know on the phone: our government's efforts to recover Zahra's body have been genuine. It's the other side that has to decide if an opening from the West is worth paying the price over. They buried Zahra at midnight last night. To me, that suggests they've decided.'

'And you don't know why Zahra was willing to risk her safety to return to Iran?'

'I don't know,' Laine said, smoothing her napkin over her lap. She was wearing a sleeveless dress in muted gold, Nate's favorite color. A thin gold rope wound about her neck, another on her wrist. His eyes sparked. These were gifts he'd given her. 'But from what I've heard, Zahra was convinced she would be able to secure her stepdaughter's release from Evin. She had a card to play. I don't know what that card was, I'm sorry I don't know more.'

It was Nate's turn to question her.

'Are you? Why?'

She examined him – his face, the nervous set of his shoulders.

'I took a wrong turn,' she told him. 'I'm trying to correct it.'

'Implicating Esa, you mean? The false report you convinced me was true?'

'Yes,' she said bluntly. 'I've taken steps to set the record straight, I wanted you to know.'

'Why?' Nate attempted to joke. 'Has something catastrophic happened?' But he knew Esa would be stunned by the news. Laine's complaint had been a lingering black mark.

'Is that what you think it would take?'

He looked away from her curious dark eyes, ashamed of himself.

'Don't celebrate yet.' Her smile was enigmatic. 'I'm not in the least bit ill.'

'Then what?'

'The same thing I did to Esa – to you, really. I've had to taste my own poison, pay the same price. It's why I was shunted around the RCMP.'

Confused, Nate replied, 'But you have a good posting now, an enviable one.'

She shrugged, a graceful gesture of slim shoulders.

'I don't deserve it. I did some despicable things, I wasn't used to being told no.'

A reference to her pursuit of Esa, her onetime colleague and friend.

Nate didn't want to ask this because he knew it made him look weak. He *was* weak. But he had always wondered.

'I wasn't enough? I couldn't erase Esa from your thoughts?'

She smiled sadly. 'You shouldn't have had to. You were more than enough, I should have told you long ago.'

She rose from the table, reached for her coat, collected her handbag.

Nate rose as well.

As a means of stalling her, he asked what she made of Zahra's interest in the coronation. Laine tipped back her head.

'At a guess, I would say that was the card she had to play.'

She shrugged into her coat. She made no mention of her second meeting.

'Where are you going now?' Nate asked. His voice rasped in his throat.

She gave him the smile that could bring Pharaohs to their knees.

'I have a room at the Chateau.'

She left without looking back.

Nate paid the bill. His restless thoughts drifted to Rachel. After a moment, he followed.

Sehr received the news about Zahra's burial with dismay. A drilling rain persisted outside the windows of her office, a suitable accompaniment to her mood. She called Rachel to give her an update on her efforts, Rachel swore in response. Sehr liked her for her genuine outrage. Rachel charged at walls and tilted at windmills. She wouldn't have accepted the smooth assurances of Sehr's government contact that Zahra's death was a function of realpolitik and what could anyone do? Zahra had chosen to go to Iran, confident of her powers of persuasion, or confident of her trump card.

Sehr told Rachel the rest, hoping she'd be impressed at what Sehr had managed to uncover. She didn't want Rachel to think of her as the frantic woman at Esa's bedside in the hospital, which was where their second meeting had taken place. Or as the prosecutor too compromised to keep her job.

She admired Rachel's dogged devotion to the truth. More than that, she admired her quickness of mind in calculating risk and deciding a course of action. She couldn't have made the choice Rachel had made at Algonquin, she wouldn't have had the courage. Even now the thought of Esa in such danger made Sehr's blood run cold.

She wanted to be Rachel's friend. She didn't see the difference in their worlds as an obstacle. The two women had something in common.

They were linked by Esa Khattak.

She would ask about him when she'd finished with the subject of Zahra, it would make the inquiry seem natural.

'We checked Zahra's phone records. Before she left for Iran in January, she made six calls to the same number, a number registered to Mehran Najafi. The number was disconnected just after Zahra arrived in Tehran.'

'Any idea what the calls were about?'

'What's interesting is their location. The calls were made to a business in the city of Shiraz. Mehran had a stake in the business.'

'Shiraz – the city near Persepolis? Why does that matter?' Rachel sounded doubtful.

Sehr didn't think it was worthwhile to get into the background. Her answer was to the point, based on information Rachel had shared about the Iranian Yellows.

'It's in the south, maybe a ten-hour drive from Tehran. It's the business that's interesting – it's a jeweler's shop.'

Rachel's voice broke up for a moment. When it came back, it was louder.

'Sorry, I'm driving back home. Did you say jewelry shop?'

'Yes. My contact told me Zahra made a trip to Shiraz one week after arriving in Tehran. She stayed for two days and came back.'

'Did she go to Shiraz to meet Mehran?'

'Not that I know of. Mehran hasn't been seen in weeks. Zahra didn't meet him in Tehran or anywhere else. And there's no record of him having re-entered Canada.'

'The Iranian Yellows have never been out of the vault,' Rachel mused. 'I'm wondering about this exhibition for the Chinese. What exactly was on display?'

Even as Rachel asked the question, Sehr knew the person best suited to answer it was Esa. She could ask about him now as part of the flow of their conversation.

'Esa could find out for you, Rachel. You should let him know what we've found.'

'I will. But I think I'll have to do more than that.'

She explained her plan to travel to Iran. The investigation was becoming too dangerous for Esa to pursue on his own. Larijani was onto him now. She worried he would end up like Zahra. He needed her at his back. She left out the details, but made her point clear.

Sehr felt sick as Rachel laid out the reasons for her decision. She had been anxious enough on Esa's behalf. Now she had real reason to be afraid.

When Sehr took too long to comment, Rachel finally offered, 'I wouldn't be much of a partner if I let him risk himself alone.'

Sehr's eyes widened. The conversation had become much more personal. She'd never before considered the depths of Rachel's attachment to Esa. And she realized that whenever Esa needed help, Rachel was the one he called. She was the one he wanted at his side. He hadn't asked after Sehr.

'Promise you'll be careful,' she said hoarsely. 'It's equally dangerous for you.'

Rachel shrugged this off. 'I can't go anyway until I get a visa. Nate's been looking into it for me.'

They discussed the leads in the case for a few more minutes.

At the end of the call, Sehr said, 'Tell Esa to come home.'

She hoped Rachel would understand. And would pass on her message.

44

Forty Days of Mourning

No beatings, no interrogations, no Joojeh, no Piss-Pants, no son of a cleric. No word from the outside world, no word from the inside world. I'm here alone, scraping out the days with my fingernails. I haven't spoken to another soul. If it was Darius or Ali or Omid, Mousavi could have done something for them – but what am I saying, am I crazy? Locked inside his house, Mousavi can't even do anything for himself. He couldn't save Khanom Sobhani, citizen of a foreign nation – there's no chance he can save me.

My apologies to Jason. I understand now what it means to be erased, what it is to see no one, hear no one, to retreat into the darkest places inside yourself – to forget your own face, your twin sister's face.

I'll be the Kurd who died in Kahrizak of some mental disease, missing my teeth and my sanity. Joojeh brought me a bottle of pills weeks ago.

I struggle not to take them.

45

Winterglass in the spring. If anyone had told Vicky D'Souza she'd be invited to cross its threshold one day, she wouldn't have believed it. Rachel had sidelined her from the interview with Franklin Yang, but Vicky's warning had proven true. Rachel wanted help – both in digging into the background of the Yellows, and in terms of finding out more about Winfield Park. She'd had to share what she'd learned in order to count on Vicky's help. But first she'd treated Vicky to another lecture on the risk to Khattak, if Vicky were to publish her story prematurely.

Remembering it, Vicky drew a breath and gave herself a pep talk as she perched on her tiptoes to ring the bell.

They can't shut me out, I'm useful. This will give me the chance to prove it.

And then, more wistfully, *Maybe they'll learn to trust me.*

Nathan answered the door. He was unsteady on his feet and looked disheveled, his longish hair uncombed, a golden-brown fuzz shading the line of his jaw. He wasn't drunk, he didn't smell of liquor, more of some aromatic spice like cedar or sandalwood. Indian background notwithstanding, Vicky couldn't tell the difference.

He led Vicky through the magnificent great hall to a spacious retreat at the back of the house. Here wood-encased, cantilevered windows offered an enchanting prospect of the lake. Woodbine and tangled dog rose framed the windows, an extravagantly wild garden grown on the crumbling roof of the Bluffs. A bright gold light spilled from the clouds, illuminating Rachel's progress, at a table hewn from a single block of wood.

Rachel was sipping cocoa from a porcelain cup so transparent, Vicky could see the dark swell of liquid inside. She sat down on a chair patterned in vivid chrysanthemums, taking in the laptop on the table near Rachel.

She gave her mouth a moment to catch up with her thoughts. Otherwise, she would have pointed dumbly and said to Nate, 'You *live* here? In this spread from *Architectural Digest*?'

Rachel seemed undaunted by her surroundings. She'd even tucked up her long legs on her chair.

Nate offered Vicky the choice of tea or hot chocolate, Rachel gave him a deadpan look.

'Don't forget the espresso.' When he'd left, she said to Vicky with a casual sweep of her arm, 'You get used to it.'

A fuzzy warmth spread through Vicky's thoughts. Could it be that Rachel was starting to like her? It sounded like an invitation.

'Did you get it?' Rachel asked.

She meant Winfield Park's home address. Vicky withdrew a slip of paper from the pocket of her vintage handbag.

'What about you?' she asked. 'How did your research on the Yellows come along?'

'No luck with the Yellows, or with Jeb Taverner. And I can't find a single article online about a private exhibit for visiting dignitaries. If you think about it – how and why would the Central Bank risk moving any part of the treasury? I'm still making my way through the book.'

'May I?'

Vicky helped herself to Nate's laptop. She had a reporter's knack for details and for inventive queries. She tried several dozen search terms before concluding that Rachel was right. The exhibit was a dead end. If Max hadn't been reeling from the news of his mother's burial, they could have asked him to check the Farsi-language papers.

'Any luck there?' She nodded at the tome supplied by Franklin Yang.

Rachel showed her the page that featured the Iranian Yellows.

Vicky whistled at the size of the stones. She'd be thrilled if someone managed to scrounge up half a carat on her behalf. These were 120- to 130-carat stones, yellow because of their size, christened cape and silver cape stones.

'I've been thinking about Zahra's sleeve,' she said to Rachel.

Rachel's sour response told her this wasn't a particularly inspired observation.

'All right, I know. The initials on her sleeve: ADTVBM. But doesn't that tell us the last set should also refer to initials? JBT? Can you show me the picture Inspector Khattak sent you?'

Rachel swiveled the laptop in her direction, opening a dormant window.

Her look at Vicky was quelling. 'You can see it. You can't save it.'

Vicky pretended she didn't mind.

Khattak had photographed the writing on the wall in the house of the Greens.

Vicky zoomed in on the name. It did look like Zahra had written 'Jebby Taverner.' But tacking up the wallpaper again could have smudged the charcoal. She flicked to the second photograph, the one that resembled a coffin.

Could someone have killed Mehran Najafi? Had Zahra been searching for his body? Is that what the coffin meant? They'd had to rule out the possibility of Zahra having meant Lot 209 with the discovery of Arlotte Tushingham's authorship of the book on the national treasury.

She clicked back to the writing, magnifying the relevant section, the swoops and flourishes of Zahra's hand.

'Rachel.' She could see it clearly now. 'Does the book have an index? Did you check?'

'Not yet,' Rachel said. 'Why?'

'Because I think it *is* JBT. J. B. Taverner, not Jebby, not Jeb. Look it up.'

Rachel flipped to the back of the book, using the pen behind her ear to bookmark the page on the Iranian Yellows.

'There's a glossary. A chronology of kings,' she added doubtfully. 'Did you know Fabergé's in here? God, what tiny printing.' She flipped another page, running her fingers down a list of names. 'Tamerlane, Tatars, Taverner. It's here!' She flashed Vicky a jubilant smile. 'No, wait. It's not Taverner, it's Tavernier, no first name. Could that be it?'

J. B. Tavernier.

Vicky tried Googling the name as Rachel flipped back through the book, searching for the reference. The name 'Tavernier' was listed a dozen or more times.

Nate joined them, bearing coffee on a small enameled tray. He seemed to catch the mood, his gold eyes brightening as he looked from Vicky to Rachel. He seated himself next to Vicky, who swallowed her coffee so fast she scalded the roof of her mouth.

'Jean-Baptiste Tavernier,' Rachel said. 'A French merchant who documented his travels to India in the mid-1600s. Is this the man we're looking for?' She chewed on her lower lip. Vicky noticed that Nathan watched her.

She pulled up the search results on her screen, working her way down the list.

'He was a traveler,' Rachel went on. 'But he was also a jeweler.' She was following up on the index pages at random. 'He made six journeys to the East, visiting India and Persia. He wrote a book about his experiences – *Travels in India*. He was quite an expert on pearls. Here!'

She slapped her hand on the book. 'Check out this page on pearls in the royal treasury.'

Nate moved his chair closer to hers. He read the section on the pearl treasure chest aloud.

'I'm not sure what we're contemplating here. A jewel heist? A theft from the inside of Iran's most heavily guarded bank, followed by an attempt to smuggle the jewels out of the country on a yacht on the Caspian Sea?'

Rachel paged through the book, ignoring Nate.

'Tavernier visited a diamond mine in 1642, the Golconda mine in India. He's famous for discovering a massive stone, the Diamanta Grande Table. I have to say, it sounds pretty fantastic.'

'The Great Table Diamond,' Nate translated into her ear. Rachel gave him a funny look.

'Have you heard of this thing? It's not like it's the Kohinoor or the Hope.' An instant later, she contradicted herself. 'Jesus God, look at the size of it!'

Vicky was reading the laptop screen as swiftly as Rachel flipped pages in the book. She had the tingling sense they were onto something.

'Tavernier saw the Table Diamond for sale in India, a stone of superlative quality. Very rare, pale pink – he estimated its weight as two hundred and forty-two carats.' Vicky allowed herself a smirk. 'That, my friends, is a very big stone.'

Rachel picked up the story. 'The Great Table Diamond belonged to the Mughal emperors of India. When Nader Shah raided India in 1739, he's said to have captured the diamond. Then it disappeared for a time. It was next seen by a gemologist named Harford Jones Brydges, who visited Shiraz in 1791. The prince of the court wanted Brydges to find a buyer for his diamonds, so he showed him a stone called the Darya-e Nur. Brydges said it matched Tavernier's description of the Diamanta Grande Table exactly. Brydges had a copy of Tavernier's sketch.'

'A clear stone of the first water, pure in color and table-cut,' Vicky supplied.

'Great Holy God,' Rachel muttered. 'You're not going to believe this.'

She held up a color plate in the book.

'There's a reason Zahra strung those initials together, there's a reason she was looking for Meen and Tushingham. They made an unbelievable discovery.'

Vicky stared at her, surprised. And a little bit worried. Rachel wasn't given to hyperbole.

'The mineralogists from the ROM *authenticated* the Great Table Diamond. The stone Brydges saw was the same stone Tavernier described. But somewhere along the road, the stone was split in two: an ornament called the Darya-e Nur.' She pronounced the name carefully. 'And a smaller stone set in a tiara worn by the wife of the Shah. That piece is called the Nur-el Ain, the Light of the Eyes. The Darya-e Nur and the Nur-el Ain are a significant part of the royal treasury.'

'Oh my God,' Vicky whispered. She was staring at Nate's laptop.

Puzzled, Nate said, 'This gets us no further forward than the Yellows did. How could anyone break into a vault of the Central Bank?'

Vicky enlarged a window on the screen. Rachel looked at it and shrugged.

'Zahra's drawing of the coffin, yes, I know. I studied it so much I went cross-eyed.'

'No,' Vicky breathed. 'This isn't Zahra's drawing.'

Rachel frowned. It was the same image Khattak had sent from Esfahan. The wooden box with a corner lopped off, shaded with parallel lines.

'What are you talking about? Of course it is.'

Vicky pointed to the description, her heart hammering in her chest.

'This is Tavernier's sketch of the Diamanta Grande Table.'

There were only five diamonds in the world that rivaled the Darya-e Nur. Two formed part of the British Crown Jewels. A third was the Orlov, held at the Kremlin. The fourth and fifth, the Nizam and the Jubilee, were privately owned. Tushingham and Meen's authentication of the Great Table Diamond had been heralded as an earth-shattering discovery. It attached a fabulous history to the stones.

Rachel reviewed their discoveries: the reference to the Yellows, the letters on Zahra's sleeve, the sketch of the Diamanta Grande Table, Zahra's visit to Shiraz.

It wasn't easy to separate the facts from conspiracies and rumors. The question Nate had raised remained: How could anyone have stolen a priceless treasure from the Central Bank?

Rachel continued to read. The next time the Darya-e Nur was worn in public was by Reza Shah in 1926. The founder of the Pahlavi dynasty had worn it to his coronation. In 1968, on the final crowning of a Shah of Iran, Reza Shah's son had followed suit.

Rachel stopped abruptly. She read the paragraph again, wanting to be sure.

Mohammad Reza Shah had worn the Darya-e Nur as an ornament in his *kepi*.

Otherwise known as a military cap.

Nate took the book from Rachel's hands. He was studying the color plate illustration of the Darya-e Nur. A blazing pink beauty now a flawless table-cut diamond, it was mounted on an embellished frame and garnished with hundreds of smaller diamonds and a sprinkling of rubies. Lion and sun symbols surmounted the pink stone, a small feathered crown appearing above it, a setting designed in the 1800s.

One of the facets of the pink stone was inscribed in Persian with the name of a former ruler: *The Sultan, Sahib Qiran, Fath Ali Shah, Qajar 1250.* Or A.D. 1834, the year of Fath Ali's death.

Nate seemed dazed at the thought of it.

'Impossible,' he said. 'And easy enough to check if any part of the treasury is missing.'

Rachel was well ahead of him. She studied the elaborate setting of the pink diamond, tumblers falling in her mind. This was about people, the people Zahra Sobhani had made a point of consulting. She was beginning to understand why.

'I don't think that was Zahra's trump card. You have to connect the chain of events.'

After the first sip, Vicky had let her coffee grow cold. Now she moved away from the laptop, taking in the view of the Bluffs through the cantilevered windows, the light spinning above the layer of clouds.

'I don't follow.'

'You have to put them in chronological order. While she was in Toronto, Zahra made several calls to her husband. She tried to track down the authors of this book, presumably to ask questions about the diamond. She paid a visit to Winfield Park, which reminds me, we need to see him. Then she left for Iran to track down Mehran, first in Tehran, then in Shiraz. After she went to Shiraz, she was able to obtain a meeting with a representative of Iran's Supreme Leader. Suppose you're right. Suppose it wasn't possible to steal the Darya-e Nur without raising a national outcry. What if the diamond isn't missing?'

It was barely ten in the morning, and the others seemed exhausted – Vicky fed up with not knowing the answers, Nate trudging along as if he hadn't slept in weeks.

'I'm sorry, Rachel. I still don't understand.'

Rachel managed a diffident smile.

'Franklin Yang told us Winfield Park is a gemstone cutter. Chances are there's a gem cutter at the jeweler's shop in Shiraz as well.'

And when they still looked blank, Rachel tapped the book.

'What if the diamond isn't missing?' She said it in a whisper. 'Suppose there was a *substitution*. Suppose the Darya-e Nur in the Central Bank is actually a replica. It would explain why Zahra wanted to find the coronation footage. She'd want to compare earlier and later versions of the stone.'

She pointed to the illustration in Tushingham and Meen's book.

'It says here, it's impossible to remove the Darya-e Nur from its setting without damaging the diamond. What if someone was able to replicate the ornament, setting and all? And that's why Zahra wanted to meet with Winfield Park, to find out if it could be done. It also explains why no alarm was ever raised. No one knows about the switch except the person who arranged it.'

Rachel could tell Vicky wanted to believe her. A jewel heist, a murder, an international conspiracy – it was the story of a lifetime. It would catapult Vicky's career into the stratosphere.

But Vicky was quick to point out the holes in Rachel's theory. And that made Rachel realize how seriously Vicky took her work. She wanted to publish the truth, she wasn't given to aimless conjecture.

'Remember the book's introduction. Tushingham and Meen discuss the security precautions taken to protect the crown jewels. Back then, they were only allowed to examine the jewels for a few hours a day, in full view of the guards. Imagine how much the bank has updated its security since the 1960s. How would a switch have been managed?'

Rachel's enthusiasm was undefeated.

'It can only have been in one place: the exhibit for the Chinese delegates. We have to find out what Zahra knew about that exhibit. I can get the boss on that, right away.'

She flushed at the admiring look Nate gave her.

'It's possible,' he said. 'Barely.' He glanced at Vicky. 'And quite a story, better than anything I could give you.'

Vicky's eyes were on fire. 'You have to let me have it. When we're done with this, I mean. When Inspector Khattak's safe.' More diffidently, she added, 'Haven't I earned your trust by now?'

Rachel considered this. She was warming up to Vicky. She

would invite her for a walk along the Bluffs. She took Nate's company as a given.

She answered honestly. 'I can't promise, but if it's the right thing to do, you'll have it.'

'It explains a great deal,' Nate cut in, oblivious to the rapprochement between the two women. 'It would have been a hell of a trump card for Zahra to play. If she could prove there was a substitution, she could easily have gotten a meeting with a representative of the Supreme Leader. She'd have something to trade for the release of Roxana.'

Rachel hadn't thought that far ahead. Now she remembered the woman who'd fought so bravely for those who were still detained, only to meet her fate at Evin.

Why? Rachel asked herself. Coincidence?

So many years after the stolen election and the uprising of the Greens, Rachel didn't believe Zahra Sobhani's activism had inflamed the sensibilities of the regime.

As fantastic as Rachel's theory was, if she was right, Zahra had been in a position to expose someone who couldn't afford to be exposed: the person who'd stolen the Darya-e Nur, Iran's imperial treasure.

Whoever that person was, they'd wanted Zahra dead.

46

Winfield Park wasn't who Rachel expected to meet. She'd imagined a man in his sixties with a posh voice and a pin-striped suit, distinguished by a monocle of dubious reliability and a tendency to perch his weight on a silver-headed cane. She realized she was picturing the Monopoly man.

Maybe because he was a well-known gem cutter, or because of his somewhat stodgy name. Or perhaps because he lived in Lawrence Park, an affluent neighborhood centered on Mount Pleasant. It presided over the lake, touting green views instead of winds, an important distinction in a city so frequently riven by winter. Quiet roads wound about a thickly wooded ravine. The air was cool, the afternoon light fleeting, the tree branches shaking off the winter.

Park's home was tucked back from the streets on the upper slope of a hill. It had sweeping views over a park with carefully tended hedges. An avenue of fairy-drift lime trees bordered a flagstone path, the house a copper-roofed jewel floating above the trees. A maid admitted them to the house, leading them to a great room that functioned as a gallery.

Here the ceiling was a smooth, gold maple, shining upon a row of narrowly aligned glass cases, whose contents seemed to sparkle. Rachel thought first of marbles. They glittered on miniature pedestals, reflecting a prismatic light. At the back of the room, a long light unspooled through a company of windows, over the leaves of trees whose branches creaked like hinges. The back garden descended into the ravine.

'This puts your little cottage in the shade,' she mumbled to Nate.

He grinned. He was posing as a consultant to the police; she supposed since he acted as an unofficial resource, it was a reasonable description of his efforts. Winfield Park nodded at them both as he crossed into the gallery.

He was a diminutive Asian man in his late forties, elegantly dressed in a plum sweater and black slacks. His smile was cautious, his manner circumspect. His blue-black hair lay across his skull like a cap. His face was unexpectedly bony, a contrast to his delicate hands. An enormous marquise diamond blazed from one finger of his hand.

Park had built his reputation on the replication of world-renowned gemstones. Rachel would lay odds she was staring at a replica of the Star of Africa behind his head.

Nate settled himself into the background, passing from case to case as Rachel drew closer to Park. A scent like powdered dust rose from the fine knit of his sweater. He explained he'd just come from his workshop, and she wondered if he'd chosen this remote lot for his home to minimize his neighbors' complaints when he used whatever kind of tools were involved in the faceting of gemstones.

'You said on the phone you wanted to talk about my meeting with Zahra Sobhani.'

Rachel withdrew Zahra's date book from her purse.

'You met with her on January 11. Did that meeting take place here?'

'Yes. She wanted to see my collection. I thought she'd be impressed by the Tavernier Blue.'

When Rachel's face looked blank, Park went on to add, 'The Tavernier Blue was the original iteration of the Hope Diamond – a huge blue stone that stunned the world. It's been conclusively proven that the Tavernier rough was cut first into the famous French Blue, a stone worn by no less a personage than Louis

XIV. The Hope Diamond was then cut from that stone – and is there a diamond more famous in the world?'

This was a question Rachel couldn't begin to answer.

She flicked a quick glance at Nate. He raised his eyebrows as she followed Park to a case in the center of the room. Here the stones were lit by cunningly positioned cabinet lights. They gleamed on their pedestals like tiny pulsing hearts.

The pieces were curated, detailed credits rested on silver salvers beside each stone. Park indicated a violet-blue stone that would have fit nicely in Rachel's palm. Two smaller blue stones were stationed to either side, each with its own description. To the naked eye, the color of the stones was similar, while the faceting of each was unique.

'This is the Tavernier Blue,' Park said with quiet pride. 'The precursor of the Hope.'

'And was Zahra impressed by it?'

Park frowned. He led them away from the Blue with noticeable regret.

'She was preoccupied, so alas, no. Though she did pay some attention to the sketch of the Tavernier Blue.'

Rachel looked back at the card beside the Blue. It featured a reproduction of Tavernier's sketch of the stone in each of its iterations. The style of the illustration was identical to Tavernier's sketch of the Diamanta Grande Table.

'Mr. Park, was this the only sketch that interested Zahra? Did she ask about any of your other replicas?'

Park plucked the note card from her hands.

'She was far more interested in how I made them and what I did with them. I use cubic zirconia, you know, and I do original research on the pieces for the most accurate projections of size, weight, and appearance. Faceting one of the more famous stones is a process that takes me months, sometimes years – and that's if the preliminary modeling has already been done.'

Rachel looked for the Darya-e Nur, trying not to get distracted by a felicitous display of opals – if she'd had a fondness for such things, she liked the sporadic fire of the stones. Park noticed her interest.

'I cut my teeth on opals.'

From his droll delivery, Rachel guessed it was a well-tried joke. Nate strolled past her, no longer directionless, murmuring names as he passed.

'The Florentine, the Beau Sancy, the Moussaieff Red, the Black Orlov, the Mogok Ruby, the Great Table, the Nur-el Ain. A most impressive effort, Mr. Park.'

'A lifetime of labor,' Park rejoined. 'But certainly not love's labor's lost, I take great pleasure in crafting these pieces.'

Rachel followed Nate to a case sheltered before one of the windows. On the top tier of the display, two stones were exhibited, each with a detailed history. One was a sketch Rachel had come to recognize: the little wooden coffin, or the Diamanta Grande Table.

'Zahra must have asked you about this.'

Winfield Park hitched up his shoulders in a fastidious gesture.

'She compared both sketches. She took quite an interest in the Great Table.'

Rachel examined his replica. She'd been expecting a regal diamond of enormous proportions mounted in a setting befitting the crown jewels. The pale pink tablet lying on its bed looked like a flat glass slab, disappointingly lacking in glamor.

She moved on to the Nur-el Ain. The oval-cut brilliant was more along the lines of what she'd imagined as a stone worth killing for, with its glittery, exquisitely worked facets.

'It reminds me of the Pink Star,' Nate said to Park.

'The Steinmetz Pink – the *Vivid* Pink? I assure you, apart from weight, the two stones have nothing in common. The Steinmetz is a South African stone, different in color, cut, and quality.' Park flicked a hand at an imaginary speck of dust on his trousers, the gesture transmitting his scorn. 'The Nur-el Ain is without question the superior stone. Its history alone is riveting.'

'You chose not to replicate the tiara?' Nate asked, undeterred by the snub.

'A platinum tiara engorged with a number of utterly pedestrian baubles? It wasn't worth my time. As it happens, settings are prohibitively expensive to manufacture – my interest resides in the rarity of the stones.'

Vicky had pointed out something similar in her summary of Winfield Park's biography. He'd been quoted in the *Lapidary Journal* as disdaining attempts to amplify stones of superlative natural quality by mounting them in pedestrian settings. The cut, he'd argued, allowed the stone to reveal its inner beauty, treasure enough for the discerning. Thus the master cutters of the Steinmetz had reduced the stone's weight by fifty-five carats to allow for a superior cut.

Rachel studied Tavernier's sketch. She viewed the Nur-el Ain from both sides. There was an empty space beside the pink tablet.

'I imagine these replicas require a lot of skill. They must excite a great deal of interest.'

Mollified, Park nodded at Rachel.

'Museums and private collectors are particularly interested. I have an exclusive arrangement with the mineralogy galleries at the ROM.'

'I don't see the Darya-e Nur.' Rachel quoted from her reading, '"A stone unrivaled in history". Did you choose not to make a replica of it?'

'Why would I leave out half of the Diamanta Grande Table? Of course I made a replica of the Darya-e Nur. And in time, I'll make another.'

Rachel caught her breath.

'Why would you need to, Mr. Park? Where's the replica you made?'

His shrug was down-to-earth.

'Who knows why collectors want what they want? They made

me a most generous offer, I sold off the piece.' He gazed fondly at the display case. 'They do seem a little diminished by the absence of their companion.'

Nate interrupted his reverie.

'Who was the collector?'

Park looked at Nathan as if he'd muttered an indecency.

'In your position, Mr. Clare, you should know most collectors prefer to remain anonymous. I have no idea who purchased the piece.'

Rachel wasn't buying it.

'Someone brokered the sale. Someone must have arranged for payment and delivery. You must have a name for us.'

'As to that, I don't know if I should say. I shouldn't like to get my intermediate into trouble.'

Rachel had been wondering why Park didn't push back on her questions. And why he hadn't asked her the nature of her interest in the Darya-e Nur. Maybe this was the reason. Maybe he didn't want the police digging too closely into his private business. Could be there were tax implications. She circled around to a different question.

'But these –' She jabbed a finger at the unsold replicas. 'These were cut from cubic zirconia. The Darya-e Nur as well? Couldn't anyone tell the difference at first glance?'

Park surprised her by laughing.

'What are you imagining, Sergeant Getty? The originals are part of the Iranian crown jewels – how would anyone be in a position to make a comparison?'

'But could you tell them apart?'

He seemed to be sizing up Rachel for the first time. He'd been happy to discuss his process, now he seemed more like an expert gemologist, his head tipped back, his canny eyes considering.

'I could, yes, so could other professional jewelers. All it would take is the proper tools. But this is irrelevant, Sergeant Getty.'

'Oh? Why is that?'

'A replica of the stone wouldn't be enough. You'd need a jeweler with the craft and skill to duplicate its frankly marvelous setting. He'd need a few hundred residual stones at hand. There are four hundred and fifty-seven diamonds and four rubies of exceptional quality mounted above the Darya-e Nur. I wouldn't have the stones, I really don't know who would.'

But Rachel had a very good idea.

'The name of your agent, Mr. Park. Since you can't help us with the name of the buyer.'

'It isn't a conflict for me, but it may be a conflict of interest for her, given her position. You'll have to leave me out of it. I've told you, I don't want trouble.'

'I can't promise anything of the kind. I'm investigating a murder.'

Winfield Park relented, either out of self-interest or because Rachel's words had prompted a momentary concern.

'Charlotte Rafferty arranged the sale. She's the head archivist at the ROM.'

Park walked them to the door, pausing beneath a chandelier hung with hundreds of shimmering pendants, arranged in concentric loops. The marble floors gleamed in its light. Nate wondered if Park had designed it. Park confirmed Nathan's guess.

'It's perfection,' Nate said simply. 'Like the rest of your work. I'm not surprised the ROM arranged a partnership.'

Park preened at the words. Now that he'd given up Charlotte Rafferty's name, he'd entered a new phase of conviviality. He withdrew a crystal-edged card case from his trouser pocket and slipped a business card into Nate's hand.

'Should you find yourself in need of a commission, Mr. Clare.'

Nate thanked him.

'I shouldn't let your flattery go to my head,' Park added. 'I aim for accuracy with my replicas, but there are some things I cannot replicate.'

Rachel looked up at him from the bottom step.

'What do you mean?'

'The Darya-e Nur.' He waved one hand in the air, swatting at an insect drawn to his cologne. 'I wasn't able to reproduce the inscription on the tablet. Charlotte said the buyer wouldn't notice, and even if he did, he wouldn't care. The diamond had sentimental value.'

When she related this story to Vicky over a dinner of Thai noodles and spicy shrimp, the young reporter was furious.

'You make me dredge through archives, but you don't invite me to see the world's most fabulous gemstones? I mean, the Hope Diamond, Rachel. How could you let me miss it?'

Rachel shrank down in her chair.

'One shiny bauble is the same as another to me. I didn't know there'd be a roomful of them. To be honest, I really didn't pay them much attention.'

'Except for the opals,' Nate put in with a smile. 'Don't think I didn't notice you gawking at the opals.'

'I would have liked to gawk at the opals!' Vicky protested.

The three of them grinned at each other. They'd found a common groove.

Rachel said, 'I'd like to know why the inscription on the Darya-e Nur doesn't matter to the buyer. And I'd also like to know why Charlotte Rafferty didn't tell us any of this.'

'You're missing the point,' Vicky warned, around a mouthful of noodles. 'Who has a sentimental attachment to a chunk of the crown jewels? I don't have a sentimental attachment to the Kohinoor. Yeah, give it back to India, but that's about as much as I care.'

'A former royalist?' Nate suggested. He managed his chopsticks with the elegance that was second nature to him. 'Someone who was at the coronation?'

Rachel snorted. A bit of sauce leaked from the side of her

mouth. Embarrassed, she dabbed at it with a napkin.

'A jewel thief in his dotage? And why the Darya-e Nur especially? Why not the tiara or the emerald belt? Why not the Shahi Sword or the scepter? They seem like good choices.'

Vicky helpfully produced Franklin's book.

'You carry that everywhere now?' Rachel asked, deadpan. Vicky blew her silky black bangs out of her eyes, a gesture that was simultaneously endearing and insulting.

'Look at this tiara,' she said, pointing. 'Yes, the Nur-el Ain is just one stone, but look at the additional stones you'd have to reproduce. And the tiara weighs two kilograms, it's not the easiest thing to transport. By comparison, the Darya-e Nur is small and discreet.'

Rachel opened another carton, searching for wontons to soak up the sauce on her plate.

'The setting,' Nate pointed out. 'Four hundred and fifty-seven additional diamonds, four rubies. That seems difficult to reproduce.'

'No,' Rachel said in a tone of discovery. 'I don't think so. Vicky's right, it's discreet. And the diamonds in the Darya-e Nur ornament are tiny. The setting is intricate, I'll grant you, but where did Zahra go in Iran?' The wontons were forgotten on her plate. She compared the delicate grace of the Darya-e Nur to the excess of the tiara. 'Zahra went to see a jeweler.'

'But the stone would be ruined if it was removed from its setting,' Nate objected.

'I know.' Rachel's smile was smug. 'That's the whole point. The stone *wasn't* removed – the entire ornament was replaced. And that's what Zahra could prove.'

47

Khattak booked his passage on the Royal Safar bus line, not needing another warning. He hadn't slept, he hadn't rested – he could only think of the others trapped in Larijani's hands.

Get out of Iran or you won't be leaving.

He arrived in time for the first bus to Tehran. He hadn't known how to thank Nasih, he'd simply embraced him. He could tell that Nasih understood.

'We are many,' Nasih had said in Farsi, explaining his well-judged silence, perhaps also explaining the delivery of the letters. Nasih was a supporter of the Green Movement. And Esa remembered Ali had told him there were others.

Khattak had retrieved his phone, checking the brick in the wall as a reflex. His correspondent had ceased to write him. Or perhaps Nasih was no longer willing to risk delivering her letters, if he was her courier.

Khattak was alarmed to see Taraneh at the bus terminal at first light, the clouds inaugurating a baleful sky behind the wings of the building. When she met him at his bus stop, he realized the extent of Nasih's connection to the others – for only Nasih could have told her of his plans.

En route to the stop, Esa had received two messages from Rachel. One was a set of photographs from a book called *The Crown Jewels of Iran*: it included color plates of the Nur-el Ain tiara, and of an ornamental brooch known as the Darya-e Nur. He was stunned to realize Roxana had pointed him to the diamond, just as she'd pointed him to the wall at Omid's house.

I slip through the crack to find you, borne along on a sea of light.

In English, the Darya-e Nur was called the Sea of Light.

Rachel had also included photographs of pages that related the story of Jean-Baptiste Tavernier. Her second message announced the arrival of her tourist visa. After making sure she knew what she was getting herself into, Nate had booked her on a tour due to arrive in Tehran in two days. She'd suggested a few tasks for Esa in the interim.

The first was to find out some background on the exhibit for the Chinese; she wanted to know which pieces had been taken out of the Central Bank's vault for the private exhibit. And she'd suggested he pay a visit to the bank to determine for himself whether a substitution of the Darya-e Nur had been made. He was on his way to Tehran to accomplish these tasks, along with one of his own. He wanted to learn what he could of Zahra's burial. The news of her burial had come as a shock. It was something he wished he'd had a chance to discuss with the others, but Larijani's intrusion had changed things.

He found Taraneh waiting beside his bus in a short black coat and a head scarf tied with more rigor than he'd come to expect from her. He glanced around for a sign of Nasreen. Taraneh had come alone, and the impish smile he associated with her was missing.

'I don't think we'll meet again,' she said without preamble. 'I'm sorry to see you leave.'

Clouds had gathered above their heads, bands of dark lace feathered with traces of gold. He saw signs of weariness in her face. She would have spent the previous night worrying over Ali's and Omid's safety. She was taking a risk meeting him here now – a risk that endangered them both. He couldn't bring himself to tell her what she must already know.

'Have Omid and Ali been released from custody?' he asked instead. He was conscious of his fear now, in a way he hadn't been before.

The driver of the bus opened the door to begin admitting passengers. The queue Esa joined began to move, Taraneh moving along with them.

'He kept them all night, but they're home now, though perhaps a little worse for wear.'

She held up a hand to his face, then thought better of it as a woman in the queue clicked her tongue. 'You're all right?' she asked him. 'They didn't harm you? Larijani told Ali he'd interrogated you.' A faded echo of her impish smile settled on her lips. 'You were clever. You said exactly what Ali guessed you would say. He didn't contradict you. They wouldn't have been released otherwise.'

'Were they beaten?' Khattak asked, dreading the answer.

Taraneh looked away. She shrugged.

'I'm thankful Darius is safe. Ali would never have let them take him again.'

It was an indirect answer – her way of articulating unpalatable truths.

'And you – or the others? Were any of you harmed?'

She studied him, a faint concern reflected in her eyes.

'You're wondering about Nasreen.'

There was no point in denying it. 'There's something she's holding back.'

'She wakes up every day missing part of herself. Is that the only reason you worry?'

The bus driver honked his horn. There were two passengers left in the line ahead of Esa. He had this moment to speak, and then it would be over, he wouldn't be returning to Esfahan. He felt a tremor that was part nostalgia, and part residual fear.

'The wall at Omid's house is a danger to you. You could end up at Kahrizak, or find yourself somewhere worse.'

'There isn't anywhere worse.'

'Listen to me, please. Convince the others. What good are any of your efforts if you're locked away or made to disappear? Promise me you'll do something about the wall. Larijani is watching you closely.'

He mounted the first step of the bus, his ticket in his hand. Taraneh considered his words.

'It's the last thing we have that was Zahra's.'

'Take a picture,' he said roughly. 'And go on to finish her work.'

'You say this yet you're abandoning us.'

He didn't flatter himself that this explained Taraneh's subdued demeanor. He remembered his days as a student. A buoyant invincibility had bubbled up from within, sustaining the efforts of his young group of friends, their safety assured, their principles secure. But as friends dropped out, as interests and career paths had diverged, he'd felt rudderless and ill at ease, wondering if he too should fall into safely trodden ways.

There was something to be said for companions in arms. He could understand why Taraneh would feel more alone now in the efforts of her group, despite how little Esa had contributed to their cause. For a brief time there'd been someone who believed. And he wondered if he would write her from Toronto.

'I'm going to Tehran to see this through, I'll let Ali know what I find. If you see Roxana's mother, please let her know I was thinking of her. And Nasreen –'

He bit back the words. His knowledge of Nasreen was confined to what he imagined her to be, his attraction an ephemeral thing, meaningless against her pain.

'And Nasreen?'

Taraneh took his hand in her own with a gentle disregard for convention. The warmth of her compassion wrapped around him. He didn't know what loss or littleness she had seen in him, but she didn't let him answer, quoting the poet Hafiz instead.

'"You still listen to an old alley song that brings your body pain".'

The poets had an answer for everything.

He read Rachel's notes closely on the long ride north, overtaken by the fear Larijani would reappear. He knew it was a mistake to be complacent. He'd have no recourse to judicial process in Tehran. And an international incident wouldn't help his situation at home, no matter what Touka had promised him.

Visiting popular tourist sites such as the National Jewelry Treasury was an uncontroversial option if Larijani was still on his trail, delving into Zahra's burial much less so. He'd begin with the exhibit, and he'd be as quick as possible. He agreed with Rachel's conclusion that a substitution of the Darya-e Nur was only possible if the ornament had been part of the private exhibit. Suppose the pieces fell into place. The substitution would have been planned far in advance: brokering the sale of the replica, arranging the transport of the stone. It would have taken time to duplicate the ornament's elaborate setting – the hundreds of diamonds, the paired rubies. A sophisticated level of craftsmanship would be required to imitate the original: the diamond was surmounted by Iran's imperial symbols, a pair of rampant lions under a fiery sun.

He studied Rachel's photographs with interest. The history of the crown jewels was fascinating, the story of the Canadian mineralogists' detective work in tracing the journey of the Great Table exactly the kind of legend that should apply to such a stone. He imagined Rachel and Nate in Winfield Park's gallery. Nate's interest would have been piqued, he had the taste and means by which to indulge a fondness for rarities, whereas Rachel's quotient of skepticism would doubtlessly have tempered the appeal of Winfield Park's treasures.

He thought of Zahra and Mehran. He was working up a possible scenario in his mind. From what he knew of Zahra, Roxana's rearrest would have left her without peace. She would have been agitating for information on her stepdaughter, long before she arrived in Tehran.

Rachel thought the phone calls between Zahra and Mehran were concerned with the theft of the Darya-e Nur, if theft there had been. Khattak thought otherwise.

Why had they assumed Mehran cared so little for the fate of his daughter?

A statement in one of Roxana's letters had stayed with him.

My father's strength infuses me.

If Mehran had spent time in Iranian jails – not for political crimes but for periodically finding himself out of favor – his fears for Roxana's well-being would have been formed from firsthand knowledge. He would have told his daughter stories of his time in prison, stories that supported her through her detention, lessons that forged Roxana's strength.

Her letters exuded a quiet toughness.

If she was what her father had made her, perhaps the phone calls between Zahra and Mehran had been dedicated to a different end: two parents conspiring together to secure the release of their daughter. Mehran had been detained for suggesting the Mossadegh letters mentioned a conspiracy to steal the Iranian Yellows, an impossible, unproven rumor. But what if the rumor had sparked the idea for the real theft?

Rachel had expressed the theory that Mehran was responsible for the substitution of the stone. But suppose Mehran had merely uncovered the theft, and shared his knowledge with Zahra on his last trip to Toronto. She'd persuaded him to participate in an exhibit at the ROM, to donate a photograph from his collection. It would have given them leverage over Charlotte, so they could demand to know who the buyer was. It was possible Mehran had trailed the buyer to Shiraz, and Zahra had followed in his footsteps. If Zahra had stepped up her activities in Tehran, she might have done so because Mehran had gone missing. The question was why – how? And why had

Zahra thought herself secure enough to take photographs at Evin? Someone must have assured her of her safety. Someone must have told her it was worth the risk. But who would Zahra have trusted with her life?

He felt the stirring of his blood. There were things he could do, answers he could dig for without endangering the others. And he would be putting himself back to work, dusting off skills grown stale from disuse.

He'd been cautious since he'd chosen the police as a career. Careful and measured consideration was the only way he knew to answer the assumption of Muslim rage. He was clean-shaven, he didn't regularly wear a *topi* or any other signifier of his faith. He prayed behind a closed door. He was light-skinned and green-eyed, passing in his public engagements, not easily pigeonholed. Whether he enjoyed living his life on these terms when he could have been at ease, expressing the different sides of himself, the things that enriched him, enriched, he believed, the fabric of his nation, was a separate question.

There were issues that engaged his sympathies, his intellect, his heart. Zahra Sobhani's murder, Saneh Ardalan's disappearance, Roxana Najafi's imprisonment – these coldly callous acts to which there was no recourse – enraged him to the heart of his core beliefs.

If one could be enraged by the loss of a favorite sports team, shouldn't his anger rise at the entrenchment of a scheme whereby no innocent person was safe, where self-determination was a crime punished by the vagaries of an opaque and impervious judicial system?

He thought of parents who begged at the prosecutor's door, the bribes paid to minor clerks for information on the missing, the mothers who collapsed at the morgue, praying not to find their answers with the coroner.

He thought of journalists and artists languishing in cells varied only in the nature of their persecutions. His mouth tightened. He had underestimated the courage required to be an activist inside Iran. Larijani had shattered his sense of himself with a single, ominous threat.

He was glad to feel his blood stir in response. It was the cresting of his humanity, something he hadn't lost, something Rachel shared with him.

He texted her an encrypted message. He needed to study Zahra's photographs again. He asked her to send them back.

Dry hills, blue mosques, dusty roads, sparse bits of green, and a blind, inarticulate sun that reddened the foreground as the miles drifted by. Khattak was offered tea and cakes on a punctual basis with a hopeful smile from the driver's assistant, whose cologne announced his presence long before his arrival, brandishing a tourism-enhanced samovar on a cart. A shaḥ with twirling mustaches and a pompous, high-stacked cap gazed torpidly at Esa from its surface.

A movie played on a shared screen, the arms of the chairs equipped with private headphone jacks. Some of the passengers dozed lightly, others followed the film. Khattak made extensive notes on the case in a specialized shorthand. By the time the Royal Safar had reached the terminal, he'd decided which of his leads to pursue. He proceeded from the ring of the terminal, tipping the driver and his assistant.

Two-note horns, diesel fumes, and catcalls rose in an antiphonal symphony to greet him. He wasn't fond of Tehran, a city gridlocked with traffic and shrouded with pollution. He had a hazy view of the Milad Tower, from which he could orient himself in the streets of a rapidly expanding metropolis. Smoke, pollution, clouds of dust and noise – the marks of a visit to Tehran, though the ashen sky freshened by a sharp tang of frost lessened the prospect of spring.

His taxi moved from the city center to less densely trafficked neighborhoods. Here, market stalls disclosed Nowruz preparations, the pavements cluttered with potted flowers in electric shades of yellow and pink, and baskets of new spring grass, their emerald blades grown tall and thick. Market stalls promised painted eggs in turquoise, the green sprouts of onion bulbs, glass bowls teeming with goldfish, and offerings of hyacinth and honey.

The city was expectant, buoyant, though it would empty soon for revels in the countryside, the traffic dying down. He checked into his hotel, offering his passport at the reception desk, whose walls, ceilings, and floors were paneled in an earth-red marble against the backdrop of French provincial furniture. He'd traded the charm and familiarity of Nasih's guesthouse for the generic imperturbability of a five-star chain. He'd chosen it for a reason: he would blend in among its crowd of eager tourists, making it easier to disappear.

The hotel was fifteen minutes down the road from the Central Bank. He took a quick shower, changed into fresh clothes, and called up the hours of the local library on his phone. He wore his black blazer and combed back his hair, hoping that a more presentable appearance would result in the librarian's willingness to assist with his search.

His drive took him through the affluent neighborhood of Elahieh, past a row of white high-rise buildings fronted by diplomatic clubs. Those who thought of Tehran as a city of black-clad mobs were clinging to an archaic picture of the past. The residents of the wealthier suburbs lived a double life away from the prying eyes of the Revolutionary Guards. Elahieh was characterized by foreign sports cars, expensive liquor, plastic surgery, and beach-ready bodies.

The library Khattak sought was a nondescript building of negligible distinction that lingered in the shadows of Elahieh – an inconspicuous relic of a time before the redevelopment boom. It sat in a garden overgrown with briars that poked through a rime of snow on the crest of a featureless hill.

The driver of his taxi offered to wait, Esa urged him on his way. He didn't want his presence to linger in anyone's memory, though he hoped his precautions were unnecessary. He was met at the reference desk by a librarian with a ruddy face and an expression of mild anxiety. The librarian introduced himself as Ramin Rajaee, a stutter in his voice. He listened patiently to Khattak's request for anything the library might house in its collection on the National Jewelry Treasury, known locally as the Jewelry Museum.

'British tourists like to visit it,' Ramin said. 'It reminds them of the Raj. But we primarily archive newspapers and magazines at this location. You would do better to visit the museum, they sell a book that documents the highlights of the collection.'

Khattak was calculating how to bring up the exhibit when Ramin's face lit up.

'Just a moment. There was recently an exhibition of part of the collection – how many weeks ago, two or three? The National Museum of Iran hosted a cultural exchange with a delegation from China. It was not a public exhibit by any means.' His clever eyes interrogated Khattak. 'It was meant as a display of prestige.' Wryly, he added, 'Our national treasures were sampled like so many items on a smorgasbord, the background to a diplomatic dinner.'

Khattak tried not to overstate his interest in this.

'Who approved the pieces for the exhibit?'

'I wouldn't know, and I doubt our archives would tell you. You're welcome to take a look, if you like. I'd be happy to search the records for you. As you can see, we don't have much regular custom.' He shrugged. 'You can draw your own conclusions about what we're permitted to preserve for posterity. Can you read Farsi?'

Esa nodded. His practice with Persian poetry would stand him in good stead.

Ramin motioned Khattak to a recessed reading room on the main floor. Khattak had been expecting dusty binders with newspaper pages preserved in plastic sleeves. Instead, he was treated to a display of sleekly lined-up computer monitors, one at each patron's station.

The librarian retreated to his reference desk, where he used his browser to search for articles on the exhibit. He made minute notations on a pad at his elbow. These he transferred into Esa's care with a satisfied glint of accomplishment. The librarian had noted down four articles in four different papers, each with its own take on the creatively named 'Clasp of Civilizations' exhibit. The Farsi title was considerably more ponderous, assuring the dignity of both sets of delegates.

Khattak read each article closely, a process that took him some time. A fulsome piece in the hardliner paper *Kayhan* discussed the inimitable nature of the treasure. Khattak scanned the pages for a more precise account of the exhibit. He found it in the final article given to him by the librarian.

The highlight of the exhibit had been the Kiani Crown. Khattak was shocked to read the crown had traveled from the safety of the vault to the lightly guarded exhibit. Its twenty-one emerald plumes curved above a second spray of diamonds, the heart of which was an eighty-carat emerald of exceptional clarity. This was to say nothing of the crown's pearl pavement, its heavily jeweled headband, or the thousands of stones that formed its perimeter and plumes.

Reading this, Khattak shook his head. Who would have insured the transfer of the crown? He read further and had his question answered: a complement of Revolutionary Guards.

The Kiani Crown had pride of place in the private exhibit, perhaps more acceptable to the present regime than the Pahlavi Crown of the deposed dynasty. It was accompanied by the jeweled mace of Fath Ali Shah, a symbol of the Shah's copious authority. Its diamond-sheathed surface glinted from a background of delicate green enamel. It was accompanied by a *jiqa*, an aigrette or ornamental brooch, that had been a favorite of Fath Ali Shah. Khattak had seen the *jiqa* in portraits of various shahs, crested by three black heron plumes, the stamp of royalty. He read on.

A handful of additional aigrettes had been scattered about the display, along with a selection of turquoise-studded cups. No other crowns or tiaras were listed, and none of the regalia of state had been removed from the Central Bank. No Shahi Sword, no emerald belt, and certainly not the Naderi Throne. Almost as an afterthought and with very little fanfare, the author of the article listed the Darya-e Nur.

Khattak read it over three times to make sure.

The Darya-e Nur was unlike anything else in the collection. Perhaps its close association with the Pahlavi shahs had merited its offhand dismissal by the journalist in question. There was no mention of the legend of the Great Table Diamond, and no indication that the Nur-el Ain had formed part of the Table Diamond together with the Darya-e Nur.

The librarian wandered over to Khattak's monitor.

'Did you find what you wanted?' he asked.

'It was of great interest,' Esa replied. 'It's unfortunate there were no photographs of the exhibit, it should have taken the world by storm.'

Pleased by this compliment, Ramin pointed to the minuscule numbering at the top of the page. It indicated the article continued at the back of the relevant section. He found the page for Esa. It featured a full-color set of photographs. But as quickly as Esa's anticipation rose, his hopes were dashed.

Primacy was given to the Kiani Crown. It was as resplendent in the photographs as Esa had imagined. The rest of the photographs were of delegates in various stages of affability. Gifts were proffered and exchanged. Thirteen or fourteen men struck a congratulatory pose. At one end of the group, a man in a sharp black suit had turned his face from the camera.

Khattak recognized him anyway.

It was Barsam Radan.

He asked Ramin, to be certain.

The librarian squinted at the printing, incurious as to Khattak's familiarity with the name.

'Yes,' Ramin said. 'It was Radan who arranged the exhibit. His personal guards secured the transfer.'

Khattak arranged for photocopies of the articles to be made. An ugly picture was forming in his mind, its outline hazy but certain of its details clear.

The Darya-e Nur had been placed on display outside the heavily guarded Jewelry Museum. Coverage of its presence as part of the exhibit had been limited to a passing mention. It was the only item in the exhibit not to be photographed.

And Radan had arranged both the exhibit and the transfer of the jewels from the treasury.

He was getting closer to the truth, he could feel it.

What if Radan had arranged the substitution of the stone? Who among his guards would have dared to challenge him?

He asked Ramin a final question.

'The cost of arranging an adequate alarm system for the Kiani Crown at a private location must have been steep.'

Ramin was reading the article over his shoulder. His answer was dismissive. The exhibit had passed from his thoughts, he was likely hoping Khattak's departure would allow him to close up early. Khattak was the last patron to occupy a carrel.

'Why would you need an alarm when you have the Revolutionary Guards?'

On his ride back to the hotel, Khattak outlined his discoveries in a message to Rachel. It was imperative she find out who had purchased the replica from Charlotte Rafferty. The day after tomorrow, all official business and buildings would be closed for Nowruz. If he was to have a look at the Darya-e Nur at the museum, it would have to be first thing tomorrow. The museum was closed on weekends, Wednesdays, and public holidays.

Tomorrow was Tuesday. He had roughly a two-hour window, and the window was in the afternoon. Which gave him time to contact Touka to ask for her help.

48

Touka waited for Khattak at a tiny restaurant wedged between a pharmacy and a grocery. Spring was in retreat, columns of clouds arranged with military precision over the Alborz Mountains. The bite of frost was in the air. The restaurant's outdoor seating was closed, its patio umbrellas folded in a corner like a stack of used-up Christmas trees. The interior wasn't much warmer, the diner-style seating supplemented with embroidered cushions in a dull burgundy, half-hearted stars limping along the borders. It was a cheerless place, but the food was good.

She had ordered helpings of pomegranate stew for Khattak and herself. His smile, when he saw her, transformed his face, brightening his eyes, relaxing his self-possession. He was dressed in casual slacks and a windbreaker zipped against the wind.

Touka had worn her new blue coat and made an effort with her hair for his benefit. A fringe of white decorated her shoulders like a cape. She had also applied lipstick in a shade adventurously named 'Kiss Me Coral.'

She urged him to eat, he told her what he'd discovered, sliding the pages of the newspaper article in front of her. She should have put the pieces together for herself. Of course Radan was involved. And it answered a question that had puzzled them both: Zahra's ability to gain an audience with a representative of the Supreme Leader. Zahra would have been careful not to give away her whole hand – perhaps, she would have named Radan and indicated something had gone amiss with the exhibit. Then she would have offered to provide evidence to back her claims.

In return, she would have demanded Roxana's release.

Something had gone wrong in that short period between Zahra's meeting at the Supreme Leader's office and her visit to Evin prison, and that was what they needed to determine. Touka was curious about one thing, though.

'What are you hoping to gain from following in Zahra's footsteps?'

Khattak eyed her directly, his attention on her face. She hadn't known green eyes could be so penetrating. She felt a bloom spread over her skin. She was certain it clashed with her lipstick.

'I want Radan held to account, and I want Zahra's body returned to Canada.'

'Is that all?' Her fingers unclenched from her fork. She was astonished to find herself flustered by an attractive man's attention.

'No.' His gaze didn't falter. 'I also want to secure Roxana Najafi's release.'

Roxana's letters were a trust. He didn't want to fail her.

As Khattak told her this, Touka saw she'd mistaken his reserve. He was passionately engaged, and he was telling her this for a reason. It wasn't Khattak who would have to demand co-operation from figures in the corridors of power. He expected Touka to do it. She should have thought of that before she had threatened him – coercing his assistance.

'You seem angry,' she said.

His reply was blunt. 'I've had the smallest taste of what these men can do. I won't leave Roxana behind.'

When they'd finished eating, he ordered tea. It came in scarlet glasses, adorned with the face of Nader Shah.

'You got me into this,' he said without preamble. 'So we should finish this together. My partner is coming. We'll work our leads to get what you need, you'll have to do the rest.'

Touka straightened her back, ignoring the twinge of pain in her hip.

'I can't promise you anything.'

But she knew she would do her best. She had caught something of his commitment. In the shadowy realms of her experience, she admitted the feeling was rare.

The Central Bank of Iran was a gleaming glass tower, an icon of Tehran's skyline. Under the aegis of a wintry sun, its blind glass eyes gazed at the streets with a basilisk glare. A green marble wall disported the name of the bank: Khattak read the logo first in Farsi, then in English. He glanced across the street, searching for a tail. No one paused to watch him, everyone in a hurry to be about their business.

He checked again to be sure, then he proffered his admission ticket to a smartly dressed guard who scrutinized him with an air of indifference and waved him through. He had chosen to arrive in the middle of a pack of tourists, a diminutive group of Malaysians, whose cameras and gentle smiles were at the ready. He swept along in their train, through a gallery crowned by arches, where a canopy of chandeliers framed a line of splendid columns. Their candle cups were white, the spindles peacock blue. Portraits lined the gallery but Khattak's attention was soon claimed by the treasures on display.

Khattak had purchased a catalog of the exhibits with his ticket. He proceeded down the central aisle where the imperial crowns were arranged in a row: the Pahlavi Crown beating like a ruby heart, the Crown of the Empress Farah, and the Kiani Crown, star of the private exhibit.

Khattak studied the crowns with a quiet sense of enthrallment. The beauty of each piece was linked to a vivid history. He pictured emperors in Delhi, the heirs of Safavid shahs, raiders from Afghanistan, each adding to the royal treasury to the best of their wits and ability.

Hemmed in by the Malaysians, Esa found himself between the Imperial Globe and the Naderi Throne, two dazzling artifacts in a hall of splendors. He paused before the Naderi Throne, used at the 1968 coronation of the Shah as an emblem of empire, excess, and sovereign preeminence. He imagined the throne as a prop for the film version of the story of the Taj Mahal, so apropos to a Mughal setting. The dynastic shahs had had an open hand with their treasury: the Naderi Throne defied description.

He moved next to a scattering of sun-gold stones on a tray: these were the Iranian Yellows. They were grouped in clusters on the floor of the diamond cabinet. So exquisite was their faceting, he couldn't imagine a substitution – they had to be the originals. The rumor had been only a rumor, and it was unlikely to have been started by Mossadegh.

Khattak looked around. The Malaysians had squeezed past him to a pair of cabinets that displayed the royal tiaras, the Nur-el Ain among these. Obligingly, he took a photograph of two women posing so the tiaras appeared to rest on their heads. Smiling, he handed their camera back, taking a closer look at the Nur-el Ain himself.

The pink diamond at its heart blazed at him, a superlative stone that had no equals. He knew he was looking at Tavernier's stone, so brilliant was its allure.

He moved in a systematic fashion down a third aisle to a small case lit from the inside, where a single ornament reposed on a soft white bed.

Here, at last, was the Darya-e Nur, the greater half of the Diamanta Grande Table. Though it was the largest known pink diamond in the world, the stone could have fit in the palm of his hand. His fingers curled with the desire to touch it.

Was he imagining that it shone less brilliantly than the Nur-el Ain? Was it an effect of the lighting, or did he discern a dullness to the pink stone? When viewed from a different angle, the stone wasn't quite flat – the diamond seemed to bubble, perhaps the result of irregular step facets. A dozen or so small diamonds surmounted the tablet and held it in their grip. Removing the Darya-e Nur from their grasp would cause irreversible damage.

Khattak pretended to a preoccupation with his catalog. The Malaysians bumped around him, full of smiling apologies. He used their presence as a cover for tying his shoe and examining the stone from below. Though he tried, he couldn't spot the Persian inscription that marked the original. It was either hidden by the bed, or the ornament he was viewing was an imitation.

He circled the case several times, but there was no means by which he could be certain. The catalog failed to clear up the matter, it mentioned the inscription without specifying its location. Khattak was at a loss.

One of the Malaysians posed near the Darya-e Nur. The flash of his wife's camera left a dazzle on the diamond. It lit up like a windowpane after a strike of lightning.

And Khattak had seen something.

The woman took another picture of her husband, and the flash lit up the Darya-e Nur for a second time.

Khattak saw it again.

He remembered the camera on his phone. He photographed the ornament repeatedly with the flash on. Finally, a guard came to tell him to step away.

Esa complied, squatting before the Darya-e Nur to study it with his naked eye.

None of the camera flashes had revealed a trace of Persian script, even on the south-facing facets. But he'd discovered an anomaly in the symbols of the Safavid dynasty, a pair of rampant lions that mounted the tablet on either side of the crown.

The setting was said to include hundreds of diamonds and four perfectly matched rubies, each pair of rubies forming the eyes of a lion. Two rubies glowed up at Khattak from the lion on his right. But on the left side, the lion's eyes were mismatched. One was a winking ruby, the other a plain crystal.

The legendary stone was a fake.

49

Charlotte Rafferty refused to grant Rachel a second meeting, claiming the pressure of work. Undaunted, Rachel waited outside the staff entrance until the ROM closed for the day, hoping Charlotte wasn't the type of employee to work at her desk after hours. When Charlotte finally joined the crowds heading to Union Station, Rachel fell into step behind her.

She took stock of Charlotte's expensive Ferragamo handbag, her red-soled, spike-heeled boots, and the stylish new haircut Rachel bet had set Charlotte back four or five hundred dollars. Charlotte Rafferty wasn't taking the subway. She strode to the curb to hail a taxi.

The hot dog and falafel carts that clogged the streets during lunch hour had packed up for the day, giving Rachel a clear view of her quarry dashing past other pedestrians. A man with a terrier on a red leash gave Charlotte a nasty glare as her boots trampled the dog's lead. She dodged him with a muttered apology. Just as a taxi slowed down along the busy street, Rachel gripped Charlotte's arm from behind.

Recognizing a lost fare, the cab sped away through the lights. With a visible flash of rage, Charlotte Rafferty turned back. When she recognized Rachel, her mouth tightened, but she didn't look afraid. Rachel put that down to the ice-cold blood running through Charlotte's veins.

'A moment of your time,' Rachel said. Her grip remained implacable.

Charlotte gave an ostentatious sigh. Rachel's hand slipped

from the cloth of her coat. She guided Charlotte over a mound of snow, directing her back to the doors of the atrium. She wasn't expecting to be let in, she wanted privacy for her questions.

'I have a dinner, and now I'm going to be late for it.'

'Not with Winfield Park, by any chance?'

The harried energy of the other woman went quiet. Two patches of heat flared in her cheeks. She pulled her handbag around to her chest like a shield.

'I'm afraid I don't understand.'

'No? I've already spoken with him, Ms. Rafferty. He's told us about the Darya-e Nur, which I'm guessing is the reason you didn't tell me about Zahra Sobhani.'

As quickly as an actor entering a new scene, Charlotte adopted an attitude of gritty sophistication, slitting her eyes, tilting her head so her hair fell around her face. Rachel wondered if she planned to extract a lorgnette from her bag. Maybe she should call the other woman 'Madam.'

A fine rain began to mist the streets, adding droplets to Charlotte's hair and spangling her mulberry coat. Her shoulders twitched, she dropped the pose.

'What do you want?' she demanded.

'Answers to my questions. Who bought the replica of the Darya-e Nur from Winfield Park? He told me you brokered the sale.'

'I don't see how that's any of your business.'

'I can very easily make it my business to get Revenue Canada to take a look at your finances, Ms. Rafferty.' Rachel had every intention of doing so anyway. 'I can also make it my business to report you to the board of the ROM for what is clearly a conflict of interest – brokering deals between patrons of the museum and third parties.'

Charlotte grimaced. A trace of scarlet lip gloss caught on a strand of hair, leaving a thin line of color along one cheek. She didn't notice.

'It wasn't a conflict. The buyer isn't a patron of the ROM, not exactly.'

'Who?' Rachel insisted. 'Who are we talking about?'

'Mehran Najafi. I honestly didn't think twice about it. He asked for a list of respectable gemologists – gem cutters, in particular.'

'Recently?'

'No, sometime last year. He's a well-known collector, I introduced him to a number of gem cutters, he focused on Winfield Park.'

'Was that the extent of your participation?'

Charlotte hesitated. She was wondering how much Rachel knew. Rachel set her straight.

'All of it, or my next call is to Revenue Canada.'

'I don't know how to describe it. He was thrilled to discover Winfield specialized in replicas, but in a way that didn't seem personal. He wanted me to persuade Winfield to sell him the entire set of Great Table Diamond replicas. He said Winfield could fashion more.'

She expelled her breath in an angry huff.

'People with money have very little understanding of how art is created. It's a sensory process, but it's also a skill.'

Rachel was surprised to find she understood this. Zach had told her the same thing.

'Winfield wasn't willing to part with it – the Diamanta Grande Table is the largest pink diamond known to history. Fashioning the replica was a labor of love.'

'Then why did he sell Najafi the Darya-e Nur?'

Charlotte Rafferty's gaze darted away.

'Mehran had been generous in the past. He assured me if I could convince Winfield to sell him the Darya-e Nur, he'd bequeath his entire collection of nineteenth-century photographs to the ROM. He put some pressure on me,' she admitted. 'He went over my head and told my boss the same thing.'

Which explained why Charlotte didn't consider her actions a conflict of interest. The bequest would have created a flurry of anticipation among Charlotte's higher-ups.

'What was Zahra's interest in this?'

Charlotte's hands moved involuntarily. The Ferragamo bag slipped to her elbow.

'I couldn't quite figure it out. She knew Mehran had purchased the replica. She didn't think he was the end buyer, she was trying to reach him in Iran. When she couldn't, she came to me looking for the name of the man who had financed the buy.'

'Who was it?'

'I didn't know.' And at Rachel's obvious skepticism: 'I'm telling you the truth. I thought Mehran was the buyer.'

'Did you find out why he wanted the Darya-e Nur?'

Charlotte gazed longingly over Rachel's shoulder. A taxi was making its way down the street. She flagged it down with her free hand.

'He said something about a sentimental fondness for an emblem of his country. And that's really all I know about the entire matter.'

She made for the stairs, Rachel let her go.

'Ms. Rafferty,' she said. Charlotte pivoted on her heel. 'What did you get out of the arrangement? I can see the benefit to the ROM, but what about you?'

Charlotte's smile was brittle. 'Do you have any idea what my salary is at the ROM? Or the hours I've put into this place?' She dismissed its crystal façade with a grimace. She placed one elegantly booted leg inside the taxi. 'He offered me a major commission on the deal.'

The door closed on her razor-edged smile. 'Believe me, I earned every penny.'

50

Zach walked in on Rachel in her bedroom, hastily throwing things into the beat-up black Samsonite she'd unearthed from their parents' basement. She'd told him of her plans, and he was worried. But it wasn't a decision she'd made lightly – a small part of her wondered if in the end it came down to weighing what Khattak meant to her against her brother's need of her, or the place of each in her life.

She brushed uselessly at her eyes. She would do anything for Zach. But how could she respect herself if each time she was presented with the consequences of doing her job, she backed away out of fear? She hadn't done that at Algonquin, she wouldn't do it now. It hadn't been easy, but she'd made her choice.

'Do you really have to do this, Ray?' Zach settled himself on a corner of her bed, stretching his long legs out. A childhood photograph of the two of them together occupied a corner of her night table. He picked it up with a grin.

'Thank God you gave up that mullet, the ponytail suits you better.'

Rachel smacked his leg with a sweater she had rolled into a bundle.

'You have all my contact information.'

She sat down on the bed beside Zach. The time had come to tell him, and she knew it was going to be tricky. She wished she had more time to talk to him about Lillian, but she had to prepare for all scenarios. Though she was confident she'd be home soon, she still had to account for plane crashes, road accidents, unexpected violence – the random phenomena of life.

She opened her night table drawer and extracted an envelope, which she handed to Zach. He'd just come from a shower, and his hair was a rumpled mess. He hadn't added his normal jewelry and eyeliner. He looked like a gangly teen, uncomfortable in the arrangement of his bones.

'What's this?'

'Nothing's going to happen to me, but you never know when you travel.' She took a deep breath. 'This is a copy of my will and my life insurance. If anything does go wrong, I don't want you to worry about what will happen to you, you won't end up on the streets.'

She didn't add the word *again*, but it hung in the air between them.

'Everything I have, I've left to you. It's enough to see you through a year in this place, or you could sell it and make your own plans.'

Zach's golden-brown eyes had gone wide. A strange expression crossed his face: a mixture of shame and disbelief.

'Why are we talking about this?'

Rachel gave his arm a squeeze of reassurance.

'You're not a kid anymore, you need to understand how things are done.' She nodded at the envelope. 'There's also information in there about my funeral arrangements.'

'When did you do all this?'

Zach's face became sullen. She knew it was because he couldn't, at this moment, face the reality she was describing.

'Not long after I found you. I'm a police officer.' She spoke briskly, hurrying over the words. 'In my line of work, it's important to make these kinds of plans.' She'd had no reason to make them before she'd found Zach. Finding him had changed everything. She stuffed the envelope back into the drawer. 'My lawyer's number is in there, too.'

She still hadn't told him about their mother. Her back to him, she heard her brother choke back the knot of emotion in his throat.

'Don't make any plans to do away with me.' She said it with a grin, trying to lighten the moment. Zach tugged on her ponytail from behind.

'Ha!' he joked. 'All your worldly goods are mine. Does that include the hockey memorabilia? I've always liked your poster of the Soviet series.'

The photograph of Team Canada during the epic 1972 series hung over Rachel's bed.

She glared at him. 'Touch it and die.'

Grinning, he locked her suitcase and lifted it from the bed while Rachel collected her purse. She glanced at his open bedroom door. The tree-within-a-tree was coming to life beautifully, the leaves at the top of the branches worked in squares of gold. Brilliant shades of green outlined the lower branches.

'Christ, that's gorgeous. You should have done it on canvas, you could have sold it for a fortune.'

Zach looked pleased. Though Rachel's arts education was limited, she'd always supported her brother's efforts, able to tell the real thing from when he was fooling around.

'Think about greeting cards, maybe. Or a calendar. I bet they'd sell out.'

Zach had no pretensions about his art. He wanted it to be seen and experienced.

'Maybe,' he agreed.

Rachel still hadn't reached for the door handle. She knew what she'd left undone, just as she knew she couldn't leave it like this. Her nightmare scenario was returning from Iran to find her brother gone.

She turned and faced him, tipping her head up to meet his eyes.

'I've got something to tell you about Mum, and I think it will probably upset you.'

The words had the effect she'd feared. Zach hunched his shoulders, his whole body tight.

'We don't need to make this anything big, I'm just afraid –' She waved one arm in a futile gesture. No one in the Getty family was a particularly skilled communicator. She wasn't sure how to go on. She steeled herself for his reaction. 'Mum came the other day while you were out. She asked me to send you back to her and Da. I wanted you to hear that from me.'

Zach's eyes rested on his sister's face, a hollowness in them that made Rachel ache.

This wasn't the way.

At last with a sigh, he asked, 'Why does that make you afraid?'

Rachel knew the answer. She just wasn't sure she wanted to share it with Zach.

'I'm afraid she'll convince you, somehow. Or make it seem like I don't want you here, and you'll be doing me a favor by leaving. That's not true.' She locked eyes with her brother. 'I've wanted you here for so long.'

Tears welled in her eyes. She blinked them back furiously, not wanting Zach to witness her weakness. Rachel Getty didn't cry. She wouldn't be much use to her brother if she did.

She chose her next words with painful consideration.

'I'm afraid she'll do something to make you leave for good. It's … been a lot, Zach. I can't face that again.'

She busied herself by checking for her passport in her purse, shocked when her brother grabbed her shoulders and kissed her on the top of her head.

'I won't do that to you again.' His tone was matter-of-fact. 'It's you and me, Ray, yeah? You and me against the rest of the world.'

It was something she'd taught Zach to say under their father's roof. She gave him a crooked smile.

'You and me against the rest of the world. That's good, you remember that.'

He opened the door for her, grabbing her suitcase in one hand.

'I'll be here when you get back,' he promised. 'You need to learn to worry a little less.'

In the heated interior of Nate's superb Aston Martin, Rachel felt the tension in her body dissipate. She was more afraid of her parents' negative influence than she was of agents of the Iranian regime – what did that tell her? She loved her father, she loved her mother. She understood their weaknesses much better than she'd done as a child. A decade of police work had taught her compassion. It had taught her to empathize even when harm was done to her.

She loved Zach more than any other person in the world, and he was back now. Her breathing slowed. He was back and safe in her home. She had to remember that.

She gave Nate a sideways glance.

He looked cool and competent at the wheel. He smelled like cinnamon and comfort, his straw-colored hair soft and rumpled. She fought the impulse to reach out and touch it.

Clearing her throat, she said, 'I need you to do me a favor.'

His eyes brushed her face.

'Anything, Rachel. What is it?'

She fetched her lawyer's business card from the interior of her purse and placed it near the gearshift.

'If anything should happen to me, I need you to look out for Zach. Help him with things, help him make arrangements.'

'Are you thinking of what happened to Zahra?'

Like Sehr, he'd tried to discourage her from going. But once she'd spoken about her role as Esa's partner, he'd done everything he could to assist her. She'd chosen not to speak of Larijani's threat, afraid to lose his support, but she knew someone had to stand by Zach, in case things turned out badly.

Rachel waited until he'd negotiated the exit to Pearson airport.

'I don't want him to suffer what Max Najafi is suffering. Just let things be, I'm okay with that. Tell him I said so, and tell him –' Her voice choked again. She didn't know what was wrong with her, why her emotions were so scaldingly near the surface.

Nate moved one hand to cover hers, the warmth of his hand surprising her. She clung to it. There'd been so few people in her life to offer help.

'Of course I will, Rachel. Nothing's going to happen, but if it does, you have my word I'll keep an eye on Zachary.' He made his voice light. 'I've had a lot of experience minding young people – I've managed to keep Audrey in one piece.'

This was something they had in common. The role of standing in for absent or incapable parents. She flashed him a look of gratitude. They didn't know each other well enough for her to have asked him for something so onerous or so personal to her. But who else was there who would help her brother, if she and Khattak were tracked down by Larijani?

And maybe she wasn't being honest with herself. Maybe there was more to her feelings for Nate than she was willing to own up to.

The trip, her mother, Zach, the case – it was making her crazy. She needed to get some of her worry and frustration out on the ice. Instead, she was about to spend fourteen hours on a flight to a new country, where if she was to believe news reports, fundamentalist Ayatollahs and bloodthirsty bomb-makers lurked behind every tree. Luckily, she'd done plenty of research on Iran, her interest stimulated by the photographs Khattak had sent her of his travels.

She'd spend part of the flight analyzing the case and the rest of it asleep, refreshing herself for the adventure that awaited. She realized she was still holding Nate's hand. Her cheeks burned. She made a show of pulling her notebook from her purse.

'You're making a list of things for me to do while you're gone, aren't you?' he said in a deadpan voice.

'Ha,' she said. 'One of these days I'll have to deputize you.'

But she thanked him with genuine gratitude when he dropped her at the terminal. He'd wanted to come in, Rachel had refused. There was something in Nate's eyes she wasn't used to seeing in a man's eyes, and she didn't know if she was ready to respond. He was attractive, talented, and famous. That wasn't anything she needed to be mixed up in.

He tried to speak, she cut him off before he could.

'Thanks,' she said. 'Thanks for being a friend.'

She gave him a cheery wave and marched off with her bags.

51

Interrogation

'You'll never get out of here alive. Everyone has forgotten you, no one knows where you are. You'll die in this cell alone.' 'No beating today?' 'Why torture a condemned man? Your execution has been announced.' 'So somewhere, someone will know. They'll know all about me, they'll be working for my release.' I say this as if I've scored a point over Hogsbreath. He has the last word, anyway. 'No one will know until long after you're dead.'

52

Rachel proceeded through customs and her baggage check without incident. She was welcomed at the gate by the leader of her private tour group, a woman named Samira Zand, who seemed surprised at Rachel's minimal luggage. As a matter of course, she straightened Rachel's long coat and fiddled with her head scarf.

'You must be tired,' she said with a pleasing lilt. 'Let me take you to your hotel.'

Rachel was booked at the Hotel Shah Nameh, an arrangement made beforehand between Nate and Khattak. As she was rushed through the airport, four other tourists were collected. A Danish couple in their sixties, and two unrelated British travelers, both with narrow frames and a tendency to make barbed remarks, even about things that pleased them.

Rachel's head was pounding from the flight, her mouth tasted sour, she needed a shower and a nap. Her impressions of the journey to the hotel were a blur: a busy, modern terminal with the requisite degree of chaos for those collecting arriving passengers, busy highways packed with traffic underlined by disharmonic sound. A muddy blue sky, through whose hazy filter, the craggy outline of the Alborz Mountains could be glimpsed. And a stunningly modern metropolis hurtling toward the future.

Noise and smoke and the unwanted overtures of her fellow travelers combined to make Rachel's head throb to the point of bursting. She was an unseasoned traveler, not given to complaint, but neither had she been ready for her journey. For half the flight, she'd worried over Nate and Zachary. For the second half, she'd conjured up nightmare scenarios for herself of gulags and dungeons – scenarios that seemed preposterous in the bright light of day and the friendly welcome of the Iranians she encountered.

'Here.' Simon, one of the British travelers with a pair of china-blue eyes and an impressively posh accent, offered Rachel a bottle of water. 'You're looking rather pale. It's easy to get dehydrated on these long flights. You need to compensate for it.'

She sipped from the bottle gratefully, breaking out some aspirin to accompany it. She felt sorry for her fellow travelers. The first four days of their itinerary had been commandeered by Nate's extra generous donation to the tour guide. They were headed south to Shiraz first, and then in an equanimity-destroying turn, all the way north to the Caspian Sea. She supposed Khattak would find a way to tag along as he'd determined the itinerary.

An hour later, refreshed by a catnap and a shower, she made her way to the restaurant on the third floor, where she'd arranged to meet Khattak. She stepped from the hotel's corridors into an enchanting garden teeming with Persian blues: the courtyard was lined with glazed tiles forming geometric patterns of delicate nuance and detail. A series of fountains surrounded by palms burbled in the center of the courtyard, and all along the perimeter, bistro-style tables with garden chairs were stationed beside sterling silver samovars. She could smell the fresh bloom of gardenias and honeysuckle. Hibiscus plants in pink and scarlet flamed throughout the court.

When her eye fell on Khattak, she couldn't mask her delight. He came forward to greet her – for the briefest moment, she thought he would hug her. Instead, he reached for her hand, squeezed it, and let it go.

'Rachel,' he murmured. 'Thank you for coming.'

She'd forgotten how much she liked his voice, how much she'd missed hearing it in person. He looked well, better than she'd seen him in the aftermath of their last investigation, gaunt and hollow-eyed and sorrowful. The weeks in Iran had done him good. His face had filled out, his eyes were no longer smudged by shadows, but more than that, she recognized something familiar. Khattak was on the hunt. And it brought out his finest qualities.

A strange sensation settled in Rachel's stomach. A moment later she recognized it as happiness. It was good to be in Khattak's company, good to begin their familiar rites together.

They caught each other up on details over a long, late lunch. Rachel had no problem having a meal with Khattak and then dining again with her tour group an hour later. Her stomach was empty, and she wanted to try everything on the menu. Toronto had no shortage of excellent Persian restaurants; it was something else to sample the cuisine in its native setting.

'First stop: Shiraz,' she told him at the end of their meal. 'Overnight train, I'm afraid, so tomorrow's a wasted day.'

Khattak leaned back in his chair, crisp and cool in his navy shirt and slacks, and very much occupied by the question of Zahra's death.

'Not necessarily,' he said. 'You'll see some of the sights of Tehran during the day, and in the evening, I'll join your train. I have a name and address for the jeweler in Shiraz. I'm afraid you'll have to stay with your group until the afternoon stop on their itinerary, but I think you'll find it worthwhile. After 2:00 P.M., slip away from the group and meet me here.' He passed a slip of paper to her. 'Call a taxi. We should be done in time for you to rejoin your group for dinner.'

Rachel eyed him thoughtfully. When Khattak had left for Iran, he'd been bleakly unforgiving of himself for the way events had unfolded in the woods of Algonquin. Added to this weight was his estranged relationship with his sister, a front on which there'd been little progress. Together with his suspension,

Khattak had been at odds with himself: directionless and burdened by remorse.

Khattak in Tehran was the boss she remembered: sharp-witted, clear-eyed, focused on the task ahead, with a well-structured picture of the end goal, more confident and determined than she'd seen him in weeks. She found herself grinning at him over a tiny glass of tea so whimsical, she felt as though she'd joined the Mad Hatter's tea party. Khattak noticed. He smiled back at her.

'You can order Nescafé here. Or Turkish coffee, if you prefer.'

Holding her cup, Rachel wangled a dainty finger at him.

'Perish the thought,' she said. 'I like to blend in with the locals.'

At five foot nine with her ruddy cheeks and athletic physique, this was somewhat unlikely. Khattak laughed, and she joined in. She asked him what he would be doing while she occupied herself with her tour group. He told her his plan to review the photographs she'd sent back to him, to see if he could find something he'd overlooked.

'Great,' she said. 'Meet me in the dining car on the train. We can talk over anything you find.' She glanced over at the well-dressed couples meeting in the courtyard. 'Any tips for me? What to do, what not to do or say?'

Khattak thought this over.

'Ask a lot of tourism questions. But don't mention anything to do with the government or the prison. And don't mention human rights.'

He didn't need to tell her not to bring up Zahra.

'I'm not sure where they're taking you tomorrow, but if there's any flexibility to your itinerary, suggest they take you to the National Jewelry Museum. You should see the Darya-e Nur for yourself. You've been on its trail longer than I have, and you know its history better.'

He passed her the museum catalog he'd kept in his pocket.

'Good night-time reading. Get some rest, the next few days will be busy.'

At night, in the privacy of his room, Khattak had time to reflect on why he'd allowed Rachel to come to Iran. Her presence wasn't necessary – he could have taken the trip to Shiraz on his own, met with the jeweler, made a last push to find out Zahra's fate and reclaim her body without exposing Rachel to a man like Larijani.

But he recognized Rachel as a competent and able officer, she'd proven her skills on numerous occasions – she had the right to make her own choices about the risks she took, and with Rachel at his side, the odds had changed in his favor.

And at a fundamental level, he admitted, in addition to her skills, Rachel's presence alleviated his sense of loneliness. He enjoyed her company and her openhearted take on their work.

Unaware his face had softened into a smile, Khattak called up the photographs of Evin on a laptop he'd borrowed from the hotel. The newspaper clippings were spread out on the desk beside him. He scrutinized the photographs one by one, dividing them into grids and using the zoom function to examine each of the faces in the pictures.

He did this several times to no effect.

A room service waiter brought him fresh coffee.

The voice of a downcast Persian musician wafted through his open window, a late breeze stirring the hair that had grown past his collar. He went into the washroom to bathe his face with cold water, changing into his nightclothes. He took the time to pray.

Refreshed, he began again, shifting between two sets of images.

Ten minutes later, he had it.

He scanned the newspaper images for further details.

The information he sought was missing.

Twenty-four hours later, he and Rachel were sitting across from each other in the dining car of the overnight train to Shiraz.

Rachel had regaled him with her adventures of the day, providing a lively account of her fellow tourists. The Danish gentleman had taken a fancy to Rachel, crowding her personal space. She'd taken refuge behind one of the Brits, an able foil to the Dane.

'Simon Graves is quite nice, really. He seconded my request to be diverted to the museum. And he gave me cover.' She smirked over a bowl of lemon sorbet. 'I guess the Danes like 'em strapping and tall. Funny, that. His wife is a bit of a thing.'

'And? What did you think of the museum?'

Esa was biding his time, his discovery hot on his tongue. He wanted to hear Rachel's account first.

'I thought Park's replicas were mind-blowing – but Holy Christ in heaven! I goggled at that throne for a good twenty minutes.' She shook her head back and forth. 'I saw it in the book, but when you're standing before it, you can't believe there's that much treasure in the world. I'd love to get my hands on the Shahi Sword.'

'Anything else?'

'The Darya-e Nur, the Nur-el Ain.' She shook her head again, disbelieving. 'Why aren't the crown jewels better known to the rest of the world? Nice setting, too, by the way. One of those chandeliers could pay off the rest of my mortgage.' She dumped her silver spoon into her empty dish. 'The Darya-e Nur,' she said reflectively. 'I tried your trick with the camera, I couldn't see an inscription. Doesn't mean it wasn't there, on the underside of one of the facets.' She flashed a grin at Khattak. 'But I'll tell you this: one of those lions is definitely missing a ruby. Amazing they got away with it, but I suspect that's because the stone is almost invisibly tiny. You'd have to know about the substitution to even register the fact that a ruby is missing.'

Khattak's jaw eased. It was a relief to hear his suspicions confirmed.

'I think it's more likely that a substitution is unthinkable. No one could have dreamt that Radan would plot such a theft, so no one bothered to look.' Mulling it over, he added, 'Then there's the fact that the stone was only ever under Radan's care. No one would have dared to question his authority – not with the power he holds.'

Rachel smiled at the heavily mustachioed waiter who came to clear their plates, hoping he hadn't caught Radan's name. She found the implications of Khattak's statement terrifying.

'Then we'd better get to the bottom of this quickly. Did you find anything else, sir?'

Esa had printed a copy of the photograph that had captured his attention. Together with the newspaper account of the private exhibit, he passed it across the table. Outside the windows of the dining car, the sky was a lapis blue, stars streaking across its surface. The train hummed along on its tracks, an underground rumble through the dark.

Rachel compared the two photographs.

'Not seeing it, sir. You'll have to tell me.'

Khattak pointed at a face in the crowd at Evin. It was one of the men with sad, weathered faces. He drew an imaginary line to the face of one of the delegates at the exhibit.

'There's no listing of their names,' he explained. 'But isn't that the same man?'

In the first photograph, the man was dressed in shabby clothes, his hands looked rough and worn, his beard was grizzled along his heavy jaw. In the photograph at the exhibit, his face was smooth, his curling hair combed back, he was dressed in an expensive suit, and he had the bearing of a man of importance. There was a sty in his left eye. It was also there in the photograph at Evin.

'It's the same man,' Rachel concluded. 'Do we know who he is?'

'He blends into his surroundings, wherever he happens to be. A mourning father at Evin, a high-ranking delegate at the exhibit.'

'So what are we saying? Barsam Radan arranged the exhibit to enable the theft of the Darya-e Nur? The unknown man was there to collect it? It doesn't explain his appearance at Evin the day Zahra was arrested.'

'Is it possible Zahra went to Evin to meet him?'

Rachel placed one photograph over the other. 'Then why was Radan there? We don't have the answer to that. We need to find out who this man is. Who can you ask?'

'Touka Swan. The Green Birds. Someone's bound to know. And if not, they're better equipped to find out.'

Rachel shifted the photographs again.

'Do you see that, sir?' She handed him the photo from Evin. 'Do you see what he's doing?' Rachel tilted the photograph so she could see it.

'Look at his eyes, the angle of his head. He's looking for someone in the crowd.'

Khattak did a double take. As usual, Rachel was right.

'Do you have all the photos from Zahra's camera?'

Khattak paused. 'Yes, I think so.'

'Take another look. Maybe we can figure out who he's looking for.'

'You don't think it was Zahra?'

'I think if he knew Zahra would be at Evin with her camera, he wouldn't have been there that day.'

53

Rachel slept well on the train. She woke to a hearty breakfast and the unrestrained chatter of her tour guide. Samira's words floated into the ether. Rachel was thinking about the photographs, wondering if she'd guessed correctly at Zahra's intentions.

Zahra knew about the Darya-e Nur. She informed the representative of the Supreme Leader. She showed up at Evin prison a few days later. She was arrested at Evin and never seen again. Her body was buried without ceremony.

Why? Why had she gone to Evin? What had convinced her to do so?

Rachel's questions remained.

Their first early morning stop was the Nasir al-Mulk mosque, a construction lovingly described by Samira as the Pink Mosque of Shiraz.

'You can choose between the Shah-e Cheragh and this. Many favor the ruins of Persepolis, but to me, these two sights are the greatest Shiraz has to offer. The more discerning will favor the mosque above the glamor of the Shah-e Cheragh, but I'll leave you to decide for yourselves.'

Samira treated them to a quick history of a region described as the heartland of Persian culture. Shiraz was the city of wine and beauty, of nightingales and poets, where Hafiz and Sadi were buried, their gravesites places of pilgrimage – the city of courtesy and courtliness, of gardens, mosques, and architectural treasures, the crowning jewel of which was the late-nineteenth-century Nasir al-Mulk mosque.

'This will be our first stop,' Samira said with an air of maternal indulgence. 'So the photographers among you may catch the light. Then we're off to Shah-e Cheragh, and you can tell me your conclusions: Which of the two is better?'

Rachel found this a bit demanding given their by-the-numbers tour of Tehran, but she was to change her mind in the prayer hall of the Nasir al-Mulk. Stained-glass windows paraphrased the light, their forms minutely articulate across a row of carpets. Patterns danced over tulip-shaped columns, a bridge to the concave arches of the *panj-e kasih* composition.

A rippling sea of turquoise, swimming in sun-warmed blues, formed the main floor of the gallery. Quietly aglow in the sea of blue were the reflections of pink-and-gold tiles. Columns floated above the floor, illusory and immemorial. Light, color, form, pattern, soundlessness, and space – though Rachel had no decided form of worship, she'd never seen a space as hallowed.

She was dwarfed by it, undone.

Simon stood quiet and thoughtful at her elbow.

'I don't see how the Shah-e Cheragh can top this,' he said. 'Maybe we should have begun the other way around.'

The Danish couple had found a place on the carpets, the other Briton set up a tripod to capture a panoramic view. Rachel had never seen anything like it. She'd imagined Iran as a place of violence and turmoil. Even the treasury hadn't prepared her for the sublimity of the mosque.

'A perfect cohesion of light,' Simon said.

Rachel nodded. She wandered off to a corner, struggling with a puzzle. Her thoughts of Iran had been limited to a scowling Ayatollah, to a region in turmoil, and lately to the nuclear negotiations. What she hadn't imagined was this ample tranquility, this amphitheater of joy.

The dignity of the mosque tore at Rachel's heart. Her lens was correcting itself. There was something to be learned from the cosmic radiance of her surroundings. Her mind was seized by a painful imagining: What must it be like to know your civilization possessed of such celestial beauty, and to find yourself the object of diminishment?

She was roaming the deep places of the soul. And she wondered if this soaring elevation of spirit was the essence of Esa Khattak, or if it was an epiphany personal to her. She felt quickened by it, lighter for it, something she would keep to herself, to be examined later on her own.

She passed the rest of the tour in a daze. The glittering turrets of the Shah-e Cheragh, the succession of colleges and mosques and robust bazaars, the gently unfurling plane trees that encircled a square of teahouses, the families about their business like any family in any other part of the world.

She met Khattak in the jewelers' district with something like relief. To investigate a death was her safe and comforting reality. When Khattak asked about the Pink Mosque, she couldn't speak, embarrassed by the way her thoughts had leapt about, evanescent in their conclusions. She hadn't snapped a single picture. The experience had been too intimate for that.

Gruffly, she turned the subject to the jeweler at Mehran Najafi's workshop.

'You think he'll cooperate, sir?'

'It depends on what he knows – how deeply involved he may be.'

The address Touka Swan had given Khattak was of a tucked-away shop in a corner of the jewelers' arcade. Windows gleamed with jewelry in turquoise and silver and gold. A sprinkling of rough carnelians occupied a glass counter. Behind the counter, an elderly man stooped over a cash register, concluding a transaction with a woman in a chador. His hands trembled as he passed the woman her change, his face had the pallor of someone who spent long periods of time under fluorescent lighting.

'Rachel.' Khattak indicated one of the showcases that lined the small shop. It featured several intricate pieces: three-tiered necklaces, engraved collars and cuffs in gold, a plume of ornamental brooches thick with blue and green gemstones.

'No rubies,' he murmured to Rachel. 'Indicative of a shortage?'

His business concluded, the jeweler turned a face of welcome to them. One side of his face dragged down, leaving his mouth with a permanent twitch. He exchanged courtesies with Khattak, identifying himself as Sharif Syed. A ripple of laughter drifted through the arcade, followed by the shrieks of birds that swooped through the bazaar.

To Rachel's surprise, Syed switched over to a precise and formal English.

'I was hoping to purchase something unique to Iran,' Khattak began. 'Something with the weight of history behind it. A friend of mine suggested your name as a specialist in reproductions.'

Syed looked uneasy. From his pocket, he unearthed a pair of spectacles with enormously thick lenses. These he perched on the tip of a nose that had once been broken. A tang of smoke drifted into his shop from the arcade, carrying the scent of burning cloves.

'Does your friend have a name, Mr. Khattak?'

'Mehran Najafi.'

The jeweler went even paler.

'I don't think I know that name.'

Khattak nodded at Rachel. She handed him the catalog from the Jewelry Museum.

'Come,' Khattak said politely. 'I'm not interested in Mr. Najafi's role in your business. I only wish to inquire whether you fashioned a replica of the Darya-e Nur for him.'

There was a stool behind the counter. Sharif Syed collapsed his weight on it, sweat breaking out on his forehead.

'It wasn't a crime,' he said faintly.

He expressed no curiosity as to how Khattak had come by his information. A blind terror had seized his thoughts. He pushed the catalog away as if warding off an unknown evil.

'I know it wasn't,' Khattak agreed. 'I want to know if you completed the work.'

Syed fumbled with the scarf he had tied at his throat.

'I'm not – feeling well. You must go.'

Khattak reached over the counter for Syed's wrist.

'Rachel,' he said. 'See if you can find some water.'

When Rachel had brought a bottle of water, Khattak helped Syed to sip it. He held Syed's wrist until his pulse stopped racing.

'Please don't be alarmed. We won't be reporting this conversation.' He shot a quick glance at Rachel, who was supporting Syed. 'We're detectives from Canada, we're trying to find out what happened to Zahra Sobhani. She came to see you, didn't she?'

Syed nodded weakly. He slumped back into Rachel's arms.

'Not here,' he wheezed. 'Take me to the back room.'

A feeble gesture indicated a narrow door in the corner.

'Shall I shut down your shop?' Khattak asked.

Syed nodded. He fumbled the keys from his pants pocket, extending his hand to Khattak. Moving quickly, Khattak secured the outer door of the shop as Rachel helped Syed to a sofa in the room behind the shopfront.

Rachel glanced around, making note of the jeweler's tools and his ready supply of rough. Though cramped, the space was well-organized, with a natural flow from a jeweler's bench to the melting surface and polishing area, to a sink at the back near a roller stand. An assortment of tools was arranged on the jeweler's workbench. Small hammers and welders, tweezers and magnifiers, jeweler's loupes, a group of gemological pliers. There were also microscopes and grading instruments.

This was clearly where Syed performed his work. A finely tooled necklace worked in sapphire and gold rested on his desk, a pair of binoculars beside it. A security camera above the door was aimed at the shop, Rachel didn't see a safe.

Khattak sat beside Syed, offering reassurance. After a time, the jeweler regained his poise. He sat up on his own, brushing Khattak's hands away with a testy gesture.

'I shouldn't be speaking to you.'

'No one is following us,' Khattak assured him, though he couldn't be sure of his words. Since his departure for Tehran, he'd been watching for a tail and hadn't spied one. That didn't mean it wasn't there. 'No one knows of our interest in Zahra. Tell us what we want to know, and we'll leave you alone. Did Mehran and Zahra come to you?'

Like Rachel, Syed kept an eye on his security camera. His shop was deserted, Rachel had dimmed the lights.

'Yes, he came. He asked me to do the impossible – to imitate the Darya-e Nur. I don't know how familiar you are with the stone. I told him it would be impossible to replicate such a rare pink diamond of its size. There's nothing similar in existence. And if there was, Najafi could not afford it. He said that wouldn't be a problem.'

'Why not?'

The jeweler sighed, his chin quivering with the movement.

'He brought me a replica of the diamond. He said my job was to duplicate the setting – the sun, the lions, the ornamental brooch. He told me to use the cheapest stones – crystals, zirconium, whatever I liked. He was willing to pay anything I asked.'

From the corner of the room, Rachel asked, 'How long did it take you?'

'Too long.' The left side of his face dragged down. He held up his shaking hands. 'It wasn't worth it. It was the only thing I worked on for six months, it ruined my health.'

His voice roughened with tears. 'If Mehran is displeased with it, I don't have the money to return, I used it for my children's education.' Only one side of his face moved as he winced.

'Nothing in Iran comes easily these days. Sanctions have made our lives impossible.'

'I'm not after the money, and I don't represent Mr. Najafi. Why did Zahra come to you?'

Immediately, the jeweler looked grave.

'Such terrible things happen in this country. How do I know they won't happen to me?'

'You've done nothing wrong,' Khattak said firmly. 'And even if you had, it would be impossible for me to report you – we're in the same position. Neither of us wishes to draw attention to our actions.'

Understanding that this was true, Syed relented. He told them Zahra had come to him in pursuit of her ex-husband. She'd wanted to know where Mehran was, and when Syed had last seen him. She'd asked the same questions Khattak was asking now. Had Syed undertaken a special commission? Had he duplicated the setting of the Darya-e Nur?

Rachel flicked Khattak a glance. Their theory had been wrong. Zahra and Mehran weren't in on the plot together. If Syed was to be believed, Zahra had been chasing her husband's trail for reasons they didn't know. Khattak's voice became animated.

'Agha Syed, do you know why Mehran wanted the replica?'

Rachel watched the jeweler's rheumy old eyes. He blinked several times. His trembling hands removed the thick-lensed glasses from his nose in order to wipe his eyes.

'He said it was a gift for his daughter, Roxana.'

He hummed an eerie tune under his breath.

With a sense of shock, Rachel recognized the song Max Najafi had played at the studio.

'Everyone in this country knows of Roxana Najafi.' His lips shook. 'It was a fitting gift for a daughter of Iran. It was my privilege to do anything for her.'

Rachel and Khattak exchanged a glance. The jeweler was a tacit supporter of the Green Movement. His role had been to reproduce the ornament, he'd played no part in its theft. Preparing to leave, they thanked him. He looked small and frail in the harsh light of his shop.

'Will the other man be back again? Will he want his money back?'

Rachel and Khattak turned at the door.

'What other man?'

'The man who paid for the materials. I was able to duplicate everything except for one of the lion's eyes. I had purchased another ruby from my supplier, but this man was in a hurry. He demanded I finish the brooch early, he didn't notice the ruby was missing.' Syed's voice quavered. 'Has he noticed it now?'

'Do you know who this man was?' Khattak returned.

Syed shook his head. 'Mehran sent him. He didn't give his name.'

'But you'd recognize his face?'

Khattak reached for the photograph of the exhibit from the inside pocket of his jacket. He grabbed a stool from the workshop and placed the photograph before the jeweler, smoothing it out. Rachel brought Syed his jeweler's loupe.

'No,' he said. 'Bring me those glasses.'

Rachel found the binoculars and handed them over. Syed examined the picture.

'Well?' Khattak asked. 'Is it one of those men?'

The jeweler shook his head. But when Khattak disclosed the second photograph, Syed gave an involuntary cry. He jabbed his thumb down on the photograph.

'This man,' he said. 'In his countryman's clothes and boots. This is him. This is what he looked like. You see his hands?'

Khattak nodded.

'I always remember the hands, they're the hands of his profession.' Rachel looked up, her heart beating fast.

'What profession is that, sir?'

The jeweler made a clean breast of things, a burden slipping from his shoulders.

'This man is a captain at Anzali Harbor. He sails on the Caspian Sea.'

54

The Suite

Joojeh is back. He takes me for a shower and a shave. My legs are weak, I haven't walked in so long. He puts an arm under my shoulders and drags me down the hallway. There's a bit of tinfoil in his pocket, it's shaped like a triangle. He passes it to me, and I see that it's the corner of a Toblerone. 'The Swiss?' I gasp. 'The Swiss are here?' Joojeh speaks under his breath. 'Not for you, for a foreigner. I got to keep a piece of the chocolate, so I saved it.' I thank him copiously. To be a foreigner in an Iranian jail! And then I realize. Joojeh has accepted me. I'm not foreign, not peshmerga, not just a Kurd – I'm a son of Iran. I lick the tinfoil, wretched in my gratitude. 'What's happening?' I ask him. 'Why such kindness?' Joojeh looks me dead in the eye. 'Kindness costs nothing, rewards everything,' he says. I slip out of his arms, sobbing. I'm shuddering with grief, with joy. I look up at Joojeh. 'My sister,' I say. 'You've seen my sister?' He jerks a hand across his mouth, telling me to shut up. He pulls me up from the floor, shoulders my weight again. 'She's safe,' he whispers. 'She's working to get you home.' Home, I think, sobbing like a child. My mother died in childbirth, my father in prison. Nasreen is my only home.

55

The sun broke across the sky, divesting the land of its cover of snow, the earth below emerging in patches. They'd left Shiraz behind, trading Tehran for a train to the harbor in the north, the Caspian Sea sounding like something from a fairy tale, magical and remote, undiscoverable by ordinary means.

'We'll need to split up,' Khattak said to Rachel. 'Slip away from your group and take this side of the harbor, I'll try my luck at the other. We'll meet at your group's restaurant for dinner.'

'Did you have any luck with Touka? Or your group of students?'

The journey had tired them both. Khattak's clothes were rumpled, his face unshaven, a dark shadow upon his jaw. The sky beyond their window was flecked with streaks of red, a herald of the dawn.

Khattak showed her a message on his phone.

'Nothing from the Green Birds. Touka identified the man at Evin as Barid Rud. That's who you should be asking for.'

'I'm not sure I can ditch the tour all day,' Rachel said. 'I think Simon is getting suspicious.'

'You're not worried about your tour leader?'

Rachel tried to reassure him.

'Nate paid her well. It isn't worth her while to ask questions about me.'

'What if she reports your absence? That's something you need to think about.'

'Don't worry, sir. Nate's promised her a bonus if my impression of Iran is favorable. I think it will get me back onto my plane.'

'You've gotten close to Nate, it seems.' There was a question in Khattak's voice.

Rachel's face burned. She stumbled into an answer.

'He's not a bad assistant. When you're not around, I mean.' Khattak smiled to himself.

'High praise indeed.' He glanced over her shoulder. 'I'd better go. Your friend Simon is looking for you. Have coffee with him, it should serve to divert his suspicions.' His smile became teasing. 'You could be misinterpreting things, Rachel.'

'How, sir?' His jaunty tone made her suspicious.

'He may be another of your admirers.'

He ducked away before Rachel could respond.

She was unsettled when Simon helped himself to Khattak's seat and ordered tea for them without asking. He made up for it a minute later, when he inquired with a sympathetic look, 'You don't mind, I hope?'

To Rachel, tea was the anemic younger brother of a sturdy double-double. Since she hadn't grown fond of Nescafé, she supposed it was the safer choice.

'Did you like Shiraz?' she asked.

'I think the question is whether you did. You went missing after the Nasir al-Mulk.'

'That's not true,' Rachel protested.

'No? I challenge you to name a single other stop we made with our indefatigable hostess.'

Rachel grinned at this description. Samira's catalog of wonders was delivered in a monotone that raced to a finish before she lost the attention of her clients.

'Safavids, Sassanids, I can't keep them straight.'

Their waiter brought tea and served it with some ceremony, with rosewater-flavored Turkish Delight. Rachel munched the confection with enthusiasm. The healthy Persian breakfast of bread, cheese, quince jam, and walnuts wasn't making a dent in her appetite.

Simon observed her.

'It's a hell of a lot of money to pay if you're not interested in Iran's history.'

Rachel took another piece of Turkish Delight.

'There's only so much I can absorb, and I don't like being minded.'

Simon leaned back in his seat.

'You intrigue me,' he said. 'I could have sworn the Pink Mosque meant something to you. As for the rest –' He waved a hand dismissively. 'Who's the man you've been talking to, a secret admirer?'

This was such a strange inversion of what Khattak had suggested about Simon that Rachel had to bite the inside of her cheek to keep herself from laughing.

'Just someone I met. He has some good recommendations about what to see.'

'Such as?'

Rachel reeled off the name of the restaurant on the harbor. 'He says we should take a boat out on the Caspian.'

Simon's response was dry. 'And conveniently that's been arranged on our itinerary.' He finished his tea and rose. 'I'm not sure what you're up to, Rachel, but if you need a co-conspirator, count me in.'

Rachel stared at him without blinking. She hadn't expected him to figure her out so quickly. And she wondered why, when he'd paid just as much money for the tour as she had, he was more interested in her activities than in the tour's itinerary. Or why he would volunteer to help her. She was a Canadian police officer in Iran. She'd have to be a little more discreet, and far less laissez-faire about her movements.

When she was sure he'd gone, she finished off the plate of Turkish Delight. Her appetite undaunted, she ordered another.

Rachel's romantic impressions of the Caspian Sea were doomed to disappointment as soon as the local bus transferred them from the city of Rasht, the capital of Gilan Province, to the boardwalk of Anzali Harbor.

The first thing she absorbed was the lush greenery of the province, the humidity in the air that allowed for the fertile growth of rice paddies and tea crops. As they reached the harbor, she expected to see blue-green waters and sandy beaches covered in shells. Instead, their group found itself on a crowded boardwalk that curved around the sea's southern bed.

The sea was doused in the haze of pollution, with mountains as a chalky backdrop, and the orange winches of cargo ships in the foreground. The hulks of container ships loomed over smaller fishing vessels, the air tasted moist and salty, though the Volga and Ural Rivers fed the Caspian Sea fresh water from the north. The beaches were saltine gray.

In the middle distance, oil and natural gas platforms decked the surface of the water, partnered with drilling rigs farther out. A roll of white surf unraveled at the shore, gulls screaming as they dived among the pebbles. By any measure, the Caspian Sea was crowded.

Rachel paid attention to Samira's description of the sea's ecology. The world's largest enclosed body of water, the Caspian was bordered by five countries. It was heavily over-fished and over-drilled, bringing untold oil riches to Azerbaijan, Iran, and Russia, while its most prized export, the Caspian sturgeon, was at the point of extinction.

Families strolled along the boardwalk, their faces differing from those Rachel had observed in Tehran and Shiraz. Azeris, Russians, Turkmens, Kazakhs – a concert of languages and customs. Samira droned on about the Gilani dialect and the garlic-infused Gilani diet. Her mind half on lunch, Rachel stared down the boardwalk and despaired. How would she have time to check each boathouse along the way? What hope did she have of finding a man named Barid Rud in the course of a single day, especially with Simon Graves at her heels?

As they strolled along the boardwalk, Rachel darted off into the entrances of pilothouses and fishing cottages, using the same phrase Khattak had taught her in Farsi.

I'm looking for a man named Barid Rud.

A few of the fishermen laughed at her statement, but no one could answer, even when she showed them the photograph. She rejoined her group as quickly as she could to avert Samira's suspicion, though she felt the silent weight of Simon Graves's reproof.

Eventually, Samira led them to a restaurant on the harbor whose name was Rain, a much-prized commodity of the Caspian region, not quite as valued by foreign tourists.

'You will now have an hour to wander on your own.' She looked pointedly at Rachel. 'Make use of your free time, so you can benefit from this tour. We'll meet at the restaurant for lunch, where I promise you, not all the caviar has been exported.'

Rachel had never tasted caviar. She made a mental note not to miss it. And to deflect Samira's attention, she asked several questions about the different varieties of caviar. She attached herself so persistently, that it was Samira who finally moved away, latching on to the Danes.

As Samira turned away, Simon caught Rachel by the arm. He led her a little away from the others.

'Let me help,' he said. 'Whatever it is you're doing, I doubt an hour will be enough time. And don't tell me you're not doing anything.'

Rachel's skin went cold. From her last case to this one, it was becoming clear that her undercover skills needed work. She made a mental note to apply for additional training.

Summoning a careless smile, she said, 'I have no idea what you mean.'

'No? You've been wandering into boathouses just because you like the smell?'

Rachel cast a hurried glance over at Samira, still chatting with the Danes.

'I like to get an authentic sense of the places I visit. So I interact with the locals.'

Simon shook his head. 'Do you speak any Persian, Rachel?' He didn't wait for her to answer. 'I do. In fact, that's my job, my life's work. I'm a professor of Indo-European languages. My passion for Iran's history and culture is quite sincere. But I'm beginning to wonder about yours.'

Rachel scowled. She'd had enough of Simon's interference.

'I might not be a professor, but that doesn't mean I'm not interested in Iran.'

He looked over at Samira. He placed a hand on Rachel's wrist, giving the impression of intimacy.

'Don't mind this,' he said. 'She's watching us.' He examined Rachel's face, and when she remained determinedly silent, he sighed. 'This isn't the safest country for tourists who walk away from their minders. Whatever it is you're doing, your activities endanger us all.'

Rachel experienced an immediate pang of conscience. She hadn't considered that, carried away by the urgency of her search. But she attempted another deflection, thinking the less Simon knew, the better he would fare.

'I was just exploring,' she muttered.

Exasperated, Simon dropped his hand.

'Really? I followed you to a boathouse, to give you a little cover from Samira. You were asking for a man named Barid Rud.'

Rachel folded her arms across her chest. She squinted up at the sun.

'So?'

'Rachel, someone's been having you on. Barid Rud isn't a name. It's a pseudonym of some kind. *Barid* means courier or messenger. In this context, it might translate to "messenger of the sea". Now do you see why you might need a little help?'

Rachel bit her lip. This was a setback neither she nor Khattak could have anticipated. She looked into Simon Graves's sharp gray eyes, and realized she couldn't involve him.

'I didn't know that,' she said slowly. 'And I appreciate you telling me that, but there's no need for you to get yourself embroiled in this. If you can keep Samira off my case, I'll consider that a favor.'

They stared at each other, smiling for Samira's benefit. Simon dug his hands into the pockets of his windbreaker. It was zipped up to his throat, protecting him from the wind. Rachel tasted sea salt on her lips.

'Are you certain?'

Rachel was tempted to tell him more, but her common sense told her that even if she could trust Simon, he was right about one thing – her off-book activities might endanger the whole group.

'Thanks,' she said. 'That's really all the help I need.'

He didn't seem satisfied, but he nodded and let her go.

Rachel's search proved futile. By the time the group came together for lunch, she'd walked less than a mile along the boardwalk. She collapsed onto a bench at their table, taking care to avoid Samira.

The Danes and Roger, the other Briton, hadn't wandered far at all. Roger showed them photographs he'd snapped of the harbor. Rows of orange cargo cranes stood sentinel against the sky. Their horns combined with the cries of gulls, a background music to their hastily conjured lunch. The restaurant's appearance failed to match the tour's promise of five-star luxury. The benches were solid wood, the tables covered with plastic, the stench of fish heavy in the embroidered wall-hangings. Their server was a woman with rough, raw hands and inquisitive eyes in a richly seamed face. She broke into a torrent of speech, gesticulating back and forth with Samira.

Moments later, the mystery of the restaurant's popularity was solved. Caviar was served with a foil of bread and garlic crackers. Its peaty taste cleaved to Rachel's tongue.

'Ambrosial,' Simon murmured beside her. He seemed to have forgotten her earlier rebuff. Either that or the renewal of his interest was meant to protect them both.

He applauded softly as the caviar was followed by a garlic-and-turmeric feast: *mirza ghasemi*, a blend of garlic, egg, and mashed eggplant; meatballs in walnut-and-pomegranate sauce called *fesenjan; shami Rashti* lentil-and-meat patties, garlic-flavored broad beans, and fried garlic leaves with eggs. The meal was served with heaps of rice, grilled tomatoes, Persian cucumbers, and a salty yogurt beverage known as *doogh*. Rachel helped herself to everything, scooping it onto bread fresh from a tandoor.

'Now what?' Simon asked when they'd finished. 'Tell me you're staying on the tour. Samira's taking us on a boat tour of the marsh.'

Rachel shook her head. 'I need to get back to the boardwalk.'

Simon frowned in warning.

'Samira is already suspicious of you. You need to come up with a more sensible plan.'

Rachel pondered this. Could she risk a few hours on the marsh? Khattak wouldn't be able to reach her, if he needed help. Seeing the worry on her face, Simon made a decision.

'Play along,' he said into her ear, moving much closer than Rachel felt comfortable with. A second later, he flung an arm over Rachel's shoulders, pulling her closer still.

He spoke to Samira fluently in Farsi. With a stiff smile pasted on her face, Rachel tried to interpret Samira's response. Simon tipped his head at Rachel, squeezing her shoulder. Samira said something in reply, and he nodded.

She didn't seem entirely pleased, but there was a sardonic glint of acceptance in her eyes.

Simon brushed Rachel's hair over one shoulder.

'What are you doing?' she muttered.

Simon murmured back, a smile dancing in his eyes.

'These kinds of public displays are not tolerated in Iran. But Samira seems quite jaded when it comes to tourists – she thinks them capable of anything.'

'So?'

Simon squeezed her shoulder again. 'I've told her we want to be alone – to take a lovers' stroll.'

Rachel's smile froze on her face.

'You can't come with me.'

'Well,' he said, nodding at the view of the Caspian Sea. 'It's a choice between the devil or the deep blue sea. She won't let you leave without me.'

Simon had outmaneuvered her. She didn't know what he'd said to Samira, but Rachel was effectively trapped.

When Samira had left with the others after dithering for a moment or two, Rachel turned on Simon.

'I need you to let me get on with my work.'

Simon coolly raised one brow. 'It's because of me you were able to stay behind. Haven't I earned the right to know what on earth you're doing?'

Rachel fixed him with a glare.

'I don't know who you are, and you don't know anything about me.'

'Apart from the fact that you have a rather hearty appetite? I think I'm beginning to suspect.' And at Rachel's sudden look of fear, he added, 'Look. I've told you, you can trust me. The British Commonwealth and so on. The Queen of England is your head of state.'

Whistling 'Rule, Britannia!' under his breath, he withdrew a copy of his passport from his satchel, together with letters of introduction to Iranian universities. They listed his credentials in detail. Reading them over, Rachel hesitated.

'You *could* help me if you don't mind working in the dark.'

'Tell me a little bit, at least.'

After another moment's quick debate with herself, Rachel removed her police ID from the inside pocket of her shirt. She presented it to Simon for a glimpse, before securing it back in her hidden pocket.

'You must have heard of the murder of Zahra Sobhani?' Simon's face went still. 'I can't say much, but that's why I've come. I need to find Barid Rud.'

It didn't take him long to make up his mind.

'All right,' he said. 'Let me do what I can to help.'

When Rachel parted from Simon to regroup with Khattak at the end of the day, neither of them had anything to report. He told her most of the boathouses he'd visited displayed a portrait of the fishing vessel's captain above the register. None of the portraits were of Barid Rud.

Rachel shared with him Simon's deconstruction of Barid Rud's name. Khattak seemed disheartened by the information.

'I didn't think of that,' he said. 'We're chasing shadows.'

'Should we keep at it?'

Khattak pulled out his phone. 'I'll ask Touka if the name means anything to her. And I'll ask Ali and Omid to search as well. Between them, they may be able to find something that narrows down our search. You should get back to your group. If you can slip away before your bus trip back to Tehran, we can catch up here in the morning.' He showed her a point on a map of the harbor. 'This is the last section I need to check on my end. It's mostly international cargo ships headed to ports in Kazakhstan or Russia.'

They agreed on the time and place for their meeting and parted ways.

Rounding the corner, Rachel bumped into Samira.

'I was worried about you,' she said. 'Where have you been, Miss Getty? And why did you come on this tour? You don't seem particularly interested in the sights.'

Completely unprepared for the encounter, Rachel's hand strayed to the neck of her shirt. As they fumbled over one of her shirt buttons, she had a sudden flash of inspiration. She shook her hair in front of her face, letting her loosely tied scarf fall away. The movement gave her a chance to undo two of her buttons. Her fingers pulled her neckline lower. She had no need to manufacture a blush.

'This tour has a reputation for discretion – that's why I chose your agency. I was hoping to make some friends here – friends like Simon.'

Rachel had never tried to portray herself as a woman on the make before. She hoped she was halfway convincing. Why hadn't she worn lipstick?

Samira flashed her a look of contempt. Her gaze strayed to Rachel's neckline.

'Button your shirt,' she snapped. 'Don't insult our customs.'

Rachel's embarrassment was very real.

'Yes, of course,' she said. And then laying the groundwork for her next misadventure: 'I promise to be more discreet.' She made her voice sound inquiring. 'I've heard Iranian men enjoy meeting women from other countries, is that true? Because if it is, I wouldn't mind a little extra time on my own.'

With a snort of derision, Samira walked away.

But she didn't refuse.

56

Interrogation

'If you confess, you'll go free.' They're laughing, slapping each other on the back. My rapist isn't there. He's been relocated to the general wing where the criminals are held. I don't have to see him or smell him. This is Nasreen's doing, Nasreen has gotten me out. 'What do you want me to say?' I ask. They've written it down, a scripted confession, a video camera on the desk. There's a bowl of pistachios on the table, they let me eat some, I lick the salt from my fingers. 'What happens after I read this?' Hogsbreath nods at the door. 'Joojeh will take you to the yard. Your family is waiting at the gates. But I warn you – if you recant, you'll be back here in no time, understand?' I assure them I won't recant. Slowly, haltingly, I read the confession aloud. I admit to being a Turkish conspirator, a Kurdish spy, an agent of ISIS, a member of the peshmerga, and other contradictory identities. I repent my collusion against the regime. I confess to disgusting forms of sexual deviance. I thank the warden for the nobility of his treatment, I promise to live a life of seclusion, and to never consider politics again. I condemn Mousavi and Karroubi as deceivers and false prophets, I condemn Zahra as a spy, my voice doesn't break, though the rest of me does.

I sign a bond to the effect that I'll pay for my term at Kahrizak – I learn that I've been here fifteen months. At the word 'fifteen,' I think of poor Piss-Pants, but I wipe him from my mind. It's spring in Shahr Ray, and I'll be free to celebrate Nowruz. The confession is signed, the camera switched off. Hogsbreath shakes my hand, so does his second-in-command. Joojeh appears at the door, I'm led down the wing of detainees, where I imagine I hear the cries of the ones still trapped. Step by step, I'm led down the stairs, past the desk to the crowded courtyard.

57

At the westernmost tip of the harbor, amidst a fleet of Russian ships, Khattak found the portrait of the man he was looking for, the man with a sty in his eye.

'I'm looking for a courier,' he said to the dockworker behind the registry, a heavyset man with Kazakh eyes, a sunburned face, and hands like boiled hams. Khattak nodded at the portrait behind the man's head.

'Barid Rud,' he went on. 'I'm told I can find him here.'

The dockworker wiped his blunt fists on his apron. He set them on the counter.

'What do you need to transport and where?'

He gave no name. His name tag identified him as Aruzhan. Khattak struggled to sort out his dialect.

'I prefer to discuss my business with him directly. Tell him, I can pay.'

Khattak looked around the boathouse. A framed photograph on one wall showed Rud standing beside a ship flying Russian and Iranian flags. Its name was the Caspian Rose. He found this oddly poetic.

'Come back in an hour.'

The dockworker returned to brewing his tea.

Khattak found himself a seat on a bench with full view of the entrance to the boathouse. He watched the waves lap at the shore, the silky current sweeping back and forth. There was a scent in the air specific to the Caspian: a tang of dead fire, a greasy salinity, the stink of fish underlined by the odor of oil. And all of it draped in humidity.

Khattak loved the smell. It reminded him of his first trip to the shores of the Caspian, on a road trip his parents had made through Asia. He'd been a child then, and the long, blue languor of the sea had stretched along a pristine shore, outlined by valleys of sand. Silvery-white shells had filled the entire expanse of Esa's vision. Holding his father's hand, he'd skipped along the shore collecting shells or diving for black rocks under the cover of the surf. He'd spelled his name on the sands of Anzali Harbor with the stones, chatting with the fishermen while kind-eyed women had smiled on his efforts and stroked his hair.

His long fascination with Iran had begun that day. He felt a pang of nostalgia at this return, absent the companionship of his father. The father who'd quoted Rumi and Hafiz and Mirza Ghalib, the last great poet of the Mughal empire, using language as a vehicle of grace.

The hour passed, he returned to the boathouse. This time the dockworker gave him a resentful glance and informed him Rud was late. He was told to try again an hour later.

Khattak returned to his bench. Barid Rud, the messenger of the sea, and undoubtedly the Darya-e Nur's courier, might have gotten wind of Esa's pursuit. He might have learned of Esa's purpose in tracking him down at the harbor. Perhaps the whole effort had been futile.

He consulted his phone. There was no new information from any member of the Green Birds. A message from Touka said cryptically: *Our bird's wings have been clipped.* He considered its possible meanings.

Droplets of rain dusted Esa's hair and fell on his shoulders. A white-haired man took up a seat beside Esa on the bench, dressed in a cashmere topcoat, the scarf at his throat wrapped with a casual elegance. The watch on his wrist was staggeringly expensive. A canary diamond gleamed from his buttonhole. It glittered like one of the Yellows.

'I hope I don't trouble you.'

His eyes were the blue of gentians. He spoke with a mild Russian accent and an air of colossal prestige.

It was not an accidental meeting.

'I admire your perseverance, Inspector Khattak, just as I admired Mrs. Najafi's. You're too late, I'm afraid, as she was. I suggest you return home, you and your partner, before you encounter any difficulties.'

The well-groomed man was in his seventies. His watchful face betrayed a calculated power, his authority absolute.

Khattak was not discomposed. He'd faced deadlier men in his time.

'May I know your name? As you're familiar with mine.'

'Alexei Mordashov, a name I trust you'll forget.'

Khattak doubted it was his real name. He took a shot in the dark, assembling the facts he'd learned about Mehran Najafi's connection to a man named Mordashov.

'I assume you're here because you've an interest in the Darya-e Nur. Perhaps you're the buyer who arranged its purchase.'

The Russian forbore to answer. His fingers tweaked his diamond-head pin. He gazed out over the waves of the Caspian, his hands clasped in his lap.

'Perhaps you've heard of the Orlov, Inspector.'

The emphasis on Esa's title was a threat. Khattak ignored the warning.

'Do you mean the Black Orlov or the diamond gifted to Catherine the Great by Count Orlov? A stone stolen from India, of course.'

Mordashov's smile was granite-edged. He pointed to the phone in Khattak's hand.

'The arc of history sweeps across the globe, as easily as you sweep your hand across your phone. I refer to the Orlov in Catherine's Imperial Scepter. It resides in the Kremlin's collection, or so most believe. It retains its original, exquisite rose-cut, a specialty of the Indians. I confess to a fondness for the riches of the Kollur mines.'

Khattak wasn't sure whether to believe the man. He knew great wealth in Russia bestowed a certain impunity. He didn't know if the impunity extended to a theft from Moscow's Diamond Fund, or more questionably, to a diamond of such historic significance. There was a rumor the fabled Orlov had once fallen from the head of Catherine the Great's scepter. The jeweler who'd restored it had failed to take its measurements. Was the idea of a theft of the Orlov any more impossible than the substitution of the Darya-e Nur? Esa attempted to find out.

'A theft of the Orlov would necessitate discretion, an unfortunate state of affairs for a collector unable to place his treasures on display.'

Something hardened in Mordashov's face.

'There are few among the general public who can discern the original from a facsimile. For a man in my position, it's enough that I know.'

He studied the harbor with a wintry gaze.

'I own dozens of transport ships, including the *Caspian Rose*. None of them holds a candle to the majesty of the Great Table Diamond. The Sea of Light will find a worthy home.'

It was the smallest of slips. It suggested the diamond hadn't changed hands yet, which meant the Darya-e Nur was still in Iran. If it was stolen before Zahra's murder, why hadn't it left Iran? Was the 'clipped bird' in Touka's message Radan? Was he unable to act? And why had Barid Rud been at Evin?

'Barid Rud works for you,' Khattak commented. 'An effective way to circumvent international customs.'

Mordashov gave a low chuckle.

'My ships are inspected where and when I wish them to be inspected. Don't trouble yourself with the details, Inspector.'

'Is that what Zahra Sobhani did? She troubled herself with details? Is that why she ended up dead?'

The Russian rose to his feet with aplomb.

'Of Mrs. Najafi, I will say only this. In her understandable concern for her daughter, she overplayed her hand. She thought she could trust her husband, her husband was a fool. I would have wished her outcome to have been as painless as Najafi's, circumstances prevented it.' He made a grimace of distaste. 'There is no elegance to Radan, the result you already know. Take my advice, Inspector. Take the first flight out of Iran. And take Sergeant Getty with you, while you still have that option.'

He made Khattak a formal bow. As he moved from the bench to the boardwalk, two bodyguards fell into step behind him. From the awkward fit of their jackets, both men were carrying arms.

Mordashov had confirmed Esa's suspicions. Zahra had hoped to use the theft of the Darya-e Nur as leverage against Radan. Her ex-husband had acted as Radan's middleman, arranging for the fabrication of the replica, arranging for a buyer. But when he'd confided his plans in Zahra, she'd persuaded him to blackmail Radan to free Roxana from prison.

The Russian, through his connection to Mehran, had known the exact moment when first Mehran, then Zahra, had become a danger to his plans. Whether he'd arranged for them both to be killed before the substitution of the diamond was exposed, or whether he'd simply whispered in Radan's ear, Khattak couldn't tell. The end result was the same.

Two lives taken, Roxana locked away for good.

But Mordashov didn't have the diamond yet. It must be why he was still in Iran. Zahra's meeting at the office of the Supreme Leader must mean Radan was being watched. He hadn't been able to arrange the transfer.

So where was the Darya-e Nur?

And why had Evin been the place where Zahra was killed?

He made a swift phone call to Touka, updating her on his findings. He was jolted by her response.

'Radan is on lockdown,' she confirmed. 'He hasn't been seen at his office or at Evin. For the last ten days, he hasn't made an appearance at an interrogation. But Larijani has been recalled to Tehran. He met with Radan at his house – he must be acting in his stead.' A hint of fear entered her voice. 'You should have left Tehran when you had the chance. You can't let Larijani find you at the harbor.'

Khattak's stomach dropped.

'Why would he look for me here?'

'He isn't looking for you. He's delivering the diamond for Radan. I told you he runs Radan's errands. I'm on his tail, he's in a car headed north.'

'He could be going anywhere.'

'I think he's headed to your Russian.'

Khattak scanned the line of Russian ships. The *Caspian Rose* loomed large in the foreground, its series of winches engaged in loading the ship's cargo. Orders were shouted down from the ship's top deck.

'Why would Mordashov give me the name of his ship? Why would he come himself, for that matter, if Barid Rud is his courier?'

Touka didn't answer right away. 'His passion to possess the stone has gotten the better of him, he wants to make sure Radan doesn't renege on the deal. If Mordashov is leaving on the *Caspian Rose* – maybe it has special clearance, maybe Barid's run these routes for Mordashov before. And maybe Barid is working for them both, playing both ends against the middle. I'm guessing there's no deal without his participation. You need to get back to that boathouse and check on the ship's departure time.'

'How will that help?'

'Because you need to intercept the transfer of the diamond.'

Khattak took a moment to think this through.

'You don't think it's best to inform the Iranian authorities?'

He listened to her sigh. 'How do we know who's involved in the theft and who isn't? Radan may have partners who helped him cover up the theft. And there's another more urgent consideration. If the Iranian authorities reclaim the stone on their own, we'll have nothing left to bargain with. Either for Roxana or for my purposes.'

Khattak saw the wisdom of her words. If he hoped to achieve anything for Roxana, he needed to prevent the transfer.

But what of Mordashov's armed gunmen? And Larijani's guards? If he factored them all in, his chances of intercepting the diamond were non-existent. He said as much to Touka.

'Larijani is coming on his own – Radan wouldn't risk the involvement of anyone else. I doubt Larijani even knows what he's delivering, or that he handles the money. It's probably done through wire transfer. You'll need to get the diamond after Larijani hands it over, but *before* Mordashov's men have the chance to get it on Mordashov's ship. He'll be there by eight this evening.'

Khattak couldn't imagine how to achieve this without causing an international incident. From that point on, his options would be bleak.

His next call was to Rachel to warn her of the risks. She refused to hear him out. She told him she'd meet him near the boathouse at seven. They had no weapons, they had no plan. And they had just a few hours to make one.

Rachel's tour group had been scheduled to return to Tehran at six o'clock. Rachel had used a hefty portion of the money Nate had given her to buy herself some extra time. She'd also paid for everyone's dinner at the most exclusive restaurant on the boardwalk. She'd promised to rejoin the tour group by ten.

She gave Samira a conspiratorial wink. She'd added lipstick and eyeliner to make her outing seem more probable. Her dangly earrings caught in her hair, her scarf well back on her head.

'You mentioned an underground club?'

Samira took the money. She tacked on a warning in a hard-bitten tone.

'My tour has a reputation for discretion. I insist that you remember that.'

She sounded more concerned with the viability of her business than with Rachel's safety, a fact she underlined by giving Rachel succinct directions to the club.

Rachel smiled. She was getting better at this.

'I'll keep my adventures to myself.'

As she made her escape, she was conscious of Simon's frown.

She found the boathouse at the dock in good time, glad to be rid of her companions. She'd participated in the tour without straying all day, earning a reprieve from Samira.

Now she was in her element, clad in black, her scarf pulled low over her forehead, her eagle eyes switching between the boathouse and the boardwalk, Khattak quiet at her side.

They'd found a good spot to spy on Barid Rud's boathouse at a floating restaurant that harbored a pair of speedboats. They waited at a window of the lime-green shack. The jeweler's binoculars would have come in handy.

'Look – there he is.'

In her excitement, she elbowed Khattak in the side. He grunted, peering through the window beside her.

'Barid Rud.'

The courier stepped out of the boathouse and made his way to the boardwalk. As Khattak had guessed, he was followed by Mordashov's men. There was no sign of Larijani. They scanned both sides of the boardwalk, a hand inside their jackets. Khattak had canvassed the *Caspian Rose*'s manifesto. The ship was scheduled to depart the harbor in fifteen minutes. Mordashov would already have boarded.

Barid Rud had left himself a small window to collect the

Darya-e Nur and drive his runabout out to the *Caspian Rose*. Rachel had checked out the runabout. It wasn't large enough for three people. It couldn't accommodate men the size of Mordashov's guards. How were they planning to get to Mordashov's ship?

Khattak showed her a boat docked fifty yards away. A passenger tender, larger than Barid's runabout, also named the *Caspian Rose*. She couldn't tell if there was anyone inside the cabin. The boat was dark, its lights switched off.

'Let's take cover on the boat,' she suggested. 'It's our best hope of dodging Larijani.'

Khattak agreed. They'd still have to face down Mordashov's men, but Larijani would no longer be a threat. And if they were out of the public eye, they stood a chance of catching Mordashov's men by surprise. Khattak weighed the risks. He took a moment to decide, then beckoned Rachel to follow.

Just as they were about to break cover, a car pulled up on the boardwalk. Larijani emerged from the car, a small black case in his hand. Mordashov's men approached him, reaching for the case. Rachel and Khattak ducked down from the shack's window. Cautiously, they peered through a gap in the tin frame.

Larijani held on to the case, taking a step back. He scouted the shore with a barked-out order to Barid. Barid Rud looked around. In response to Larijani's question, he shook his head. Larijani barked the same question to Mordashov's men. They didn't speak Farsi. Barid Rud repeated the question in Russian. All four men scouted the shore. One of Mordashov's men moved closer to the shack.

'We have to get out of here,' Rachel realized. 'I think they're looking for you.'

The only way through was to exit from the shack's other side, past the spot where the speedboats were docked. Khattak went first, Rachel ducking down behind him.

'There's no cover,' Rachel warned. 'They'll see us.'

'Hold on to these,' Khattak said. There were hooks on the outside wall of the shack, out of view of the boardwalk. Khattak used them to maneuver himself farther down the floating dock to the shore. Her palms slippery, Rachel followed. When the door of the shack banged open, Rachel and Khattak were gone.

They crept under the pier along the sand, staying low to the ground. They heard the sound of Mordashov's man trudging across the sand in the opposite direction. Startled by another sound, Rachel risked a glance over her shoulder.

Larijani was staring directly at Khattak.

Could he see them?

She froze in place, digging her elbow into Khattak's back. She threw herself over Khattak on the sand, the water lapping at their faces.

'Don't move,' she muttered.

They waited. The boardwalk was eerily quiet. A minute passed. Then another. And another. She didn't dare look back again.

And then she heard the sound of a car door. And the skittering of gravel as the car drove away.

Larijani had gone.

'Hurry,' Khattak whispered back to her. They moved at a furious pace, crawling on their elbows through the sand, listening for the approach of the others. An argument had broken out between them. Rachel didn't care. She had a face full of sand, but she'd reached the tender's berth.

The tender dipped as Khattak climbed aboard. He made his way portside to the cabin, where he vanished from Rachel's view. She saw movement in the cabin and waited. A minute later, he reappeared, giving her a signal. He kept his eye on the boardwalk as Rachel leapt aboard.

She followed Khattak's course. The wheelhouse was deserted, the cabin empty. The tender could have taken a dozen or more passengers. She looked around for a weapon or a place to hide.

They could duck behind the last row of seats in the cabin or take their chances in the wheelhouse. But the most they could do in the wheelhouse was take one man by surprise.

Rachel explored the lower deck.

'We can hide down here, sir. Chances are they'll stay up top.'

'We'd better wait for them to radio the cargo ship they're on their way.'

He worked his way through the ship's compartments. He pulled a toolbox out of stowage, helping himself to a hammer and the largest of four wrenches. He passed the hammer to Rachel. The boat dipped again. They climbed back to the upper deck, scouting their quarry from the windows. Rachel checked her watch. Ten minutes past eight. The cargo ship was preparing to depart. Where was Barid Rud? Why hadn't he reached the tender yet?

She spotted him on the boardwalk. He was hemmed in by Mordashov's men, the three men arguing over the case in Barid Rud's hands. Something in his manner or something at the scene tugged at her memory. She'd witnessed a similar scene before.

Rachel bit her lip. What if they went to the runabout instead?

But she'd guessed right about the guards. They were headed to the tender. They'd yielded the case to Barid, but were shepherding him between their massive bodies. Rachel looked doubtfully at the hammer.

Barid waved the case in the direction of the boat. Rachel and Khattak drew away from the cabin windows, ducking behind the last row of seats. Their hope was that all three men would head directly to the wheelhouse. They could follow them up the stairs, catching them by surprise. Beyond that, they were relying on their wits.

Rachel jumped. Voices from the pier rose in an angry exchange. The boat rocked to one side. Rachel's stomach lurched into her throat. She swallowed back her nausea. The voices were growing louder, quick staccato commands. An answer was grunted back.

Footsteps moved up the stairs to the wheelhouse. A moment later, the engines caught. The boat hummed under Rachel's feet. She heard the heavy fall of a rope being thrown. Khattak peered up at the stairs. He shook his head. They couldn't see anything.

The radio crackled to life. A disembodied voice offered a few words in Russian. Khattak nodded at Rachel. He was holding a smaller wrench in his left hand. He tossed it to the back of the cabin. The engines gunned, the boat moved out of its berth. Footsteps pounded the stairs.

Rachel and Khattak crouched in the shadows. She was counting. One man or two?

Whoever had come down the stairs was taking his time. Pausing halfway, he flipped on a light in the small alcove between the stairs and the entrance to the lower deck.

Rachel's hand was slippery on the hammer. Her blood thrummed in her ears. Khattak had whispered a Russian phrase to her, one he'd learned from his phone.

One of the guards stepped into the cabin.

Rachel blocked his path, tugging down her head scarf, the hammer behind her back.

In broken Russian she managed, 'Please, I'm a stowaway. I want to leave Iran.'

The man scowled at her in the dark. His gun drawn, he grabbed at Rachel's wrist.

Khattak smashed the heaviest wrench against the back of his head.

His mouth formed an *O*. He sank to his knees. He wasn't unconscious. Rachel knocked him out with the hammer. The gun slid out of his hand.

The second guard lunged from the stairs. His shot went wild as the boat veered into open water. Khattak scrambled for the gun on the deck. It went sliding under the row of seats, the passenger tender crashing into the waves. Rachel lost her balance. She fell heavily on her knees. Khattak charged past her, knocking the guard sideways. The impact of the collision winded both men. They fought furiously for control of the second Russian's gun.

The boat curved a wide arc to the east. Khattak stumbled out of the cabin and onto the causeway, where he lost his footing. The Russian lunged at him. They wrestled, but Khattak was no match for the other man's size and strength. Twisting the man's arm, he was sent sailing into the water, followed by the gun. Now the Russian turned to Rachel. She flung the hammer at his head. It missed by a mile, pitching into the water.

Barid called down from the wheelhouse. The Russian shouted back. Rachel's frantic thought was for the radio. The Russian grabbed her by the shoulders, lifting her off her feet and shaking her like a doll. One large hand fastened on her throat and squeezed.

Her eyes rolled back in her head, her body went limp. She had a moment to realize she was going to suffocate before he tossed her body into the sea. She scrabbled weakly at his grip, his fingers gouged her throat. A mist of red rose behind her eyes, capillaries bursting with blood.

A noise clanged against her temples. The world went briefly black.

The punishing grip came loose, the Russian falling face down with a thud.

Rachel gasped for air, blood pounding in her ears. She blinked salt spray from her eyes, a man's silhouette appearing between the outline of the waves and the glare of the open lightbulb. The passenger boat picked up speed, the man's face swung into view.

It was Simon Graves, grinning at her in the dark. He held up a fire extinguisher in one hand. He used it to break the bulb. He jerked his head at the stairs.

'Can't have him seeing what we're up to.'

'Simon?' Rachel wiped a hand over her face. 'Simon, thank God! Look for my partner in the water!'

She dived back into the cabin, searching for the missing

gun. How far out was the cargo ship? Five minutes? Two? She scrambled under the seats until she felt a solid weight. The gun wavered in her hands. Her vision was still blurry. She took the cabin stairs two at a time, launching herself into the wheelhouse. Barid Rud turned to face her. His left eye was cloudy.

He wasn't armed. He reached for the cabin radio.

Rachel lifted her chin and aimed the gun at his chest. He held up his hands, his dark eyes watchful.

'Cut the engine,' she told him. 'I'm an excellent shot.'

He did as she said. The engine sputtered into silence. They were halfway to the platform where the *Caspian Rose* was docked. There wasn't much time before Mordashov figured out their boat had changed course.

'Simon, get up here.'

She knew Khattak could swim.

Simon hovered at her elbow.

'Can you get us back to shore?'

'I'm no expert, but I think so.'

'No time for caution, hold the gun.'

There was a loop of rope hanging from a hook in the wheelhouse. Rachel used it to tie Barid Rud's arms and legs. He swore at her in a guttural Farsi. She knocked him to his knees, taking the gun back from Simon. He switched on the engine, setting a course for the dock.

'I see him!' he shouted.

Rachel careened down the stairs. Simon had switched on the headlights. Khattak's white face loomed up against the waves.

'We're coming!'

She tossed him the life preserver she'd found beneath the gunwale. He raised his hand in weary acknowledgment. Five minutes passed before she was dragging him out of the sea. He coughed vigorously, water dribbling down his chin. Rachel found him a blanket in the cabin.

'Come up to the wheelhouse when you can.'

She checked on Barid and Simon, desperately grateful that Simon had risked following her. They were minutes from the dock. Mordashov's men were still out. Maybe for ten minutes, maybe for the night, she didn't have time to check. She scanned the wheelhouse for the case.

It was sitting on the dashboard above the wheel, a hard black case the size of an electronic tablet, square and sleek.

Rachel reached for the case behind the wheel. Barid began to swear.

'What's in it?' Simon asked her. He cut his speed as they neared the dock.

'You wouldn't believe me if I told you.'

Khattak lumbered up the stairs wearing the woolen blanket like a cape.

Barid Rud let out a stream of Farsi. Khattak answered him in English.

'I wouldn't worry about your money or Radan. But I'd get out of Iran if I were you.' He turned to Rachel. 'Is that it?'

There was an electronic lock on the case. Rachel demanded the combination. Barid Rud supplied it at the business end of her gun. Holding her breath, Rachel punched in the numbers. The clasps of the case flicked open.

A pink fire flared in the dim light of the wheelhouse.

They'd found the Darya-e Nur.

58

The day before Nowruz, snow tinseled the streets of Tehran, the rooftops sheathed with a coating of ice. A faltering bonfire gave a paltry warmth to the group huddled in the courtyard of the Hotel Shah Nameh. Except for their party, the courtyard was deserted.

Rachel drank her tea, listening and observing, as Khattak narrated their adventures at the Caspian to an attentive group of listeners: three handsome young men, and two women, one with a mischievous face, the other with an aura of abject misery, who could hardly stir herself to attend to Khattak's recital.

They had turned the Darya-e Nur over to Touka Swan. In the aftermath of a carefully worded phone call, Touka had been invited to escort Maryam Ghorbani to the office of the Supreme Leader. There, a quiet and desperate negotiation had taken place. Threats were made, concessions offered. Barsam Radan was under arrest, his trial pending. The following morning, Touka had driven Maryam to the gates of Evin. After a morning of additional negotiations, Roxana Najafi had been released to her family's care. All three women had wept.

Touka Swan had left the country the same night.

Rachel and Esa were leaving for Toronto on the afternoon flight from Tehran. The sense of danger that had hung like a pall over Esa's visit to Tehran had vanished. Touka had made her dossier of events available to the representative of the Supreme Leader. She had advised him that copies of the dossier would be given to the international press in the event of a move against persons whose interests she represented. She didn't name names, but they both knew she meant the Green Birds.

According to Touka's account of the meeting, the resumption of diplomatic relations between Canada and Iran was something desired by both sides. Iran's government wished to return to the community of nations – its treatment of political prisoners wouldn't change, but it was prepared to sacrifice Radan to move relations forward. Talk of the opening of the Canadian embassy had reignited, and Touka's masters were pleased.

And Touka had made one final, non-negotiable request in exchange for the unpublicized return of the Darya-e Nur.

Rachel was still coming to terms with the fact she'd held one of the world's most famous diamonds in her hand. She'd felt the weight of the stone's history in her palm, glowing with an arcane fire.

The Green Birds were enthralled by Khattak's story. Though Nasreen hadn't spoken, her lambent eyes were fixed on his face. Her black-and-white scarf had fallen away, a trail of swallows flitting down her shoulder.

Rachel frowned.

She was thinking of the case that had held the Darya-e Nur, the sense of déjà vu it had occasioned. She scrolled through the photographs on her phone, half her attention on Khattak's recital. She studied the prison gatehouse, the camera straps at Zahra's neck, Zahra's hands reaching for someone.

Rachel paused at the photograph of Barid Rud, on the hill outside the prison. His eyes were searching for someone in the crowd. Rachel scrolled through the photographs again. The crowd was mostly women in black chadors. A young man supported an elderly woman. And there in the background, a bearded man with a shadowed face not far from Barid Rud. Barid's eyes weren't on the man with the beard. They were on the case in his hands.

Had Barsam Radan arranged the transfer of the Darya-e Nur

on the very day Zahra Sobhani had decided to visit Evin? If so, it was an improbable coincidence.

Why hand the stone over at Evin, instead of a handoff shrouded in secrecy?

Was it, in fact, the same case?

She slipped away to another table, pulling up the photographs on the larger screen of her laptop, conscious of Khattak's eyes on her back.

The full-size photograph made it clear. It was the same case they'd found on the *Caspian Rose*: the coincidence beggared belief.

She motioned Khattak to join her.

He looked lighter and fresher than she'd seen him in weeks. Restored to himself, ready for the challenges ahead. He leaned down to study the photograph on the screen.

'Why, sir?'

He moved his fingers on the laptop's touchpad, running Zahra's photographs as a slideshow. The sequence told a story. It told them Zahra hadn't been at Evin to demand the release of Roxana. She'd been there to photograph the transfer of the diamond. If a handoff had been attempted, she'd missed it, but she'd photographed the parties involved: Barid, Radan, and the man with the case. Khattak couldn't see his face, but he guessed the man was Larijani.

He lingered over a photograph he hadn't studied as closely, the one of Zahra's car.

Rachel saw it, too. The driver's door was ajar in this photograph, but closed in the others. Khattak flicked through the slideshow again.

His hand balled into a fist.

Rachel looked up at him.

His face had lost its color.

'I think I know,' he said to Rachel. 'I think I know why Zahra was there. Could you distract the others?'

Rachel nodded. She moved to the other table.

'Nasreen,' Khattak called. 'Will you take a look at this for me?'

He'd examined the photographs piecemeal, over brief periods of time. Seeing them with fresh eyes, with the knowledge of who Barid Rud was, the photographs told a story. Radan's presence at Evin, Barid looking for the man with the case, the letters Zahra had written on her sleeve, the case itself.

And the woman in the head scarf bordered by a flight of birds.

Esa's hands were clammy, he felt perceptibly ill.

He remembered a dark night in the woods in winter, and how long it had taken him to arrive at a decision, seconds strung like particles falling through infinite space.

He showed Nasreen the photograph.

'You were with Zahra at Evin, you drove her there.'

Nasreen let her scarf fall to the ground. Khattak stooped to collect it. It was the same scarf she'd worn in the photograph, its tail end captured by the lens.

'You told me you were closest to Zahra, you were the one she talked to.'

'Because of Saneh.' Her voice was expressionless. 'He was the subject of her second film. It surprised me.' She touched fingers that looked cold to her brow. 'She could spare as much passion and energy for Saneh in Kahrizak as she could for Roxana in Evin.'

She reached over and deleted the photograph from Rachel's laptop.

'No one was meant to know.'

'No?' Khattak's lips were stiff. 'Then why write me the letters?'

Her smile was bleak. 'You said the letters were from Roxana.'

'That's what you wanted me to think. But how could Roxana have shadowed me in Esfahan? I suppose I knew she couldn't have.' He didn't wait for an answer. 'Why was Zahra at Evin that day?'

Taraneh glanced over at them from the other table. She made a move to rise, Rachel stopped her.

'Tell me,' Khattak said. He brought the force of his personality to bear, advancing his face to within inches of hers.

A muscle beside her eye twitched. Her face was filled with secret knowledge.

'Zahra knew Mehran was involved in the plan to steal the Darya-e Nur. Radan got the idea from the rumor about the Mossadegh letters. He knew he could use Mehran's shipping business and his connections in Canada. He pressured Mehran to arrange the substitution and find him a buyer. Apparently, Mehran had mentioned a man named Mordashov many times. He had regular dealings with him. So Zahra told Mehran to go ahead with Radan's plan. She thought they could turn the tables on Radan, using the theft to ensure Roxana's freedom. She was certain it would work, and she was right.'

'It didn't turn out that way. Zahra was murdered at Evin.'

'I know that.' Nasreen's breath came out in little puffs. 'Radan was suspicious of Zahra's return. He knew Mehran would be influenced by her, so he had them followed. When she traveled to Shiraz, it became clear she knew Radan's plan.'

'So Radan had her killed to pre-empt her? Why not release Roxana to buy her silence?'

'He knew it wouldn't end there, Zahra wouldn't stop. She'd have used her leverage to free others.'

She was telling him Radan's thoughts with an insider's knowledge of them.

'Zahra had a card to play, she didn't need to go to Evin – why did you take her there?'

In the icy light of the morning, Nasreen's face was rigid with strain.

'Radan came to me.' She fluttered a hand at the others. 'We've been under surveillance since the election. When Zahra sought us out, he kept all of us under watch. I was vulnerable because of Saneh – he used my brother against me.'

Horror rose at the back of Khattak's throat.

'I tried to use him, too. He wanted Zahra at Evin under any pretext. He needed to discredit her before she could expose him. That's what he told me he would do.'

'How would going to Evin discredit her?'

'Zahra was always careful. She went through appropriate channels to secure the release of detainees. Even for Roxana, she worked within the system.' She shook her head sadly. 'She was too well-known for Radan to detain her without cause. And other branches of the regime were watching her – they would demand to know why Radan had provoked an incident at such a critical moment in Iran's international relations. But if Zahra crossed the regime's red lines – if she was caught taking photographs of Evin – Radan would have had a legitimate excuse.'

'Why did shutting Zahra down matter so much to Radan? A rumor of the theft was just a rumor. She couldn't prove it.'

Nasreen looked down at her hands. 'You know how corrupt this system is. Everyone is looking for a chance to climb up on someone else's back. Radan has many enemies – they'd be only too happy to bring him down. The theft of the Darya-e Nur would be just the ammunition they needed.'

'So you persuaded Zahra to go to Evin. You took her there. You were working with Radan from the first.' The words formed like rust in his mouth.

'I persuaded *Radan*. I told him Zahra would only come to Evin if he transferred the diamond right outside its gates. And he would have to find a way to leak the news of the transfer to Zahra. She would have her proof, she'd be willing to take the risk.' Her words were despairing. 'I needed those photographs just as much as Zahra did. I needed a way out from under Radan's thumb. I convinced myself I could do both – arrange to photograph the transfer, and somehow keep Zahra safe.'

Khattak's face became grim.

'It was criminally naïve to believe Radan would go along with your plan. He could have faked the transfer – he didn't need to bring the Darya-e Nur.'

'He did. Mehran had told Zahra the names of the parties involved. If she didn't see them at Evin, she wouldn't have gotten out of the car. And Barid wouldn't have come for anything less than the diamond. Zahra was prepared, in any case.'

She meant the writing on Zahra's sleeve, Khattak thought. The initials directing them to the Darya-e Nur.

'She didn't trust you to follow the trail of the diamond if she was arrested?'

Nasreen's eyes filled with tears. They streaked her cheeks with a misty precision.

'She trusted me. She feared I might be arrested as well. So she told me to stay in the car. The letters on her sleeve were for the security camera. She knew they'd be passed on to the Greens. When the guards came, she ripped them from her cuff to protect herself.'

Khattak's response was harsh.

'You must know you sent her to her death.'

Nasreen's voice was hollow. 'Once she'd taken the photographs she needed, I meant to pull her from the crowd.' She met Khattak's gaze without evasion. 'But I always knew Radan would reach her first.'

Khattak's face was ashen.

'Then why do it? Why betray her to Radan?'

Nasreen's lips formed the rictus of a corpse.

'He showed me a video of my brother's torture. I still hear the screams in my sleep.'

Khattak had difficulty speaking. His thoughts were filled with a retrospective rage at the futility of Zahra's death. She had always been headed to this moment. Her life's work, her unfaltering purpose – always destined for this.

And Roxana, the Green Birds, the starred students, Saneh Ardalan, the prisoners of conscience held around the world, their lives sacrificed on the altars of false gods –

A few miles from where he took tea in a courtyard, screams sounded against the walls of a prison, darkening the skies. A graveyard scarred the hills, witness to the truth.

Khattak knew of no way to measure these realities, or to grapple with their contrasts. He felt an unbearable pity for Nasreen, even as he felt the weight of judgment. Unsure of what he was offering, he touched her wrist with his hand.

Her natural warmth had deserted her. Her face was a death mask, the wraith-like smile sketched on her lips, her head bowed in prayer, her fingers like claws against her throat.

'Why did you write me the letters? If you were playing Radan's game, why did you lead me to the truth?'

'Zahra once said only our hands could pull back the curtains on the truth. I had to do something to honor that.'

Nasreen dug her fingers deep into her neck, raising crescent-shaped indentations with her nails. Khattak gave an inarticulate cry.

'Don't,' he said. 'Don't.'

She didn't listen.

'When Radan arrested Zahra at Evin, Barid lost his nerve. He thought he'd been photographed on Radan's orders – he thought it was a double-cross. He didn't wait for the transfer, he left without the diamond, and that gave me a chance to set things right – to redeem something for Zahra and myself. I wrote the letters to send you after the diamond. I wrote them in such a way that even if Radan found them, he wouldn't guess it was me. He wouldn't know what I was doing. I *wanted* you to bring him down. I'm good at treachery it seems.'

There was nothing Khattak could say to this. Zahra's life or

Saneh's – it was a terrible, poisonous choice. As he'd once had to weigh Rachel's life against his sister's.

'Do the others know? Weren't you putting them at risk, too?' He gestured at the Green Birds.

She avoided a direct answer, saying instead, 'Do you remember seeing the word *Allah* on Omid's wall? Didn't you take a picture of it?'

He nodded. It was among the images Rachel had sent back to him. He found it after a moment's search.

'Look at it again.'

Khattak studied what he'd read as Arabic letters. He allowed his vision to cloud.

She'd written in the Arabic style, but the word she'd written in English was *RUN*.

59

The Gallows

They were never going to set me free, though Nasreen must have tried. She's my twin. I've felt her agony every hour, every minute at Kahrizak. Each time I bled, she bled. Each time I cried, she wept, like Joojeh is weeping now. As he blindfolds me, I tell myself he didn't know. He's a kind man, and Kahrizak exercises its cruelties on guards as well as inmates.

The rope is rough, the blindfold steeped in tears. They've rustled up a cleric from somewhere – the ubiquitous cleric of Kahrizak. My hands are bound or I'd wave him away, I don't need his pious hypocrisy. I know what Hossein stood for, they can't lie to me about him.

It's my last chance to speak, so I do.

My name is Saneh Ardalan.

I'm singing Roxana's song.

60

Khattak and Rachel walked the group of students down to the lobby, Nasreen silent at their heels. Rachel watched as Khattak embraced Omid, Ali, and Darius. He reminded them to be careful, they thanked him on Zahra's behalf. Rachel had found the young men serious and dedicated. They'd asked questions about the Darya-e Nur, a touching wonder in their eyes. Each wished he could have held the diamond for a moment.

Taraneh offered a caustic comment.

'So you're puckface48. I was expecting someone more glamorous.'

Rachel laughed. 'With a name like that? You shouldn't have been expecting anyone but me.'

Taraneh spared her a reluctant smile. She nodded over at Esa.

'You're lucky you get to work with him every day.'

Rachel's response was droll.

'You're lucky you got to work with him here.'

They met a welcoming committee at the airport. Vicky D'Souza, Nathan Clare, and surprisingly, Sehr Ghilzai. Vicky immediately struck up a flirtation with Khattak. He was hard-pressed not to respond. He enjoyed the obvious pleasure Vicky took in it.

He thanked her for her discretion, and for her efforts with the case.

'I didn't offer my services for free,' she warned him. She sauntered over to Nate. 'He's promised to get up close and personal on prime time. And then there's the little matter of an exclusive from you, Inspector.'

Nate blinked at Rachel with something like terror. To her surprise, he hugged her fiercely at the gate.

'You're back safely, thank God,' he murmured.

'And Zach's okay?' was the first thing she asked in reply.

His hands slid away from her shoulders, disappointment in his face.

'He's fine. You'll find him back at your place.'

Relieved, Rachel hugged him back.

'Thanks,' she said. 'It means a lot that I could count on you.'

Nate held her gaze for a moment, his eyes quietly expressive.

They found a restaurant near the airport and traded stories over dinner. Vicky studied Rachel with something like awe.

'So who was this man, Alexei Mordashov? How did he figure into Barsam Radan's plans?'

Khattak answered for Rachel. 'He claimed he was a collector, I asked Touka to send me some information on his background. Your research will probably turn up more. He's enormously wealthy – he represents Russian oil interests. And he's rumored to have quite a collection of illegal artifacts and gems. His connection was to Mehran Najafi, through Mehran's export business.'

Vicky's eyes widened. 'That's right. Wasn't Mehran exporting caviar?'

'And other less respectable things. There may have been more than one reason Mehran kept ending up in prison. Rachel, do you remember telling me that Max Najafi mentioned Mehran's frequent travels to Neyshabur – the birthplace of Omar Khayyam?'

Rachel nodded, as the others listened, rapt.

'Mehran was selling Persian antiquities from the Neyshabur archaeological dig. Brokering the sale of the Darya-e Nur wasn't that much of a stretch from there.'

Vicky had slipped out her notebook.

'What else can you tell me about Mordashov?'

'My own impression? He's an untouchable Russian oligarch – he's beyond the reach of the law. And from what I know of such men, this won't be his only line of business.'

Vicky scribbled furiously.

'What are you thinking? Arms dealing? Sex trafficking?'

Khattak studied her gravely. 'That's for you to find out.'

Blushing a little, she chewed on the tip of her Hello Kitty pencil. Then she turned to Rachel.

'You actually held the Darya-e Nur – tell us, what's it like?'

Rachel hesitated, choosing her words.

'It was gorgeous, Tavernier had that part right.' She took a breath, not wanting to sound sentimental. 'But compared to Zahra Sobhani? I'm sorry, I found it meaningless.'

She was depleted of energy, eager to get back to Zach. Mordashov and the diamond thoroughly dissected, their party broke up shortly after.

She saw Sehr pull Khattak aside, holding up a message on her phone for him to read. His eyes were patient on Sehr's face. Then his expression changed. To Rachel's immense surprise, he took Sehr by the arms, touching his forehead to hers.

'Thank you,' he said. 'Thank you for your part in this.'

A smile of wonder broke over Sehr's face.

Rachel squinted to read the message on Sehr's phone. It had been sent by Touka Swan.

Zahra's body had been disinterred from its burial place in the graveyard of the martyrs.

Touka had sent Zahra home.

Author's Note

The political events of this book are based upon the disputed 2009 presidential election in Iran, and the immediate aftermath of that election. To that end, I conflated specific incidents related to the protests and the mass arrest of protesters in 2009 with current events inside Iran. It should be noted that a subsequent presidential election was held in Iran in 2013, and that the 2013 election was won by the pragmatist reformist candidate Hassan Rouhani. The results of the 2013 presidential election were not contested, and though this was not a free election, it was generally considered fair by the Iranian people. The 2009 slogan 'Where is my vote?' was not reiterated in 2013. In addition, the severe repression, murder, and detention of protesters, and the widespread torture and sexual assault of political prisoners at Evin and Kahrizak prisons, were not repeated after the 2013 election. This is not to say that political repression inside Iran has been alleviated, or that there is currently a possibility for the resurgence of the Green Movement.

Green Movement leaders Mir Hossein Mousavi, Zahra Rahnavard, and Mehdi Karroubi remain under house arrest at the time of writing: they have now been detained five years. As of March 2016, there were 820 political prisoners detained in Iranian prisons. Their ranks include students, journalists, human rights activists, artists, labor activists, bloggers, and members of religious and ethnic minorities. Psychological and physical torture remain a staple of the treatment of political prisoners, including extended periods of solitary confinement.

Because of widespread fear that is actively encouraged by the security services, the number of actual political prisoners may be underreported. In addition, many of Iran's most prominent dissidents are in exile, including Nobel Laureate Shirin Ebadi, journalist Akbar Ganji, and theologian Mohsen Kadivar. Dual citizens return to Iran increasingly at their peril, while many choose self-imposed exile.

Reports from the UN Special Rapporteur on Human Rights in Iran are not encouraging. Dr. Ahmed Shaheed notes the following: Iran is in the process of drafting legislation to expand 'state influence over the legal community, media, and civil society organizations,' and these laws and practices continue to operate to the great detriment of civil society activists, precluding fair trials, due process, or accountability. The *Islamic Penal Code* in Iran is used to justify serious human rights violations by the judiciary and other officials. The penal code also criminalizes 'the peaceful exercise of fundamental rights,' for which the penalties are extreme. (See Paragraphs 3–4, and 63–72 of the *Report of the Special Rapporteur on the Situation of Human Rights in the Islamic Republic of Iran*, March 10, 2016, *A/* HRC/31/69.)

But there exists a parallel reality as well: civil society groups are well-entrenched, the literacy and education rates in the country remain high, and Iran has a vigorous, well-informed (though heavily censored) press and populace, with a strong tradition of grassroots activism. These groups give expression to a vibrant and resilient artistic, intellectual, and religious heritage: perhaps nowhere in the Muslim world has Islam's religious tradition been as thoroughly interrogated and explicated as inside Iran, with a multiplicity of views and many progressive interpretations emerging into the public sphere. More promisingly still, Iran has a century-old tradition of democratic struggle dating back to the Constitutional Revolution of 1906, resurfacing in the 1950s with Mossadegh, again in the early days of the 1979 Revolution, and most recently with the Green Movement in 2009. As a result, Iran has developed an astonishingly sophisticated political philosophical tradition that is little known or appreciated outside the country. And there are other factors to consider: Iran's sizable youth population is highly educated, increasingly globalized, and politically secular, all of which bode well for the country's future, despite the grim human rights picture.

Two other notes on historical events described in this novel: though the private correspondence of Mohammad Mossadegh and Dariush Forouhar did exist, the letters disappeared on the day of the Forouhars' tragic murder. To my knowledge, there was no mention of the Iranian Yellows in this correspondence: this is a fiction I invented. And while the Iranian Crown Jewels are real and exactly as described in this novel, a private exhibit of items from the national treasury has never been arranged, nor was a theft of the Darya-e Nur ever attempted. The Darya-e Nur and the Kohinoor/Koh-e Nur (The Sea of Light and the Mountain of Light) are two magnificent sister-stones that reputedly decorated the armlets of a Mughal emperor – a legend that embellishes the very real diamonds. I should also mention that the Orlov Diamond in Catherine the Great's scepter is the original stone.

Finally, the murder of Zahra Sobhani in this book was inspired by the real-life murder of Canadian-Iranian photojournalist Zahra Kazemi in July 2003. Zahra Kazemi was arrested by the regime for taking photographs outside Evin. In September 2016, Tehran's former Prosecutor-General, Saeed Mortazavi, publicly apologized for the deaths of political prisoners at Kahrizak in 2009. In a public letter, he asked the families of the victims for forgiveness for his role in these deaths. Responding to Mortazavi's confession, an outspoken member of Iran's parliament, Ali Motahari, insisted that Mortazavi's apology would only have merit if Mortazavi also revealed the role he'd played in the murder of Zahra Kazemi, and if he named *all* the parties involved in her murder. As of yet, no one has been held accountable for Zahra Kazemi's death.

Recommended Reading

There is a vast and daunting body of scholarship on Iran's politics, history, and religious tradition, but a few books that stand out for me are: Laura Secor's *Children of Paradise: The Struggle for the Soul of Iran*, Christopher de Bellaigue's *In the Rose Garden of the Martyrs: A Memoir*, Ervand Abrahamian's *A History of Modern Iran*, Nikki R. Keddie's *Modern Iran: Roots and Results of Revolution*, Amir and Khalil's *Zahra's Paradise*, and Omid Memarian's *Sketches of Iran: A Glimpse from the Front Lines of Human Rights*. I also recommend the United States Institute for Peace Iran Primer website (http://iranprimer.usip.org), and Robin Wright's deeply insightful articles on Iran in *The New Yorker*. For a comprehensive account of the rise of the Green Movement, there is *The People Reloaded: The Green Movement and the Struggle for Iran's Future*, eds. Nader Hashemi and Danny Postel. And for a fascinating history of Iran's national treasury, see *Crown Jewels of Iran*, by V. B. Meen and A. D. Tushingham.

Acknowledgments

With gratitude to my father, whose voice I miss, and my mother, whose voice is always with me. Though all I remember is seashells by the Caspian Sea, thank you for that drive from England to Pakistan, and for your wonderful stories of Iran.

Thank you to my amazingly supportive siblings, Ayesha, Irfan, and Kashie – wildly worthy doers of good, nurturers of dreams, and indispensable, lifelong companions. I think it's time to say it: 'This should please our mother.' Thank you to my many irreplaceable sisters for your love and unstinting support: Hema, Furby, Farah, Cake Pop Irmy, Haseeba, Uzmi, Yasmin, Semina, and Nozzie. Thank you to Ayesha and Nozzie especially for providing the early design of the 'Run' image, on short and demanding notice. And to all my family and friends for the myriad ways you've encouraged me and spread the word about my books. Thank you to the great kids in my life who can be prevailed upon to attend book launches even in the dead of winter (Rachel especially thanks you). And thank you to Uncle Munir and Auntie Aira.

Thank you, Elizabeth, for being such a wise, brilliant, and helpful editor, and for letting me tell these stories. In these troubling times, your encouragement and support offer so much hope. Thank you also to Kelley, Hector, Brendan, David, Allison, and everyone at SMP and Minotaur Books for your inspired and dedicated work on behalf of this series.

Thank you to Danielle Burby and to everyone at HSG for buoying up my dreams with such clear-headed clarity and commitment. Danielle: you give your heart and soul to my books, and I couldn't be more grateful for your faith. Thank you, Tanusri, for a thoroughly enjoyable discussion of Indian movies – and for all your incredible work. I don't know how you understand those contracts, but I'm grateful that you do. Thank you, Dylan, for keeping your kind and clever eye on my website.

Thank you to Jamie, Fleur, and Laurie at Raincoast Books, and to Dan for such wonderful support of my books in Canada, and for many enlivening conversations about books and politics. Thank you, Ben McNally, for hosting me at your beautiful bookstore in Toronto. And for the invigorating experience of Books & Brunch.

Thank you to my fellow writers who offer such generous encouragement: Mark Stevens, you are in a class by yourself. Every writer should have a friend like you. Hilary Davidson, thank you for being so thoroughly wonderful to newly published writers, I'm so very grateful! Thank you to Hank Phillippi Ryan for so much encouragement. Thank you to Marian Misters and the Crime Writers of Canada, and to Carol Stacy and *RT Book Reviews* for honoring *The Unquiet Dead*. Thank you also so much to Mystery Readers International, George Easter and *Deadly Pleasures Mystery Magazine*, and *Mystery Scene Magazine*. Nadine, Mimi, and Nikki, thank you for your kindness – I'm so delighted by your books! Thank you to Marni Graff, my very kind friend and an early believer in this series. And thank you to Len Vlahos at the Tattered Cover for featuring *The Language of Secrets*, and for sharing your incredible work with me.

Warmest thanks to Cat Acree, Azra Agic, Professor Ahmet A., Asian American Literature Fans, Reza Aslan as always, Julie Barlow, Bearpond Books, Brian Bethune, the wonderful ladies of Bibliobroads, Michelle Bosu (I miss you – that's a big ocean to cross!), Dottie Brenner, Sue Carter, Lisa Casper, the very kind Oline Cogdill, Michael D'Souza, the lovely and charming Angela Dover for so many things (Frances!), Amira El-Ghawaby,

Saadia Faruqi for buoying me up, Barbara Fister, Peter Ganim, Ihsaan Gardee, Sarah Harvey for such encouragement, Steve Hockensmith, Jilliane Hoffman, Nur Nasreen Ibrahim, Arif and Nausheen Khan, Barbara Khan at Baer Books, Nora Krug, Owen Laukkanen for such kindness, Owen and Linda L. Richards for a great panel, Jennie Lay, Hind Makki, Carol Memmott, Vick Mickunas, Soraya M., Sahar Mustafah, the lovely Joann Oh, Sumathi Pundit, the late Colleen O'Connor, whose voice will be missed, Glen P. Sherman, Sadaf Siddique, Amanda Skelton, the very kind Robin Stevenson, Art Taylor, Sarah Tranum, Asma Uddin, Stacy Verdick Case, Paula L. Woods, and especially to Jenn Northington and Amanda Nelson at Book Riot.

Thank you to Irene Lau, a kindred spirit, and to the wonderful Lonnie Propas for inviting me to the Cuffed Festival. My deepest appreciation to all the readers who regularly interact with me on Facebook and Twitter with such informative and enthusiastic feedback. Thank you to the book clubs which host me, and the wonderful women behind them. Thank you to the chapters of the American Association of University Women who invite me to speak. Thank you especially to Tabassum Siddiqui, who so warmly helped me share my point of view on 'q' with the lovely Piya Chattopadhyay (Tab was also my fabulous partner in crime at MGM), and to the amazing Shelagh Rogers at CBC Radio for a fantastic interview.

Thank you to the incredibly talented Saladin Ahmed for reading my books, and for your kindness and generosity in encouraging your thousands of followers to do so, as well. (If you're not following Saladin on Twitter or haven't read *Throne of the Crescent Moon*, you don't know what you're missing.)

Thank you to the lovely and talented writers' group in Toronto: Sajidah, Uzma, and Rania – I can't wait for your books and stories! There's a romantic comedy in my immediate future, right?

Thank you to Tony and Craig for being such wonderful

neighbors, and to Jonas and Cati for so generously allowing the sheer magic of Shiloh and Gordy into our lives.

Thank you to Quincy Drinker for so many frank and fruitful discussions about the representation of communities of color in fiction. I love talking about books with you. Keep writing, my friend, your voice matters.

Thank you to RJ and Janice Rosa, who not only take such excellent care of my brother, but who are also so kind to me. Jan, I'm in awe of your intellect and compassion, and am deeply grateful for the mentorship of such a distinguished luminary of the law. Thank you also to *all* of Irfan and Uzma's friends for such kind and enthusiastic interest. (And for making the trek from Buffalo. In winter.)

Thank you to Richard Doughty for featuring me in a publication I've admired for as long as I can remember, and for telling so many enchanting stories about the Islamic civilization. And thank you to Piney Kesting for such a stimulating discussion of art, history, and culture.

Thank you to Ian Iqbal Rashid and Jennifer Kawaja for writing me the kindest, most meaningful letter on my books I've ever read. And thank you to everyone at Allison Shearmur Productions, especially Allison Shearmur and Lillah McCarthy, for taking a chance on these books, no matter how our journey turns out.

On Iran

My deepest gratitude to M for such a generous and emotional discussion of Iran's past, present, and future, and for reliving the protests and the arrest for the sake of this book. Thank you to M for speaking so candidly about those frantic hours, for describing the Sonata – and for the desolation and hope you spoke of so eloquently. So many of your words made it into this book.

Thank you to the beautiful and much-loved N for your

invaluable research on the murder of Zahra Kazemi, may God grant her peace. And to F, F, M, and M for answering so many questions about names, locations, forms of address, and language. Juju is Joojeh thanks to you. To B, for a long and immensely helpful discussion of the Shah of Iran's legacy, and for the stunning archival photographs. And again to F, for knowing when to send a timely photograph.

Thank you to S, for advising me so thoroughly about cyber and satellite communications inside Iran. And to N, for your thoughts on Iranian etiquette and customs.

To A, for graciously granting me an interview on your legendary work in the field of human rights. It was an honor and privilege to meet you. To S, role model and daily inspiration, for such magnificent clarity and courage. To H, for showing me such courtesy at your institution, and for what I learned from your ordeal. And to those friends and colleagues, formerly in prison or currently in prison, praying for the day of release. You are many, and you are remembered.

Thank you, Nader, for so many things. Your seminal book on the Green Movement, the countless sources you directed me to, the dozens of books you loaned me, the constant elucidation of Farsi, the endless encouragement that this was a story worth telling, and most of all, for your encyclopedic knowledge of Iran's politics and history. Thank you for answering a library's worth of questions. And for being the kind of person whose faith in a magic green bracelet never wavers. You are always the light of my eyes.

And finally my deepest gratitude to my *susraal* for treating me like a daughter, sister, and aunt from the day we became a family. And for all the cups of tea you made for me with milk. Your love and understanding have meant so much. Thank you for the gifts of Hafiz and the Qur'an.

About Us

In addition to No Exit Press, Oldcastle Books has a number of other imprints, including Kamera Books, Creative Essentials, Pulp! The Classics, Pocket Essentials and High Stakes Publishing > oldcastlebooks.co.uk

For more information about Crime Books go to > crimetime.co.uk

Check out the kamera film salon for independent, arthouse and world cinema > kamera.co.uk

For more information, media enquiries and review copies please contact marketing > marketing@oldcastlebooks.co.uk